Catalan Women Writers
and Artists

Catalan Women Writers and Artists

Revisionist Views from a Feminist Space

Kathryn A. Everly

Lewisburg
Bucknell University Press
London: Associated University Presses

Associated University Presses
2010 Eastpark Boulevard
Cranbury, NJ 08512

Associated University Presses
16 Barter Street
London WC1A 2AH, England

Associated University Presses
P.O. Box 338, Port Credit
Mississauga, Ontario
Canada L5G 4L8

The paper used in this publication meets the requirements of the American National Standard for Permanence of Paper for Printed Library Materials Z39.48-1984.

Library of Congress Cataloging-in-Publication Data

Everly, Kathryn A., 1967–
    Catalan women writers and artists : revisionist views from a feminist space / Kathryn A. Everly.
        p. cm.
    Includes bibliographical references and index.
    ISBN 0-8387-5530-5 (alk. paper)
    1. Catalan literature—Women authors—History and criticism. 2. Catalan literature—20th century—History and criticism. 3. Rodoreda, Mercá, 1908—Criticism and interpretation. 4. Varo, Remedios, 1908–1963—Criticism and interpretation. 5. Roig, Montserrat, 1946—Criticism and interpretation. 6. Riera, Carme—Criticism and interpretation. I. Title.
    PC3906 .E94   2003
    849'.9509352042—dc21   2002026177

For my grandmothers,
Ruth and Lauretta

Contents

Preface

FEMINIST CRITICS HAVE CONSTANTLY STRUGGLED WITH THE IRRESOLV-
able duality of female identity and patriarchal language. Just when
it seems clear what we mean by women's voices and women's
words, we are reminded that those very words that make up the
expression are part of the larger signifying problem. In an effort to
get away from what is becoming something of an annoying skip on
the soundtrack of feminist theory, current studies have tried to explore the idea of the complicated construction of the gendered subject. Instead of locating the speaking subject in a concrete
culturally defined position, the feminine voice has emerged in contemporary theory as being located outside of culture, outside of society, outside of what is acceptable and "normal." Thus, the idea of
women living in everyday exile from language, from expression,
from true appreciation as human beings comes to represent what
the women in this study seek to remedy. Even though this book
deals with art and literature, the themes are about us, women, still
in many ways searching to be included in a society that categori-
cally pushes us to the margins.

Certain themes reappear in the works studied here, such as
motherhood, marriage, sexuality, and creativity. These are complicated epistemological concepts that cannot be changed by the passing of a law but require serious reconsideration of gender roles and
female desire if there is ever going to be a shift in the way we think
of these experiences. Catalunya during the second half of the twentieth century provides fertile ground for women to express themselves in new and intriguing ways. A tradition of liberal politics
paired with a distinct language gives Catalan women a concrete
place from which to begin to examine their position in the larger
society. The experience of exile caused by war and the metaphorical exile caused by gender-based societal unrest share many common characteristics including isolation, confusion, entrapment,
and eventually a liberation of the individual. This space of physical

9

and ideological liberation is where the women in this study find the
means to create literature and art that redefine the feminine experience.

I have decided to use the original Catalan versions of the texts
when possible to promote the language and maintain the tone the
writers intended. However, I have included in the bibliography at
the end of the book the titles in Castilian for those readers who
would like to read the works in a language other than English and
perhaps closer to the original. Not all of the works have been translated to Castilian or English, so for the sake of continuity all English
translations are my own.

I would like to thank the following people who made my research
in Barcelona possible and extremely enjoyable in the fall of 1998:
Laia Miret for her help in gaining access to materials at the Fundació Mercè Rodoreda, Meri Torras for her enthusiasm and the
loan of books and materials on Montserrat Roig, Carme Riera for
granting me an interview at her home, and for their warm hospital-
ity and friendship, Inés Delseny and Cristóbal Pera.

For their help and inspiration I am most appreciative of Virginia
Higginbotham, Naomi Lindstrom, Vance Holloway, Katherine
Arens, and Jacqueline Barnitz. I am indebted to the Study Abroad
Office that granted me an International Fee Scholarship Award
from the University of Texas at Austin for research abroad as well as
to the Department of Spanish and Portuguese. I am also eternally
grateful to Walter Gruen for his assistance and generosity in granting permission to reproduce the works of Remedios Varo. The Arxiu
Mercè Rodoreda housed at the Institut d'Estudis Catalans in Barcelona has granted permission to reproduce Rodoreda's works. I
thank them for their help and hope to aid in the promotion of Catalan culture and literature.

I would also like to thank my colleagues at Syracuse University
for their support and friendship, especially Gerry Greenberg and
Amy Wyngaard. A final and most sincere word of thanks goes to
my parents, Janet and Stephan, to the rest of my family and to my
husband, Chris Gascón.

Catalan Women Writers
and Artists

Introduction:
Metaphorical Exile in Catalan
Art and Literature

La dona, per a mi, és l'estimuladora màxima, la portadora i rev-
eladora de *la meva part fosca*. [Women, for me, are the ultimate
stimulus, the bearer and revealer of *my dark side*.]
                                                    —Federico Fellini

Gender is the repeated stylization of the body, a set of repeated
acts within a highly rigid regulatory frame that congeal over
time to produce the appearance of substance, of a natural sort
of being.
                                                    —Judith Butler

It's hard being a woman. It's like being a female impersonator
every day.
                                                    —Rita Rudner

THE CONCEPT OF POLITICAL OR EMOTIONAL EXILE WITH ITS TIES TO
estrangement and dislocation has proved a provocative theme in
peninsular letters. From the heroics of the exiled Cid to the inner
confabulations of grandeur and chivalry of perhaps the most famous literary Spaniard, Don Quijote, the estrangement from country and self allows for a fresh vision of the nation, of creativity and
of individual identity. Unamuno's exile to the island of Fuerteventura in 1924 led him to voluntarily continue his exiled status in
Paris. His experience inspired him to write *De Fuerteventura a
París: Diario íntimo de confinamiento y destierro vertido en so-
netos* [*From Fuerteventura to Paris: an Intimate Diary of Confinement and Exile Poured into Sonnets*] and expresses a need for
the artist to articulate and share this ambiguous state of being and
nonbeing. Later in the twentieth century Juan Goytisolo, perhaps
the most avid writer about the experience of internal exile, chal-

13

lenges the notion of Spanish nationality in *Juan sin tierra* [*John the Landless*] and *Señas de identidad* [*Signs of Identity*]. Both novels redirect traditional ideas about exile and place the lost individual firmly on Spanish soil who intellectually struggles with feelings of abandonment, chaos, and fear.[1] Many of these novels help us understand the effects that war, social upheaval, and political change exert on the individual. The experience of exile creates a space from which a displaced individual finds the necessary freedom to reimagine him or herself. Paul Tabori provides a comprehensive worldwide historical and semantic account of the political exile experience but doesn't enter into questions of an ontological nature.[2] Paul Ilie takes the examination of exile one step further as he investigates the emotional repercussions of an exiled state. Ilie's work analyzes the literary malaise after the Spanish civil war, which he links to the plight of writers both outside and inside the national boundaries.[3]

However, the brand of exile that I propose in this study is different. Remedios Varo, Mercè Rodoreda, Montserrat Roig, and Carme Riera have produced works spanning seventy years that redefine the situation of women in a changing society. The common link between these visions is that of feminine exile from dominant culture. The sense of alienation found in the works of Varo, Rodoreda, Roig, and Riera points to women artists and writers struggling to forge an identity in an oftentimes hostile patriarchal environment. María Lagos-Pope states: "Since antiquity the term exile has been associated with the idea of loss or separation."[4] The loss expressed in works by Varo, Rodoreda, Roig, and Riera is very personal and internal. The separation is not permanent, nor an immanent death, but rather an impetus to search for the missing links that will lead the female voice to her creative identity. Thus, the female experience is defined in the works in question as one of exclusion from a larger social, patriarchal experience. Ilie touches on this idea without a gendered focus: " 'interior' exile is limited to those malcontent sectors of the population in relation to the official culture."[5] The women in this study reconceptualize institutions such as marriage, family, heterosexual love, and politics from the position of an outsider, from the position of an exiled woman who has lost her sense of self in a social formula that necessarily excludes her individuality. Therefore, the imposed or voluntary internal exile of creative women within society allows for a reaction and revolutionary vision of the dominant culture. The aim of this book is to analyze and draw connections between the three writers and artist from Catalunya who experience exile in various forms. Political, emotional, linguistic, or social exile permeates the works of all four women and from this marginalized space these women confront through self-expression the silence imposed on them by dominant discourse.

The concept of exile becomes the metaphorical tie that binds the women in this study together. Exile in an amplified and extended scope that includes the political situation but reaches to the farther edges of creativity becomes a focal point for women who seek to rewrite patriarchal history, women's role in society, and women's role as writer and artist. Women and Catalans, in a much broader sense, confront not only political exile but also various forms of social, linguistic, and personal exile that force them into a silent corner. Therefore, the idea of a metaphorical exile that equates exile with silence on several sociopolitical levels reveals a thematic cohesion of the women's works presented here as well as the development of a feminist literary and artistic trend in Catalunya.

These Catalan women reveal in their work the impact that certain cultural and political moments of the twentieth century have exerted on women's identity and they demonstrate the development of a distinctly feminine artistic voice. The unique combination of codeveloping feminine and Catalan identities places the works of these women in a unique context that deserves attention. While addressing universal problems and triumphs of all women, Catalan literature thrives on the tension between pertaining to a national literature and maintaining a sense of regionalism. In this sense the regional exile of Catalunya from the rest of Spain acts as a backdrop provoking women to go a step further and experiment with their own sense of gender separation within their particular culture.

Writer Mercè Rodoreda and painter Remedios Varo, both born in Catalunya in 1908, engage this tension in order to come to terms with an emerging feminist consciousness in their works that share parallel themes of war, political and emotional exile, journey, and discovery. Montserrat Roig and Carme Riera, both writers born in the late 1940s, develop these themes instigated by the rupture of the Spanish civil war and elaborate on the beginnings of a feminist consciousness found in the works of their predecessors, Rodoreda and Varo.

The Catalan question of regional identity and how it effects literary and artistic production has gained in popularity with the growth of cultural studies, which is a theoretical discourse covering various aspects of literary, linguistic, sociological, anthropological, and historical analyses of culture. The interdisciplinary nature of cultural studies allows for permeable boundaries between art forms and analyses. The question of exile therefore can be isolated in a specific individual's experience or expanded to represent Catalunya's struggle with regional identity, linguistic instability, and geographic marginalization. The blossoming of alternative voices that reveal not only historical hegemony but also produce enlightened rereadings of human interaction comes to the forefront of Catalan women's art and writing in the second half of the twentieth century. This study looks at alterity as a form of ideological exile that becomes a positive space from which women can reimagine themselves within highly constrictive social codes. Therefore, instead of concentrating on the oppressive nature of the gender bind, I hope to show that the act of voicing the silent gender flourishes in both visual and verbal forms and has guided the artistic production of these four women.

Inevitably the question of emotional exile suggests the problematic position of identity. How does exclusion shade an individual's perception of the world? Several of the female protagonists in the novels by Rodoreda, Roig, and Riera find themselves outside of a dominant discourse: Natàlia in *La plaça del Diamant* [*Diamond Plaza*] lives secluded from the political machinations of the Spanish civil war, yet these mold her experience. Natàlia Miralpeix from Roig's trilogy considers love a fabrication that she cannot understand, yet her reconstruction of *The Odyssey* demonstrates a counterpoint to traditional romantic paradigms. Àngela from Riera's *Qüestió d'amor propi* [*A Question of Self-Respect*] places herself outside of and in control of the epistolary genre in order to manipulate the essence of the letter, language, and authorial intent. From the position of emotional exile that these characters exemplify we can infer the following questions: What experiences constitute the subject's ideology about life? How is this ideology rooted in certain moral values, social obligations, and in gender and class difference? The principle question then revolves around gender difference, but within the written texts and Varo's iconography other questions bleed into and blend with the primary social difference of gender.

Therefore, female subjectivity will be explored as a position rendered by experience and fed by a necessity to explore and exploit the idea of women's social roles.

Michel Foucault implies that the prefabricated and highly susceptible construction of history leaves open the possibilities of alternate discourses. These alternate voices must then be unearthed and salvaged from the cacophony of dominant discourse. The alternate history or underside of dominant discourse is what French writer and feminist Marguerite Duras labels as a provocative danger, or the "blackness" and "darkness" from which women write.[6] Duras alludes to the ideological space of exclusion from which women approach language. Unable or less equipped to draw on rich literary tradition, women begin from nothingness. This shadowy underside of history from where women began and continue to explore the development of the feminine narrative voice in Catalunya emerges in the works studied here.

Foucault's genealogy of ideas that posits the reemergence throughout chronological history of specific ideologies can be seen as a parallel to the idea of a multiple subject position as formulated by Julia Kristeva.[7] The importance of the subject becomes tantamount when trying to pinpoint the value of the exiled or marginalized experience. The subject in process or on trial rejects the notion of one monolithic discourse, or as Foucault states, one absolute Truth. Notions of truth and subjectivity become diffused into a blurry field of language that is never constant, always constructed and therefore always a product of a prefabricated discourse. Kristeva and Foucault decenter the speaking subject as they propose to unearth the hidden side of meaning: Kristeva through the semiotic and Foucault through a study of genealogy. The decentering of the speaking subject opens up spaces of rupture in meaning, allowing alternative voices a position. In a sense, these theorists celebrate the alterity of an exiled vision in that it provides an alternate viewpoint. This notion is important for Catalan women who search within tradition to exorcise not one alternative but rather variations on historical themes.

Kristeva's semiotic deals with the movement and fluctuation of meaning in language.[8] Alterity exists within the semiotic where the unspoken resides and waits to be exposed. Foucault's genealogy also relies on movable meanings, not of language but of historical concepts, ruptures in time and space that emerge repeatedly throughout what we call a chronological cycle. Therefore, the rhythmical emergence and recess of meaning operate in language as in history. Granted these ideas pertain to different areas of inquiry, namely sociolinguistics and philosophy, but they do come together in a meaningful way when approaching texts from an interdisciplinary standpoint. The similarities reveal the project of dismantling monolithic discourse and opening up possibilities of multiple expression by multiple sources. Rodoreda, Varo, Roig, and Riera embrace the possibility of multiple histories by retelling canonical tales, inserting a female point of view into historical discourse, and rewriting previously unchallenged stereotypes. Rodoreda challenges monolithic biblical themes in her short stories while Varo uses humor in an underhanded criticism of surrealism. Roig's rewriting of certain classical literary traditions is mirrored in the way she deconstructs the nuclear family based on a heterosexual model. Riera takes on literary genre as an absolute; her manipulation of readerly expectations reevaluates the roles of writer and reader, giving her female protagonists the power of the pen.

Several excellent monographic studies exist on the works of these individual women.[9] However, the lack of a comprehensive study that pinpoints the similarities and differences between these important writers and artist is the void that I hope the present study will adequately fill. In order to understand completely each woman's contribution to the literary canon, her individual accomplishments must be viewed in light of the larger development of women's presence in art and literature. Therefore, the movement toward a fuller understanding of women's experience within the Catalan tradition depends on each individual contribution yet gains form through a nurturing symbiosis of expression and consequent analysis. Furthermore, the present body of criticism often cites the notion of alterity or marginality as a creative space from which women specifically can criticize dominant culture. The notion of exile or an exiled person directly addresses difference and inclusion as problematic yet coexisting terms. The gray area of how to express a unique feminist voice while integrating feminist ideology into the existing structural discourse has consistently rumbled ominously beneath literary and artistic feminism of the latter part of the twentieth century. However, seen together as a representative whole, the works of all four women in this study draw from an ideological formulation of exile, embracing difference as an identifying mark. Together, they create a feminist discourse that breaks the silence by embracing exile as a privileged space and by maintaining a keen and critical viewpoint of dominant (patriarchal) culture.

Mercè Rodoreda (1908–83) is perhaps the most canonical writer in this study, but much of her work still demands critical attention. Besides a prolific career as a writer, Rodoreda spent several years exiled in Geneva dedicated to the visual arts. Her watercolors and drawings housed in the Institut d'Estudis Catalans provide revealing insight into the nature of her written work. Because of her skillfully crafted narrative and often jarring but lyrical writing style, she has the reputation as the first woman to develop Catalan literary language. Carme Riera explained Rodoreda's importance in a recent interview: "Mercè Rodoreda tiene una enorme importancia porque en realidad crea la novela catalana moderna. Y por tanto, en este sentido es la más importante de los escritores" [Mercè Rodoreda is extremely important because really she has created the modern Catalan novel. And therefore, in this sense, is the most important writer].[10]

Her best-known novel, *La plaça del Diamant,* tells the story of a young woman struggling with the tragic effects of the Spanish civil war while yearning to understand her own sense of self. The success of the novel led to Italian, Polish, Czech, Hungarian, German, Danish, Japanese, French, and English translations as well as a 1981 film version directed by Francesc Betriu. Rodoreda lived most of her life in exile due to political tensions in Catalunya during the Spanish civil war. She lived first in France and then in Geneva, but returned to her native Catalunya in the early seventies just before the death of dictator Francisco Franco. Rodoreda's large body of work has received numerous awards and in 1980 she received the prestigious Catalan Literature Award of Honor.

Artist Remedios Varo (1908–63) also fell victim to the disruptive forces of the Spanish civil war. In 1937 she fled Spain and lived for a short while in France before moving permanently to Mexico. Varo spent her young life in Spain studying art at the famed San Fernando Academy in Madrid and became a visible member of the avant-garde group in Barcelona known as the *logicofobistas* or "those who fear logic." Facing difficult economic situations, Varo produced commercial art in Mexico and supported herself and her famous husband, French surrealist poet Benjamin Péret. Her marriage to Walter Gruen in 1953 brought economic stability and allowed Varo to dedicate herself fully to her personal artistic interests and develop her unique signature style. Varo's work has been seen in solo exhibitions in Spain, Mexico, and Japan. In the spring of 2000 her first retrospective in this country was held at the National Museum of Women in the Arts in Washington, D.C. Varo's oneiric landscapes populated with fantastic hybrid creatures magically fuse her early surrealist training and mature polished technique that focuses on her interests in the occult, alchemy, science, and spirituality.

Montserrat Roig (1946–91) is perhaps better known in Spain as a journalist than as an author. Her in-depth investigation into the account of Catalan exiles held in Nazi death camps during World War II won the Serra d'or Critic's Prize in 1978. Roig also directed several informative television programs in which she interviewed famous authors and politicians. Roig's loyalty to her native city Barcelona appears quite obvious in her novels as the city becomes an intrinsic part in her retelling of a specifically female history. Her body of work includes several books of essays, collections of interviews, short stories, novels, and a lifelong journalistic career in print and on television. Her dedication to political and social justice emerges as a constant theme in her work and was reflected in her activist lifestyle as a member of the Socialist Party and as a self-proclaimed feminist. In 1971 her first collection of stories, *Molta roba i poc sabó i tan neta que la volen* [*So Many Clothes and Too Little Soap and They Want Them All So Clean*] won the Víctor Català prize for narrative. Consequently, Roig went on to write several other award winning novels including *El temps de les cireres* [*Time of Cherries*] that won the San Jordi Novel Prize in 1976. Montserrat Roig left an impressive and important legacy behind when she died prematurely of breast cancer on 10 November 1991.[11]

Carme Riera (1948–) also combines an interest in journalism with her life as a professor at the Universidad Autónoma in Barcelona as well as with her fame as a creative writer. Riera, a native of the island of Mallorca, has produced a varied body of work including short stories, novels, a play, newspaper columns, and a diary of her pregnancy. Similar to Roig in her political stance, Riera affirms her dedication to the feminist cause in her fiction and constantly subverts readerly expectations in regard to heterosexuality as a relationship norm. Her continued interest in subaltern voices led her to write her award-winning novel published in 1994, *Dins el darrer blau* [*In the Furthest Blue*], an account of Jewish *conversos* whose failed attempt to escape Mallorca during the inquisition in 1687 leads to their heroic demise. This is the first novel written in Catalan to receive the Spanish National Literature Award. In 2001, Riera received the Serra d'or prize for her novel *Cap al cel obert* [*Toward the Open Sky*] as well as the Spanish National Culture Award for Literature.

The connection between these four women lies in their search for an accurate formula for female expression. Through close analyses of their texts, imagery, and stylistic technique, I show how various forms of exile create a singular feminist voice. The primary focus lies in their conception of the exiled woman and her role, both mandated by the patriarchy and self-imagined, in the family structure and in society at large. Certain historical moments color the work of all four women; however, they all express an acute sensitivity to the problematic dual nature of pertaining to a marginalized region and gender.

By writing in Catalan and dealing with issues of female socialized identity in frank and open narratives, Roig and Riera continue the textual struggle initiated by Rodoreda and Varo in search of an adequate representation of female experience. The fact that both of these women published in their native language of Catalan proves to be an act of rebellion in and of itself.[12] In the early years after the Spanish civil war, Franco had effectively banned Catalan language for public or private use. Thus the language became relegated to the secretive hidden corners of the home, to the traditionally domestic maternal feminine sphere; in effect, Catalan language was exiled from Catalunya yet survived in the feminine space of the home. Both contemporary writers bring the language out from the darkened interiors and into the light of public view to create and promote a body of feminist literary works written in Catalan. Therefore, the themes of silence and political and emotional exile that lead to finding an authentic artistic voice unite these women and will guide the analyses of their narrative. Marginalized spaces and subversions will be explored in these women's works as they move toward a common goal of formulating an alternative discourse.

Rodoreda and Varo, writing and painting within the confines of the male-dominated surrealist movement, persisted relentlessly in their efforts to embrace not only the revolutionary art form but also the innovative cultural ideology that surrealism promoted. Surrealism plays heavily on themes of political and sociological exile, and many members fled Europe during the 1940s and embraced the dreamworld as a land without borders, a nation-state for all exiled artists. Whitney Chadwick has explored the secondary role that women played in surrealism but also cites the benefits of such a revolutionary movement that provided women the chance to "revolt against the conventional female roles assigned to them by family, class, and society."[13] Consequently, women emerged from surrealism with a working iconography and vocabulary with which they were able to communicate women's silence and double marginalization. Surrealism as an artistic and literary movement illustrates well the struggle women faced to pertain as serious contributors, yet they were systematically shut out because of their gender.

Susan Rubin Suleiman has labeled the position of surrealist women as on the double margin. Within the notion of the vanguard, which lies at the margin of dominant culture, women are displaced one step further as they occupy a space on the margins of the male-dominated movement. Suleiman's careful analysis of the surrealist group and its patriarchal worldview proves the "problematic position of actual women who might wish to integrate themselves, as subjects, into the male script."[14] This position that seems to teeter on the edge of inclusion and exclusion is exactly where the four women in this study converge. Montserrat Roig perhaps best expresses the position as that of a *"mirada bòrnia"* [one-eyed gaze], which Jaume Martí-Olivella describes as the "double gaze that allows women writers to inscribe at the same time their inclusion and their exclusion within a patriarchal context."[15]

Both Chadwick and Suleiman suggest that the double marginality of women writers and artists offers them a unique position and a unique experience with which they can critique and lay bare patriarchal constructions of male and female identity. From the position of double marginality, Rodoreda, Varo, Roig, and Riera insist on acts of double subversion, that is, subversion of male-dominated literary and art histories as well as subversion of dominant discourse in general.

However, the goal of creating meaningful feminine artistic and literary expression cannot be obtained in a gender vacuum, and the obstacles that make it difficult for women to be taken seriously as writers or artists were (and still are) very real. Varo and Rodoreda gained entrance into literary and surrealist art groups primarily through association with various male lovers. In fact, the overwhelming trend in surrealist circles sidelined creative women as a muse for her more established male partner. This form of relegating artistic women to a sexual role unfortunately hasn't ceased to exist. In January 1981 critic Manuel Vicent wrote, "Montserrat Roig brought to literature, more than anything else, a pair of nice legs. . . ."[16] Robert Belton's discussion of the surrealist male gaze defines women as object in a discourse that assumes a male recipient and therefore presents the world from a male point of view. His use of the theory of a *horizon of expectations* developed by literary theorist Hans Robert Jauss proves especially helpful in understanding the common denominator of female objectification that was not only employed by the surrealists but also embraced by counter as well as dominant culture.

The *horizon of expectations* refers to the collective knowledge that a public brings to the interpretation of a piece of art or literature. Therefore, the "implicit contract" between artist and receptor depends on social, political, economic, and cultural conditions.[17] However, the task of women writers and artists within any codified social and artistic movement is to reevaluate the very *horizon of expectations* particular to their cultural conditions. These unwritten social contracts provide an ample source of material that women can explore, challenge, and reformulate according to their own experience. Rodoreda, Varo, Roig, and Riera each confront the patriarchal social contract of their particular time and undermine a system that dictates female behavior.

Several concrete political changes allowed women to entertain ideas of social change and experience a newfound independence from imposed stereotypes. An important moment for women's artistic expression in Catalunya was the blossoming of the Second Republic (1931–36) that represented social and political freedoms for women. Women were granted the right to vote in Catalunya in 1931, while 1932 brought a divorce law and abortion was legalized in December 1936. The Constitution of 1931, serving as the official document and declaration of the Second Republic, formally recognized equality between the sexes.[18] These legislative accomplishments, which the civil war would annihilate, cannot be taken for granted, especially in light of the social liberties that would directly affect the artistic development of young women artists and writers of the day.

Drawing from the freedoms implied by socially accepted liberal politics, the Catalan vanguard movement created an artistic space in the public arena where marginalization became desirable for anarchic artistic production. Therefore, women artists found themselves participating in a socio-artistic revolution and reaping the benefits of a liberating cultural movement. However, within the vanguard microcosm of social relationships, women were systematically subordinated and excluded from the existential musings of male intellectuals and artists. The vanguard movement in Barcelona not only separated men from women artistically but also separated the city culturally from the rest of Spain by maintaining an alliance to the Parisian vanguard. The dominant male culture that developed the ideology of the vanguard proved to be an obstacle for women intent on formulating a subjective artistic persona. Even though the vanguard has always been a political and social movement of counterculture, on the margins itself, for women the movement eventually came to represent just another manifestation of patriarchal control. The publications, exhibitions, and manifestos excluded women as artists, but glorified the idea of woman as muse.

The growth of the Barcelona vanguard springs directly from events in Paris during the early 1920s. The influential surrealist ideologies treat women as a mysterious, incomprehensible other as seen in the epigraph to this chapter in which Fellini describes woman as the key to understanding the male dark side. André Breton's fabrication of the woman as muse and Freud's mystification of female sexuality link together ideas negating female subjectivity. The publication of André Breton's *Surrealist Manifesto* in 1924 opened the floodgate for artists throughout Europe to dabble in areas traditionally outside of literature, painting, and sculpture such as psychoanalysis and dream interpretation. Automatism, the free association technique that Breton proposes in his manifesto, describes an oneiric, altered state of creative liberty unconscious of logic and time. Artists in these altered states required the inspiration of a female muse and doted on the submissive *femme-enfant*. Freud's studies of the unconscious and the publication of *Interpretation of Dreams* in 1900 also directly affect the emergence of the new art form privileging the untapped and misunderstood side of male human consciousness.[19] Although human unconsciousness also seemed to be sexist according to surrealist dogma, Rodoreda and Varo were able to overcome this gender hierarchy. In their later works both women exploit the surrealist fascination with human nature and explore the female experience of reality and dream states with uninhibited imagination.

Perhaps most significant to the artistic development of both Remedios Varo and Mercè Rodoreda living in prewar Barcelona is the political and social commitment that went hand in hand with artistic freedom. Despite struggling with the misogynist overtones of the surrealist movement, women were a crucial element in the pursuit of artistic freedom and experimentation. Artistic liberation and political activism fused into one common dream of a utopian republic that inspired economic equality and unlimited creative boundaries. The ambience of Barcelona in the early thirties was one of hope and revolution mirrored by the intense growth of surrealism as a liberating artistic movement, which fused the metaphysical with the mundane, the intellectual with the visionary, the political with the artistic.

However, with the onset of the Spanish civil war in 1936, liberal politics, the arts, and cultural production in Barcelona came to a complete halt. Despite the detrimental effects of war on artistic and liberal social development in Catalunya, the women in this study make a concerted effort to assimilate the Spanish civil war into a particularly feminine experience and express the hidden underside of a dominant history. Thus, the reinterpretation of chronological acts that produces an interiorization of the experience proves to be a fundamental step for these women that leads to the production of alternative versions of history.

Although Franco's iron-fist dictatorship left artistic Spain in shambles, the enthusiasm of the Republican cause in Catalunya ultimately formulates the essence of Catalan identity, which serves as a backdrop for most of the literary production in the years during and after the war. Mary Nash concludes "although the Franco regime cut off the path to freedom and emancipation, it did not succeed in completely undermining the social experience of the war years."[20] The upheaval of the Spanish civil war formulated a unique social consciousness in Catalunya while bringing women to the forefront of the defense effort. The oppression of the dictatorship followed by the watershed of the post-Franco years have served as a catalyst for women to rewrite and reinterpret an "official" history while, in the case of the writers, providing the chance to employ the once-prohibited language of Catalan that becomes symbolic of change and autonomy. Thus the subversive symbolic value of being Catalan parallels the subversive symbolic value of being a woman artist and creates the dynamics of double subversion in the works of the women in this study.

After the Franco era (1939–75) the circulation of art and literature again became intertwined with new political freedoms and this fervor spurred on the liberal artistic and mainly cinematic movement in Madrid of the early eighties known as *la movida*.[21] Montserrat Roig and Carme Riera chose not to align themselves with this specific movement that tends toward extreme sexual shock value but rather with the general political atmosphere of the new democracy, socialism, and emerging feminism in Catalunya. Therefore, their works are often politically minded as they rigorously challenge the *horizon of expectations* laid out before them in the last two decades of the twentieth century.

The study of regional literature demands extensive research in various disciplines; however, my approach will be defined by the sociopolitical circumstances in which these women produced art. The ways in which each woman approaches the lack of a feminine history reveal the determination of twentieth-century women writers and artists to break new ground and, as Hélène Cixous suggests, " bring women . . . to their meaning in history."[22] However, none of the women in this study dedicates herself to a project in search of a definable essence of women's writing style or *écriture féminine*; instead they take a more socially practical approach.[23] These women observe the trends and conflicts surrounding women, men's perception of women, and women's perception of themselves as projections of alternate histories. Therefore, what holds these four particular women together is the way they embrace alterity as a necessary by-product of emotional exile in order to undermine a dominant discourse. This emphasis on and manipulation of forms of the unvoiced or unspeakable can be illuminated through the use of various theoretical frameworks. However, in order not to label the work of the women in this study or the analysis itself as pertaining to one body of theory, I have developed an approach that draws on various ideas concerning history and the tension between silence and speech.

In the first chapter the avant-garde art movement in Barcelona of the 1920s and 1930s provides the basis for study of how the impact of surrealism affected the methods and approaches to literature and art that underwent a radical change during this time period. Surrealism questions the seemingly logical relationship between signifier and signified, producing a rupture in traditional concepts of meaning. The movement has been criticized as misogynist in light of the notion of woman as a subordinate function of the male artistic psyche.[24] While this position certainly hindered productive participation by women artists and linked them inevitably to male counterparts, the liberating ideology of surrealism actually provided a breeding ground for transgressive, subversive identities that the surrealist women adopted in order to survive artistically outside the movement. This process of self-discovery through alienation will be discussed in the first chapter utilizing the texts, watercolors, and drawings of Mercè Rodoreda and the paintings of Remedios Varo. Rodoreda's novels *La plaça del Diamant* [*Diamond Plaza*] (1962) and *El carrer de les camèlies* [*Camellia Street*] (1966) as well as several short stories reveal her mature writing style that weaves together her realist approach toward the Spanish civil war and exile with oneiric sequences and fantastic creatures. Remedios Varo, who painted with the vanguard group of *logicofobistas* in Barcelona, presents a body of work that grows considerably throughout her lifelong exile in Mexico. Varo's mature work also incorporates images of her native Spain with hybrid creatures of creative genius. The metaphysical aspect of surrealism plays an important part in Varo's later work as it allows the artist a certain liberty from the obligation of strict realistic representation. Thus, in Varo's later work she incorporates fantastic creatures, half-animal and half-human, representing the irrational side of the human mind. Her interest in alchemy as an alternative science becomes more of a symbolic continuing metaphor of the search for the unspoken, for the underside of mainstream consciousness.

In the second chapter I will discuss Roig's development of the feminine consciousness planted by Rodoreda and Varo. Roig represents a generation conscious of feminism and voices the change it promised yet she is quick to point out the failure and disillusion that can emerge from such socially constructed institutions. In her trilogy *Ramona, adéu* [*Good-bye, Ramona*] (1972), *El temps de les cireres* [*Time of Cherries*] (1976) and *L'hora violeta* [*The Violet*

Hour] (1980) Roig traces the genealogy of a Catalan family through matrilineal inheritance. These novels have been called a "counter-saga" as opposed to the traditional saga, as they tell the underside of history, the feminine side of traditionally male-ordered chronology.[25] The collection of short stories written in the early seventies, *Molta roba i poc sabó i tan neta que la volen* [*So Many Clothes and Too Little Soap and They Want Them All So Clean*] (1971), is a precursor to the trilogy and includes some of the same characters. Intertextuality in Roig's work establishes a consistency of character, time, and space that transcends the physical limitations of the written page. The short stories as well as the trilogy reveal Roig's concern with letters and diaries that document and record private (typically woman's) existence. Roig intends to publicize the inside, private sector of society. Her project to bring the private into the public sphere involves peeling back the constructed socialized layers of habit and performance that Judith Butler suggests determine our gender identity.[26] What lies underneath is often frightening because it is unrecognizable, yet Roig demythifies family, marriage, and love and offers an alternative point of view, a subversive and disturbing yet liberating account of what these institutions pretend.

In the third chapter I will explore how Carme Riera brings to the discussion yet another level of feminist consciousness. Riera looks at the same socially constructed ideas of love, heterosexual codependency, and family, but instead of a political deconstruction of the system, she manipulates language to renegotiate ideas of power and social positioning. Her intent is actually to subvert the notion of a female consciousness that in and of itself falls into categorization within certain social, political, and economic boundaries. Her epistolary *Qüestió d'amor propi* [*A Question of Self-Respect*] (1987) and the collection of stories *Contra l'amor en companyia* [*Against Love with a Partner*] (1991) present certain formulated, and therefore accepted as "normal," circumstances and then undermine the normality by manipulating the reader's expectations. Her surprise endings leave the reader questioning not only the text but also her own preconceived ideas of gender. Riera's collection of stories from early in her career *Te deix, amor, la mar com a penyora* [*I Leave You, My Love, The Sea as a Token*] (1975) and *Jo pos per testimoni les gavines* [*I Give as Testimony the Gulls*] (1977) reveal the thematic beginnings of gender questioning that will become central to the subversion of linguistic power found in her later works.

The aim of this book then is to bring international attention to a group of women writers and an artist who challenge established cultural stereotypes of women. I do not propose to explain exile in the political sense but rather to explore the possibility of social and emotional exile as a new way to look at the cohesion of a feminist voice in Catalunya. Through reinterpretations of history and the dominant symbolic discourse nurtured by tradition, these women uncover a distinctly feminine voice rising from an all too often ignored female experience. Female experience itself can be considered a type of social exile from which a voice of dissension rises to break the silence. The links between the art and narrative endeavors of these four women establish a positive force that acknowledges the tradition of gender exile in Catalunya and affirms the power of creativity. With words and images, these women combat the silence imposed on generations of women by political and emotional exile.

1

Mercè Rodoreda and Remedios Varo: Exiled Daughters of Surrealism, Insightful Mothers of Invention

> It is clear, historically and sociologically, what women brought
> to Surrealism, it remains to be asked what Surrealism brought
> to women.
>
> —Susan Rubin Suleiman, *Subversive Intent*

CATALAN NOVELIST MERCÈ RODOREDA AND CATALAN PAINTER REMEDIOS Varo both were forced into exile in order to escape the violence of the Spanish civil war. Consequently, themes of exile, longing, journey, and a search for identity permeate their works throughout their artistic careers. Similarly, both women suffered a silent exile within; for Rodoreda the violent stripping away of her maternal Catalan tongue left her without a literary voice, and for Varo a determined search to distance herself from surrealism's dominating influence led her through various thematic and stylistic phases. Both women struggle with and eventually shed the restrictive adornments of surrealism's ideology, which limited productive discourse for women in search of more authentic and profound feminine artistic identities. The recent unveiling of over eighty paintings, drawings, and watercolors by Mercè Rodoreda has revealed important connections between written and pictorial language indicative of women experimenting with various modes of artistic expression. Through both verbal and visual images, Rodoreda and Varo develop various artistic identities reflective of the swiftly changing midcentury sociopolitical scene moving from the height of the Catalan avant-garde, through the destruction of the Spanish civil war and into the deteriorating Franco regime of the 1960s and early 1970s.

30

Both women were born in Catalunya in 1908 and both spent years in France linked romantically to male colleagues who would greatly affect their artistic and literary work. Varo spent a year studying painting in Paris with her first husband, Gerardo Lizarraga, an accomplished painter himself. Janet Kaplan describes this year of Varo's life as a "tantalizing interlude" that convinced the young couple to settle in "the more avant-garde atmosphere of Barcelona" instead of Madrid upon their return to Spain in 1932.[1] Varo's early exposure to the budding Parisian surrealist movement fostered her interest in experimental art, which she intensely pursued in Barcelona. Varo later fled to Paris in 1937 with the poet Benjamin Péret, whom she had met in Barcelona, leaving Lizarraga behind. She would spend several months in Marseilles in 1941 before gaining legal passage as a political exile to Mexico, where she lived the rest of her life.

Rodoreda spent the beginning of her self-imposed exile, from 1939 until the German occupation, in a small town not far from Paris called Roissey-en-Brie. Rodoreda had decided to flee from her unhappy marriage to her uncle and leave behind her only son in war-stricken Barcelona. In Roissey-en-Brie her romantic involvement with Catalan writer Armand Obiols began and would last until his death in 1971. Rodoreda returned to Catalunya in 1973 and resided there until her death in 1983. Both Varo and Rodoreda experienced the height of the avant-garde in Barcelona and the liberating politics for women of the Spanish Second Republic. They both were victims of the terrible Spanish civil war that cost them careers on Spanish soil and sent them into exile. However, the theme of exile seen in their works deals more explicitly with the emotional distancing from a world dominated by patriarchy. The metaphorical exile of a creative woman seeking her artistic voice through a reevaluation of women's roles lies at the heart of the insightful, groundbreaking works of Varo and Rodoreda.

Both Rodoreda and Varo turned to painting as a form of artistic and personal expression. Varo discovered her talent quite young and studied in Madrid at the prestigious Academia de San Fernando where Salvador Dalí studied during the same years but was promptly expelled.[2] Rodoreda, on the other hand, had already enjoyed success as a journalist and fiction writer when she turned to painting as an alternative medium when she could not bear to write in her banned native language during the first lonely years of exile.

She discovered a hidden talent that helped her express certain fears and emotional strains when words failed her. In either case, surrealism and its problems and promises for young artists living and working in the 1930s directly affected Rodoreda's writing and Varo's artwork. To begin to answer Susan Rubin Suleiman's question about what surrealism brought to women, a careful analysis of these two women artists may help uncover the underlying nature of surrealism's misogyny that pushed women to the margin and forced them to develop a voice of their own in order to survive there. Varo's visual inscriptions of feminine identity create an intertextual proactive iconography, while Rodoreda's novels and short stories incorporate disturbing surreal images of wartime atrocities and shed light on a specifically feminine point of view concerning the emotional casualties of war.

Even though neither Rodoreda nor Varo defined themselves or their art as feminist, most contemporary critics of their work acknowledge a convincing presence of controversial, progressive thinking in regard to gender roles. In approaching their work from a feminist critical standpoint, the critic should take care to locate their developing ideologies in the concurrent artistic and literary atmosphere in which they worked. Radical feminism of the time stemmed from Simone de Beauvoir's *The Second Sex* (1949), an extreme representation of biological and psychological femaleness.[3] De Beauvoir, born in Paris in 1908 (the same year as both Rodoreda and Varo) published her landmark work in 1949 when Varo was living in Mexico and just beginning to develop her own style and Rodoreda, prior to publishing her best-known work, was painting in Geneva. Rodoreda and Varo chose not to align themselves politically or artistically with feminism, yet this should not affect a justified feminist reading of their work. Historical labels only limit possibilities of interpretation and allow history and language to dictate meaning. Perhaps these two women would have joined the more mainstream feminist movement of the 1970s or perhaps not; in either case their work stretches to the limits of and directly challenges confabulated, patriarchal ideals of femininity. In addition to questioning socially ingrained gender expectations, both women sought to develop the surrealist's interdisciplinary approach to art and crossed boundaries limiting them to only one form of expression.

Emmanuel Guigon describes the fusion of poetry and painting

that the surrealists embraced, and he observes: "Remedios seems to never have limited herself to just one mode of expression. For her the tools of the painter and of the writer are unified in breaking down our visual and intellectual customs."[4] While Guigon's statement identifies Varo's notions of transgression and subversion of traditional artistic categories, it also provides a valuable ideological link to Mercè Rodoreda's work. The importance of these two women lies in their multifaceted approach to artistic expression. Rodoreda's art production stems from a necessity to express her experience in exile through means other than her prohibited native Catalan language. Lourdes Andrade seems to speak for both women when she claims: "Remedios didn't live just one life but many, she didn't fulfill one destiny but rather multiple destinies, those of each of the fabulous characters that populate her canvases."[5] Although far from autobiographical, the works of Rodoreda and Varo expose the various subordinate roles women were expected to play. While Rodoreda's consciousness of artistic presence in literature reveals itself in the descriptions of paintings in her novels, Varo infuses her artwork with narrative or allegorical qualities. Guigon defends Varo's practice claiming that this type of art has been unfairly labeled as "pintura literaria," [literary painting] and unjustly considered inferior to other types of symbolic or abstract art.[6]

The idea of "literary painting" and "visual writing" emerges frequently not only in art and literature but also as an important dialogue in established debates concerning cultural studies. W. J. T. Mitchell brought to the forefront of cultural studies the somewhat problematic discourse surrounding verbal and visual images. His article "What is an Image," predating the book-length study, serves as a type of taxonomy of images, which Mitchell categorizes as graphic, optical, perceptual, mental, and verbal. His aim is to bring together the historically disparate ideas about visual versus mental or linguistically generated images.[7] Mitchell's article serves as a valuable point of departure for a discussion on the modern history of the verbal and the visual. He claims the "point, then, is not to heal the split between words and images, but to see what interests and powers it serves."[8]

In the same spirit, Margaret Persin moves to a more concrete example of the development of this relationship. Persin pinpoints the ekphrastic, and therefore tangentially the visual/verbal dialogue, as bearing certain social and cultural ramifications that reveal how the writer views art and chooses to represent it through language. Ekphrasis is the practice of writing artistic descriptions about the plastic arts. According to Persin, Homer's description of Achilles' shield in the *Iliad*, Keats' *Ode on a Grecian Urn*, and modern literature by T. S. Eliot, James Joyce, and Marcel Proust all prove that artists have struggled with the "seemingly irreconcilable differences in artistic discourse."[9] Writers intent on crossing artistic boundaries have repeatedly broken the rules by "communicating spatial relationships traditionally associated with visual art, through a verbal medium."[10]

Mercè Rodoreda's use of ekphrasis in both *La plaça del Diamant* (1962) and *El carrer de les camèlies* (1966) illuminates each respective text through pictorial allegory in paintings her characters analyze and thus she creates a metatextual artifact, the painting, that draws on the reader's sensibilities of time and space. The popularity of interdisciplinary art forms in twentieth-century Spain exhibited in the work of Rafael Alberti, who trained as a painter only to become a renowned poet, Antonio Buero Vallejo, Federico García Lorca, the filmmaker Luis Buñuel, and Catalan critic and poet Pere Gimferrer, sets the stage for a serious study of the paintings and writings of Rodoreda and Varo.[11] These two women, working in both mediums, bring accomplished contributions to the existing dialogue and move beyond ekphrasis to ontological questions of Self and Other in search of female subjectivity.[12]

In this chapter, I examine how both visual and verbal texts demonstrate Rodoreda and Varo's problematic relationship with surrealism and the resulting artistic discourse they developed. Varo's development from a purely imitative to an individual artistic identity reveals that she defied surrealist misogyny yet retained the oneiric motifs typical of the movement in her later painting. Rodoreda likewise incorporates surreal scenes in her novel *La plaça del Diamant* in order to disrupt linear narrative modes. Emilie Bergmann pinpoints the effects of a first-person narrator distanced temporally and emotionally from her story which "combined with elements of interior, subjectivized reality . . . suggest the possibilities of the visionary and the fantastic."[13]

An analysis of Rodoreda's artwork in relation to her literary production leads to a comparison of visual and verbal representations in the work of both Rodoreda and Varo. Spatial restructuring and iconography on the canvas seem to parallel certain linguistic innovations and metaphors on the page. Both women use ironic laughter as a subversive weapon against psychoanalytic modes of masculine discourse represented in surrealism and patriarchy in general. Finally, as a response to the question of how these women intend to reidentify themselves as artists, I will explore metamorphosis as a catalyst for both physical and emotional change found in two short stories by Rodoreda and several paintings by Varo. The connection between physical metamorphosis as a form of exile from the human body and emotional growth appears in Rodoreda's characterizations of women as well as in Varo's images. Alchemy, as an alternative science, provides a methodology for experimentation that Varo practiced in Mexico with her friend and fellow artist Leonora Carrington and this system that depends on physical transmutations symbolically releases a trapped being from a material body. For women searching to reconstruct an autonomous self outside of the female body as object, alchemy and metamorphosis serve as an effective mode of expression. However, these modes of expression are not limited to female subversion of dominant culture, for Franz Kafka used metamorphosis to the same subversive ends as do Rodoreda and Varo. The instability of the human body, that which reality affirms as constant, becomes a transgressive space and in its mutations challenges societal assumptions about identity and systematic behavior patterns. Therefore, Kafka's social commentary that questions individuality within a system parallels Rodoreda and Varo's questioning of the individual woman's place within a patriarchal system.[14]

When investigating a single theme, such as metamorphosis or surrealism, in different art forms, it can be a difficult and dangerous task to maintain the integrity of the material images as separate from the linguistically rendered mental images. For there is a fear of oversimplifying either form of composition. But, as Mitchell suggests, rather than concentrate on the characteristics that distinguish between material and mental images, a more productive methodology may be to draw on the richness of similarities between these verbal and visual images. In doing so we may construct a working, symbiotic relationship between words and forms, sentences and shapes, in order to understand more completely how we relate to the world around us.

SURREALISM, SEXUALITY, AND ARTISTIC IDENTITY

In her book *Surréalisme et sexualité* [*Surrealism and Sexuality*] (1971), French feminist Xavière Gauthier reveals the misogyny inherent in surrealism, which she claims is manifested in the liberty taken by male artists to contort and alienate the female body.[15] Several other critics of surrealism including Chadwick and Suleiman have revealed how women struggled against the definitions of surrealism to assert a positive feminine identity and eventually emerged triumphant. A specific symbolic language created by women artists attempts to subvert and redefine the distorted female sexual identity carefully developed by the surrealists. Rodoreda and Varo take advantage of their gender exile from the movement in order to come to terms with artistic and regional marginality and ultimately draw from that position a wealth of artistic discourse and a constructive means to autonomy.

Catalunya itself as a geographically and linguistically marginalized region in Spain serves as a political, social, and economic backdrop for the works of both of these women. Before the Spanish civil war, the avant-garde in Barcelona enjoyed a healthy reciprocity with Parisian artists and intellectuals who enthusiastically lectured on the revolution of surrealism. The artistic atmosphere of Barcelona in the twenties and early thirties that influenced Varo and Rodoreda thrived on experimentation, disregard for tradition, and a fiercely liberal political stance. Rodoreda and Varo were not only deeply affected artistically by the sudden creative and spiritual crisis brought on by the onset of the Spanish civil war but also by the dispossession of personal identity corresponding to the repeal of Catalan independence as a result of Franco's dictatorship.

The problematic development of an artistic identity for women within surrealism becomes clear once we identify the psychological workings of femininity formulated by André Breton and promoted so vigorously by male surrealists. Breton gives priority in his *Manifestoes of Surrealism* to experimental artistic technique or automatism and preaches unlimited liberation of the artistic mind and spirit for both men and women. His worldview revolves around artistic as well as psychic automatism, which he defines as the visualization of the human thought process. Under this umbrella term, Breton makes several references to woman and her crucial role in the creative process. Yet at the outset of the manifesto, Breton seems to contradict himself by immediately objectifying woman as one of the many mundane things to which the common man has grown accustomed; therefore he becomes discontented and takes her for granted. This apathy toward material objects includes "what women he has had, what silly affairs he has been involved in."[16] Thus, from the opening paragraph Breton clearly categorizes woman as a disposable object whose identity remains dependent upon her relationship to men.

However, it would be unfair to say that Breton simply sketches woman in one dimension; on the contrary, he develops her role as catalyst, lavishes her with compliments, and wonders at her enigmatic power to inspire the blocked poet. Breton builds up the image of woman, inflates the importance of her beauty, youth, and innocence, resulting in a complete and complex image of the Other, specifically for the self as artist. Breton describes the female capacity to soften and ease the harshness of waking reality:

> this idea, this woman, disturb it, they tend to make it less severe. What they do is isolate the mind for a second from its solvent and spirit it to heaven, as the beautiful precipitate it can be, that it is.[17]

The female herself doesn't participate in this waking reality; she eases the pain for the male artist by liberating his mind. Here Breton creates an idea of woman that is somewhat dehumanized as she is removed from experience and stripped of intellectual capabilities to fully comprehend the harshness of reality. Therefore woman lacks not only intellectual capabilities but also a reality that constitutes her experience. In Breton's terms, woman as human ceases to exist and instead an intellectualized idea of woman as muse in the service of the poet/artist takes her place. Superficially it may seem that Breton grants the idea of woman the power to inspire yet he actually sets up a transparent one-sided power play between the artist and his muse. He supposedly cannot create without her but his control of language and expression defines her and ultimately relegates her to a subordinate position. Pierre Bourdieu's model of hierarchies within a linguistic market set forth in *Language and Symbolic Power* reveals that Breton's surrealist manifestos claim that men have a monopoly on linguistic exchange. Bourdieu states:

The power of works is nothing other than the *delegated power* of the spokesperson, and his speech—that is—, the substance of his discourse and, inseparably, his way of speaking— is no more than a testimony, and one among others, of the *guarantee of delegation* which is vested in him.[18]

Read in light of Bourdieu's idea of delegated power, not only what Breton says but his poetic text subverting the traditional order of treatise-writing (in the form of a manifesto) grants him the linguistic authority and power of the avant-garde spokesman. His treatment of women passes as part of his delegated authority and therefore as part of surrealism itself. The artist, according to Breton, creates the muse in order to be inspired to produce great art or poetry, yet it is obvious that actual women have very little to do with the solipsistic work of male surrealists. For Breton, language is the ultimate power playing field where ideas are exchanged, manipulated, and subverted. He suggests that the feminine influence, created by his speech, lies in direct subordination to male artistic production. The idea of woman as muse can easily be transformed into a scapegoat for uninspired, badly written, or poorly executed art. She is whatever the male artist/subject wants her to be.

To further illustrate the point that women are not considered part of the male experience, Breton goes on to describe a gathering of his famous surrealist friends: Paul Éluard, Robert Desnos, Roger Vitrac, Antonin Artaud, Francis Gérard, and Benjamin Péret, Varo's lover. Also present are an unnamed, unidentified group of "gorgeous women." (Was Varo one of these?) In the midst of the cheerful gathering, Breton becomes pensive and laments the difficulty of cultivating meaningful friendships: "The solitude is vast, we don't often run into one another. And anyway, isn't what matters that we be the masters of ourselves, the masters of women, and of love too?"[19] Obviously Breton's thought roots itself in the objectification of the female, yet she possesses something that he feels the urge to dominate. Thus the marginalized, mysterious apparition of the female leaves behind footprints of her splendor for the beauty-starved artist to follow.

The muse inspires excitement and anticipation of artistic greatness masked in physical desire that supersedes actual contact with the woman. Breton expounded on this theme in his novel *Nadja* of

1928 in which desire and the possibility of love propel the narration and the object pursued becomes secondary to the pursuit itself.[20] The hedonism central to surrealism threatens woman's sexual autonomy as well. The pursuit of pleasure defined as sexual freedom and liberation places women in a subordinate role and allows men to feel convinced that female spiritual freedom is an erotic, physical, and emotional surrender to men. Compounding the error of this false liberation is the idea that women can actually experience true freedom through sexual excess and at the mercy of the male erotic fantasy. Nevertheless, by bringing female sexuality to the forefront of artistic discourse, the surrealists revealed the sexual hierarchy and symbolic possession of the female body that had defined patriarchal painting for centuries. Therefore, women artists struggled to generate a doubly subversive artistic identity, gaining access to their own bodies by refiguring the surrealists' prescribed roles of female sexuality.

The marginalizing effects of surrealist ideology allowed Varo to rebel against it, that is to say, surrealism itself eventually evolved into a mainstream patriarchal institution that overtly represented to Varo the limiting experience of phallocentric community. Surrealism became just another *center* from which she, as a woman, was marginalized. Linda Nochlin, a feminist art scholar, sees this systematic marginalization of women artists as a major obstacle in how women have been perceived artistically in the past. She proposes a reevaluation of how we (society) categorize art by women. Her method intentionally subverts traditional notions of what is great or valuable art and also questions the very basis of how art is judged. Nochlin redefines the entire scholarly field of art history, a radicalization that Griselda Pollock will develop in her own feminist art analysis. Both scholars agree that patriarchal notions of the romantic individual who becomes inspired to greatness through some form of ethereal intervention have played a distinctive role in shutting women out of the privileged space of social recognition. Art as artifact becomes the hinge on which the feminist argument opens: art historians must redevelop traditional definitions of masterpieces as individual accomplishments displaying moments of personal genius. According to Nochlin, canonized art pieces should be considered as testaments of specific social, historical, and ideological moments. Nochlin challenges "the naïve idea that art is the direct, personal expression of individual emotional experience, a translation of personal life into visual terms. Art is almost never that, great art never is."[21]

Nochlin applies to painting Roland Barthes's affirmation that "[w]riting is that neutral, composite, oblique space where our subject slips away, the negative where all identity is lost."[22] Nochlin's remedy for the romanticized ideal of the genius artist lies in the discursive recognition of power hierarchies embedded in visual composition and iconography of women artists. These observations made by women artists cannot be considered individual assertions of power, but rather manifestations of the cultural power struggle. The visual composition of painting that forms a readable text testifies to women's position in the dominant culture and thus confirms Barthes's observation that "the text is a tissue of quotations drawn from the innumerable centres of culture."[23] Barthes's quote poses the challenge for the feminist critic to distinguish between dominant and subaltern culture, for it seems he refers to one culture yet does suggest it has numerable centers. However, Nochlin is quick to admit that what defines power in women's art is actually the lack of power found in the majority of representations of women within artwork accepted by the dominant culture.

The powerlessness of women and the struggle for physical and emotional control manifested by usurping the existing power paradigms become a central focus in the works of Varo and Rodoreda. Rather than condemn the artist from a feminist standpoint for embracing her own victimization at the hands of the omnipotent patriarchy, these expositions of powerlessness allude to the absence of autonomy and therefore to a counterpossibility of unmasked, peripheral power. Foucault explained that power functions and is tolerated only on the condition that it mask a considerable part of itself.[24] The surrealists masked the oppressive power of misogyny with artistic liberation and progressive radical thinking, making the power play tolerable for those women involved in the artistic movement trying to create erotic images of sexual and intellectual liberation of their own.

Griselda Pollock acknowledges the inherent power structures that have formulated gendered representations and exiled females from artistic recognition. However, she points out that Nochlin, by deferring to the powerlessness of female figures and tangentially female artists, is merely succumbing to the patriarchal ideals of male possession and female lack of power. Pollock proposes a paradigm shift that is a radical reconstruction of the "disciplinary matrix" or paradigm, which no longer serves adequately to analyze the histories of art.[25] Her concern lies in the complacency of women to accept the standard paradigm norms not only of evaluating art but also of delegating power and accomplishment within western cultures. Pollock takes on patriarchy as "a web of psycho-social relationships which institute a socially significant difference on the axis of sex which is so deeply located in our very sense of lived, sexual identity that it appears to us as natural and unalterable."[26] Pollock cites as an example the acceptance of male creativity juxtaposed with the necessary invention of a female creativity. These terms become differentiated through a discourse located in a male-dominated arena where what is natural for a man automatically becomes an obstacle for a woman due to her sexual difference.

Current feminist art history criticism as pioneered by Nochlin and Pollock seeks to vindicate the underprivileged woman artist of the nineteenth century and relocate the origins of her lack of success in the artistic world from her sex to her forced alienation from educational institutions, lack of cultural exposure and general lack of encouragement to pursue a career in the arts. Women were forbidden to sketch nude male models when the artist's capacity to compose the line and form of the human body distinguished his talent in nineteenth-century European salon exhibitions. To give just one of many examples, this shutting out of women from what was considered fundamental art training must be considered in analyses of the artwork produced by women during this time.

In the light of the work accomplished by these feminist critics, Breton's *Manifestoes of Surrealism* shifts from a radical art treatise to an alienating, rigid systematic methodology. Therefore, even if Varo didn't topple the existing oligarchy of surrealism, her transgression fits Nochlin's definition as that which questions the established boundaries of codes of thought and behavior of the time.[27] Once surrealism became just another *ism,* women artists and writers moved beyond the margins of power in order to explore and uncover the nature of the role they had been assigned to play. Both Varo and Rodoreda in their artwork recognize the inadequacy of patriarchal gender distinctions and their work sets the stage for the radical departure seen in their artistic and literary descendants in the later decades of the twentieth century.

Varo's work moves from imitation of her male surrealist companions to an exploration of theme and composition and finally to a stylized intertextual world, spanning numerous paintings of fantastical spaces often reminiscent of the surrealists' fascination with the oneiric. However, two paintings executed in 1936 demonstrate Varo's intent to fit into a mold and find acceptance from her surrealist peers. *Desire* and *Painting* both incorporate the repetition of spiked waves to suggest movement and the danger latent in the erotic. *Painting* shows various bald female figures floating helplessly amid the threatening waves. Their faces are expressionless and each body varies in composition; some are hollow, one is a bird, one has an empty square where her arm should be, and one central figure exposes her breasts. The repetition of limbless, deformed female bodies plays into the deconstruction and manipulation of female sexuality and consequently the female psyche. *Desire* presents symbolic potent male sexual imagery. An ominous, dark mountain chain spouts white foam that resembles melted wax and nurtures the growth of slender green plants on each mountain peak. Kaplan draws a parallel between this painting and *On the Ladder of Desire* (1936) by the Viennese artist Wolfgang Paalen

R. Varo. *Desire* c. 1936.

that suggests Varo's imitative style and distinctly male-oriented symbolic eroticism that was necessary for her acceptance into surrealist circles. Another important painting from this early imitative stage is *Anticipation*, dated 1937 in Kaplan's book. This painting was included in the exhibition of the *logicofobistas* in May 1936 at the Galería Catalunya as documented in a well-known photograph published in *Surrealism in Catalunya* and in an article by Lucia Garcia de Carpi.[28] In the photograph we see two men sitting at a table in the distance and one lying faceup on the floor. However, the paintings exhibited on the walls behind these figures play a more important role. The first painting hanging on the left is one of the largest in the photograph and is clearly the seated figure of Varo's *Anticipation*. The bizarre female figure wrapped in a winged shroud extends one leg in the form of a key across the center of the composition that opens a closet door revealing a large planet or sun. Thus, Kaplan's date of 1937 is impossible because the *logico-fobista* exhibition took place in May 1936. Lucia Garcia de Carpi includes the painting with its Catalan title, *La cama alliberadora de les amibes gigants* [*The Liberating Leg of the Giant Amoebas*], in the list of pieces exhibited in the show. It is possible that there are two versions of the same painting, a preliminary composition exhibited in 1936 and a finished product dated 1937. Nevertheless, the composition with the trademark barren surrealist horizon and the headless female with objectified body parts places the painting stylistically with *Painting* and *Desire* that links Varo's early work to that of her male contemporaries.

Double Agent painted in 1936 marks a turning away from mere imitation to thoughtful restructuring of space suggesting entrapment and the sexual tension felt specifically by a woman artist working with surrealist iconography. *Double Agent* reveals sexual tension through ambiguous gender identity restricted to the enclosed interior space. The painting replaces the typical surrealist horizon, which suggests limitlessness, with a shrunken space where all possible exits are disproportionately small compared to the figure on the left. The masculine head and torso of this figure sporting curvy feminine legs confuses the sexual identity of the person. A large winged insect clutching onto its back threatens to strike at any sign of movement and accentuates the static pose of the figure. The gray wall decorated with huge isolated breasts and foliage growth dominates the background with the threat of over-

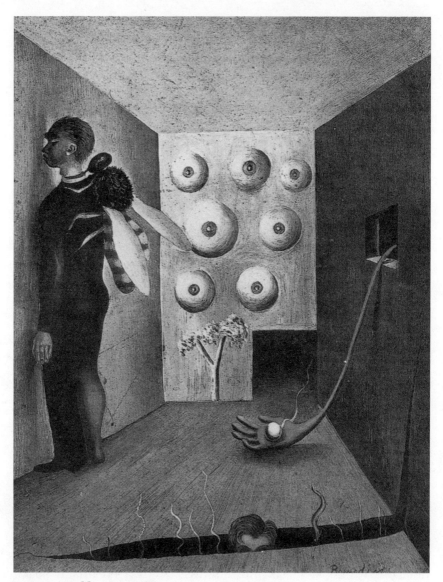

R. Varo. *Double Agent* **1936.**

bearing female sexuality. Varo interprets this female sexuality as a
sterile, gray, petrified representation of nature. The red elastic
hand entering through a dark square opening carefully cradles a
sperm-like ball as though to guard it or protect it from falling into
the crack in the floor. The erotic nature of these objects confined

to an unwelcoming space suggests a world of sexual tensions and misconceptions. The disproportionate scale and the random combination of male and female sexual images defy the label of a bipolar, purely female or purely male sexuality. Varo plays the surrealist game of exploring blatant, exposed sexuality but by combining both male and female elements she creates a startling androgynous iconography.

Janet Kaplan in her biography of Varo has related the intensity of the enclosed and trapped space to the growing political unrest in Barcelona in the year the painting was executed, 1936. However, while the tension in the painting does suggest conflict, the sexual content is striking and points to the strangely perverse notion of static female sexuality. The person trying to sneak a peek from beneath the floor doesn't emerge quite far enough to get a glimpse of the strange and disturbing surroundings. The wavy red hair could belong to Varo herself who, as the artist, appears in the tense ambiguous sexual space yet remains hidden and on the margin. The frustration of restricted movement and claustrophobia implied by her use of spatial relationships emerges as a continual theme in Varo's work.

Varo began to infuse her work with more personal symbolic and allegorical iconography that incorporated surrealist themes but intentionally focused on more profound issues of self-representation as problematic for women artists. The plethora of images in Varo's body of work concerning travel, escape, and journey have been cited by Whitney Chadwick as allegorical of Varo's desperate flight from Europe to Mexico during World War II.[29] Janet Kaplan links the consistency of this theme in Varo's work to her status as a lifelong exile in Mexico. These images do include notions of a physical departure but there also exists a metaphysical or spiritual side of Varo's continual search. Her many scenes of exploration or escape reveal the artist herself in search of creative autonomy.

The Tower from 1947 fuses the reconstruction of space and surreal pictorial narrative in a painting that alludes not only to Varo's flight from Europe to Mexico but also to her stylistic intentions to recreate the representation of woman in surreal art. The enclosed space of *Double Agent* is redirected in *The Tower* to a stagnant pond encircled by a crumbling brick wall with a rickety ladder propped against the side, suggesting the possibility of escape. A dark, empty phallic tower emerges from the pond but offers no light or refuge.

R. Varo. *The Tower* 1947.

The repetition of the three small female figures and their spatial
relation unite the past, present, and future. One woman flees from
the central space occupied by the wall and pond along a path to the
left curving toward the barren landscape. The same small woman
balances precariously atop a makeshift unmoving windmill floating
in the pond that emphasizes the stillness of the central scene. The
third repetition of the figure returns to the walled-in pond from the
right side of the composition. She is riding a tricycle along a wind-
ing path leading from the distant horizon. The apparent symbolism
of wartorn Europe suggested by the deserted tower is obvious, yet
the persistence of time and memory becomes more important in
the painting when the viewer turns her attention away from the
wall and pond and toward the fleeing and returning motion of the
figures. Varo certainly alludes to her political flight from, and the
desire to return to, her homeland through surreal iconography but
she also develops a particularly active female figure that defies the
stagnation of the crumbling phallocentric ideology of European
surrealism. The timelessness suggested by the circular motion of
the female figure breaks the canvas into three distinct moments,
yet unites the allegory of growth and change through continual

movement. Varo begins with this painting to represent woman in a new light. The movement and repetition of the female figure ironically overshadow the surreal horizon, dreamlike landscape, and juxtaposition of unrelated objects. No longer the body limbs of Hans Belmer's *Dolls* or Breton's "beautiful object," the woman in Varo's painting is mobile and active; she dominates the aging surreal landscape.

Later in her life Varo declared herself free from surrealism and often poked fun at what she considered an "old boys' club." She obligated herself artistically to leave the group in order to develop her own artistic identity, which would allow her a certain female subjectivity not found in surrealism.[30] In *Rupture* of 1955, Varo reenacts on the canvas her departure from demons of the past. Kaplan reads this painting as an autobiographical outlet for Varo who "was still working out complex issues of independence, family, powerlessness and power . . . Varo felt the disapproving scrutiny of family and neighbors as she left her husband and her country to run off with a foreigner."[31] Although Varo did leave her husband Gerardo Lizarraga in Barcelona and went with Benjamin Péret to Paris in 1937, the painting from 1955 presents a positive, productive escape. Beatriz Varo, Remedios's niece, reads the painting in Jungian terms claiming that "the search for the future and consciousness is indicated by the right side, just as we see the figure in *Rupture* descending the stairs on this side."[32] While it is certain that Varo was an avid reader of Jung, the multilayered iconography and implicit allegory of the composition also deserve attention. One observation that Beatriz Varo makes about the snails as "hermaphrodite beings, and therefore an object of attention for surrealist women"[33] links this painting to the hermaphrodite figure in Varo's earlier painting of 1936, *Double Agent*. This aspect of static sexuality allows the female painter to incorporate notions of the erotic without falling into the male-established pattern of representing the sexualized female Other. However, *Rupture* stands out as one of Varo's most complex compositions because the juxtapositions of time elements attack the viewer's sense of chronology. The figure is suspended in midstep as she breaks her stride to peer back at the disapproving faces of the past. The slow-moving snails in the foreground spatially break the focus on the figure and interrupt the rhythm of her run down the stairs. This awkward, restricted use of space that Varo creates as she depicts a figure, perhaps herself,

R. Varo. *Rupture* 1955.

fleeing from a house haunted with peering eyes, is reminiscent of *Double Agent*. Walls loom above the central figure, closing her in and hiding that which lies outside. However in sharp contrast to *Double Agent*, the figure in *Rupture* acts determinedly as the motion of the descending figure leads the viewer eventually out of the framed space. The figure in motion pulls her cloak close around her and scowls up at the faces in the windows as she hurries away.

The smirk on the figure's face in *Rupture* belies the ominous shadows, high reaching walls, fluttering curtains, and stark tree line of the composition that imply entrapment, insecurity, and fear. The surreal elements of *Rupture* such as the numerous sheets of paper fluttering out from a door left ajar, or the dry leaves that convert themselves into snails that climb a brown grass wall add the appeal of the incongruous to the composition. The papers flying out of the door chasing the figure down the steps can't possibly catch her and the pages are blank and useless. The leaves are brown and dead, the snails will never reach the top of the wall; if they do, the figure will be miles away. Thus, the surreal details of the painting represent remnants of what the figure leaves behind. She is the only unattached mobile agent in the painting. Just as the figure in *The Tower* moves repeatedly through time, this figure observes the past yet moves toward an unknown future. Her foot, poised and ready to make the final step, accentuates the motion in contrast to her stagnant and dying surroundings.

The metaphor of journey combined with an acute awareness of her own subjectivity come to the forefront in *Exploration of the Sources of the Orinoco* of 1959. Peter Engel states that this painting presents a journey that is "at once mythic and real."[34] In this late painting Varo depicts herself in a fantastic vessel designed like a man's waistcoat that apparently restricts her movement. Conflicting interests of freedom and confinement weave together androgynous sexuality with accepted social roles. A dichotomy becomes apparent: the composition expresses limited freedom, the figure travels but is confined to a small, restrictive vessel made out of a man's waistcoat. The symbolic value of the waistcoat suggests that in order to be an explorer, one must dress and act like a man. This image contains a multilayered iconography that seems to send contradicting messages of the mythic liberation of women and the very real societal restrictions. On the one hand, Varo paints a version of herself in the role of the explorer who reaches the outer limits of

R. Varo. *Exploration of the Sources of the Orinoco River* **1959.**

what is known in order to retrieve information. On the other hand, the figure sits motionless, crowded into a tiny space pulling on thin strings in order to steer the vessel. The mood is somber; her eyes are darkened and covered by a bowler hat. The restrictive space paired with the theme of exploration creates a dichotomy or a visual paradox commenting on the supposed freedom of the figure. She is belted into the vessel and the controlling strings run through her coat's shoulder buttons, tying her to the vessel and making them one in the same. The figure's mobility depends on the unnatural contraption she steers, which in turn strips her of the capacity for independent movement.

Varo's sophisticated composition recasts natural spaces as appropriated by humans. Nature exists in subordination to the definitions of the explorer, for the magical fountain housed in a large hollow tree trunk exists for us, the viewer, only because it was discovered by the explorer and consequently painted by the artist. Thus the secret source of the Orinoco symbolically reinforces a distinctly human presence in the appropriation of nature instead of standing alone or "undiscovered" as a natural phenomenon. In this metaphorical exploration of space and spatial relationships between human beings, nature and machinery, Varo tests conventional notions of human domination over natural and mechanical space. Just as the enclosed spaces in her earlier paintings confine her figures, producing a certain unsettling, claustrophobic image for the viewer, in this painting the space becomes so shrunken that it is what defines the figure. The limited movement of the boatlike contraption alludes to larger social limitations imposed on women. The man's coat, hat, and the waistcoat-shaped vessel become elements of the disguise the figure adopts in the gender role-play.

Judith Butler discusses this idea of gender identification as an imposed set of rules or a social script. She discusses the idea of "gender coherence" as the genealogy of the constructed identity. The gathering of attributes that equal one or the other gender is related to notions of power. Therefore a person cannot be a sex and Butler concludes that gender is performative.[35] Varo, three decades earlier, created an image that crosses established gender boundaries and implies that social power codes privilege one gender over the other. It is precisely these gendered codes that become mistakenly accepted and identified as natural and consequently construct the explicit power structure that Rodoreda and Varo attempt to redefine.

The social code assigned to women in Spain during the 1930s and 1940s is a central theme in Mercè Rodoreda's novel *La plaça del Diamant*. Although she did not publish the novel until 1962, Rodoreda incorporates certain surreal moments into the narrative in order to question these social codes but is by no stretch of the imagination a surrealist writer. Her work has not been traditionally categorized as surreal nor did she employ Breton's idea of automatism in her writing, and it is clear that her background as a journalist influences her meticulous, direct, and often jarring style. However, Rodoreda has been acknowledged as a writer who in some way transcends traditional nineteenth and twentieth-century Spanish realism. Mario Lucarda claims that Rodoreda's narrative "goes beyond mere realism in order to stress those more significant aspects and give them symbolic value."[36] Therefore, the surrealist techniques of disorientation, random association, and misogyny in *La plaça del Diamant* serve to express the silencing of women in society and the devastating effects on women of the Spanish civil war. Frances Wyers describes the war as distanced and on the outside in relation to the main character, Natàlia.[37] However, the narrative reveals that the war actually defines Natàlia, it controls her and forces her, against her will, to marry, to send her son to an encampment so that he can eat, and to almost poison herself and her children to avoid starvation. In other words, the war is the protagonist that acts on Natàlia, although her version of the events may not be an official historical account of battles it is just as valid and actually compliments the purely historical accounts.

Rodoreda classified her own novel *Quanta, quanta guerra . . .* (1980) [*So Much War . . .*] in its prologue as an account not of the war of artillery and technology, but as interiorized experience of disruption, displacement, and dead bodies.[38] The same can be said about the depiction of the Spanish civil war in *La plaça del Diamant*. Natàlia doesn't act but rather reacts to circumstances presented to her. As J. W. Albrecht and Patricia Lunn have pointed out, Natàlia lacks the wit to assimilate and comment on her life as she narrates, thus the novel "escapes sentimentality by forcing the reader to imagine Natàlia's life."[39] In other words, the absence of emotion and the silence comprising Natàlia's narration provide the ideological space for a metatextual rendering of the character's psychological state. Rodoreda explicitly constructs a narrator who is naïve of her own growth process until the final scene of the novel. Therefore the reader traces her development by positing in the accumulated silences a fabricated, metatextual meaning and in doing so the reader helps create the Natàlia character that the Natàlia narrator doesn't seem to identify with until the closing of the novel. Natàlia's circumstance can be considered a form of emotional self-exile. Her inability to comprehend the political situation bleeds into her everyday life as she retreats into a small confined world of isolation. One of the best examples of the reconstruction of the seemingly destructive silence and the surreal incongruity lies in Natàlia's relationship with her first husband, Quimet.

Quimet is not portrayed as a likable war hero even though he eventually dies fighting for the Republican cause; on the contrary he bullies Natàlia into marrying him, repeatedly silences her, and goes as far as to rename her Colometa, or "Little Dove," thus claiming her very identity as his own. After a bout with tapeworm, Quimet reveals a strangely inappropriate pride to Natàlia who confides in the reader that: "Quimet deia que ell i jo érem igual perquè jo havia fet els nens i ell habia fet un cuc" [Quimet said that he and I were equals because I had made the children and he had made a worm].[40] This degrading commentary becomes even more so because Natàlia accepts it without protest; her feelings and reactions are absent from the text. Her maternity, a distinctly female function, equals the expulsion of an infestation in the eyes of her husband. Natàlia's failure to express herself is a tactic Rodoreda employs in the text that forces the reader to fill in these gaps and guess what her silence means and how this emotional violation feels. Just as Varo uses ambiguously gendered figures to attract the viewer's attention, Rodoreda coaxes the reader into a dialogue with the text specifically questioning the role of female sexuality and motherhood. The reader must reevaluate Quimet's distasteful remarks and create an inner dialogue for Natàlia. The character's lack of a logical response employs the same interactive technique of surrealism's illogical pairings and oneiric settings that require the viewer or reader's participation to decipher and give meaning to the image.

Sex and motherhood are often examples of these illogical, perverse, and eerie moments in Natàlia's life. On her wedding night she fears being split in two because her only knowledge of sex is that "les dones . . . moren partides" (54) [women . . . die split in two]. Quimet makes fun of her innocence and fear by telling her the story of Queen Bustamante whose husband "per no tenir feina, la va fer partir per un cavall i de resultes va morir" (55) [so as not to be bothered, he had her opened by a horse and consequently she died]. Stephen Hart concludes: "This passage—in a humourous way—conjures up the atmosphere of the fairy tale as a backdrop for Natàlia's first sexual experience."[41] Sandra Schumm reads the passage in a similar way: "Her fear about sexual intercourse—that she will be split in half by it—and, therefore, be led down the road of tears, causes her literally to burst into tears and confess her terror to Quimet. In contrast, this metaphoric cliché that reveals Natàlia's innocence and fear is probably initially humorous to the readers."[42] On the contrary, I find this passage neither humorous nor fanciful. Quimet is the person who plants the seeds of fear in Natàlia's head with his story and he doesn't soothe her but rather laughs out loud. The propagation of misogyny and fear blinds Natàlia to any truth about her own sexuality. She is completely disempowered and convinced that her body is not her own but at the mercy of possible sexual violence.

Surrealists embraced the sadomasochistic world of the Marquis de Sade as a paragon of sexual rebellion. Yet evident in this scene from the novel is the established phallic discourse of power and subordination of women. For as Breton states: "Sade is Surrealist in sadism."[43] Gauthier in her chapter on sadomasochism from *Surréalisme et sexualité* discusses the subjugation of women at the hands of the sadomasochistic fantasy where she is represented only as body parts, for use and disposal. Gauthier describes a reproduction by Jean Benoît on an invitation to celebrate the anniversary of the Marquis de Sade's execution. A large erect phallus destroys prison walls "and bends the bars of a window-sex organ that appears at the center of womens' legs that are open, repeated, and deployed to form the wings of an eagle."[44] This disturbing image of sexual oppression and violence recreates the female body into a type of barricade to be destroyed while positioning multiple female legs to represent the wings of an eagle. The surrealist obsession with violence and aggressive sexuality took for granted the female body as recipient of their subversion. The same violence expressed through sex that necessarily subjugates the female seen in Benoît's image resurfaces in Rodoreda's description of Natàlia's wedding night. The result of woman stripped of corporeal ownership ironically results in humor for Quimet and in an homage of great magnitude to the Marquis de Sade.[45]

Rodoreda links the sexual displacement of the female body to motherhood and pregnancy as well. When Natàlia becomes pregnant she sees herself as a huge balloon that some unknown power has inflated full of "una cosa molt estranya" (63) [something very strange]. During the delivery of the baby, which she calls a "bestiola" [little animal], she is deafened by her own screams and afterward hears the far-off voice of the midwife mutter that she almost suffocated the baby. The confusion, anxiety, and fear about sex and birth seem normal to Natàlia. She accepts her ignorance with a childlike complacency, which once again forces the reader to create the inevitable emotional repercussions. The misogyny inherent in the Queen Bustamante myth and the misogyny inherent in the cultural silence surrounding such "taboos" as female sexuality and childbirth are exposed as harmful and manipulative when told from Natàlia's point of view and then systematically unresolved in the text.

In contrast to the recurring theme in Varo's works of escape as liberation and discovery, Natàlia's escape appears as a regression into a fantasy world that slowly reveals her inability to understand and manage in a world that has been completely destroyed and turned upside down. Even after her second marriage, which does bring economic stability to the family, Natàlia's fear sends her spiraling into a dark, lonely, haunted existence. She convinces herself that Quimet, her first husband killed in the war, may still be alive to find her and ruin her new life. She fantasizes about how she misses the doves Quimet used to keep in their house, which at the time she loathed and even secretly shook the newly laid eggs in an effort to kill them off. She wanders through the park telling her life story to strangers, admires the trees as people living upside down with their heads stuck in the ground, and counts herself among the living dead: "ja va començar l'angúnia . . . i el no dormir i el no viure" (164) [then the anguish began . . . and the sleeplessness and lack of a will to live]. The external influence, the devastating Spanish civil war, paired with a slow internal spiritual degeneration caused by years of emotional abuse result in her enforced silence. Trapped inside her new home, she wanders the rooms confused and disoriented. As she wanders through the house her confusion and disorientation become apparent:

¿Entrava al dormitori del nen? Paret . . . Parets i parets i passadís i parets i passadís i jo amunt i avall rumiant la mostra i de tant en tant cap a una habitació dels nens, fent martell; i cap a l'altra i altra vegada martell i amunt i avall i parets . . . vivia com si visqués tancada en una presó . . . (165–66)

[Was I entering the boy's room? Wall . . . wall. Walls and walls and hallways and walls and hallways and I went up and down and around with
the same thing and once in a while entering one of the children's rooms
and up and down again . . . I lived as if I were locked up in jail.]

In the previous passage Natàlia's mental process reveals the disorientation, confusion, and uncertainty symbolic of the social crisis in
Barcelona after the civil war. Her identity along with the identity of
Catalunya has been severely shaken. Even her name changes back
from Colometa to Natàlia. The unfamiliarity and spiritual vacancy
she experiences in her own home juxtapose traditional notions of
domesticity with the splintered, paranoid ramblings of the jailed female. Only toward the end of the novel does she break the imposed
silence by screaming out loud in the *plaça del Diamant,* the place
where she met her first husband, Quimet. By releasing pent-up
frustration, she finally recognizes her fear of death and abandonment.

Both Varo and Rodoreda make use of surrealist devices in their
works in order to unsettle and disturb accepted cultural and social
norms. Both take issue with the problematic assumptions of female
sexuality and femininity displayed by surrealists and by society at
large. While Varo steers her artistic self away from surrealism in
order to seek out more liberating self-images, Rodoreda finds that
certain surrealist motifs define her particular vision of isolation and
despair of post–civil war Spain. However, given the similarities of
Varo and Rodoreda's work, Varo's disillusion with surrealism links
her more closely to the movement than Rodoreda. For example,
the writer observed automatism from a distance while Varo imi-
tated and practiced the technique. Varo never completely leaves
surrealism out of her work, for even when she ridicules the narrow-
mindedness of the surrealists she admits to the movement's influence on her life and work.

The specific instances when both women choose to subvert the
surrealist ideology and ridicule the surrealists' appropriation of
Freudian psychoanalysis are key moments in their artwork and literary production. The humorous moments are manifestations of
an irreverent voice, countering an established phallogocentric institution. Margaret Persin affirms: "This absent yet present female
gaze and voice may manifest itself, for example, in the manner in
which a female writer offers a tongue-in-cheek version of a cultural

artifact revered by the patriarchy."[46] According to Persin, female sarcasm and wit create an artistic space where the "absent yet present" female voice can be heard. In Varo's well-known painting from 1961 entitled *Woman Leaving the Psychoanalyst* and in the final scene of Rodoreda's Lacanian drama *El carrer de les camèlies* (1967), humor serves to break the rigidity of accepted paradigms of social failure and success as dictated by Freudian-based psychoanalysis.

Pierre Bourdieu states that the effectiveness of symbolic power lies in its misrecognition or in its ability to be absorbed into social structures and practiced unconsciously by both ends of the hierarchy. Those able to wield economic, violent, or intellectual power accept the terms as an ideological advantage or potential while those who would become victims support the power structure by buying into and contributing to the same potentiality.[47] Bourdieu states that figuring into the power equation all levels of a social hierarchy maintains the balance of necessary elements. Bourdieu also claims that humor functions as part of the system, for in order to commit a symbolic act of satire in art, for example, the subject presupposes a comfortable relationship with the target material. Thus the digressions that Varo and Rodoreda create in their art and literature specifically aimed at psychoanalysis and its relationship to the surreal do little to defame or criticize the target, in this case psychoanalysis, but rather perpetuate a discourse utilizing the terms and conditions previously apparent. In this performative or citational aspect, Varo and Rodoreda propagate a psychoanalytic discourse. Butler raises questions about the complicated nature of citation, especially of hate speech, and its implications of promoting a harmful discourse under the guise of legal jargon during the prosecution process of criminal trials.[48] She cites Foucault and his ideas of ideological repression of an act fostering linguistic discourse and actually promoting the very idea that was initially censored. But, the psychoanalytic discourse that Varo and Rodoreda undermine emerges in their work recontextualized in several ways, first in the voice of a feminine subject and secondly in a noncombative yet irreverent and sarcastic tone. Therefore the incorporation of a psychoanalytic discourse does not necessarily presume to destroy it, but rather to reevaluate and recast terminology in a critical light.

Varo's figure in *Woman Leaving the Psychoanalyst* neatly dis-

R. Varo. *Woman Leaving the Psychoanalyst* 1961.

poses of a miniature male head upon leaving a psychoanalyst's office while layers of her green robe seem to fall away from her face revealing a latent identity. Cecília Ce, the protagonist in Rodoreda's novel, finally comes to terms with her own lack of origins through laughter and self-recognition when she takes refuge in her past, indicative of a more innocent time and symbolized by her adoptive parents' house. She returns to this fabricated sense of home after suffering years of abuse and sexual exploitation while trying to literally find her absent father and metaphorically acquire the Language of patriarchal society.

Varo writes of her own painting: "Esta señora sale del psicoanalista arrojando a un pozo la cabeza de su padre (como es correcto hacer al salir del psicoanalista). En el cesto lleva desperdicios psicológicos"[49] [This lady leaves the psychoanalyst throwing the head of her father into a well (as is correct to do upon leaving the psychoanalyst). In the basket she carries psychological waste]. The figure exits from a door marked "Dr. F. J. A." that, according to Kaplan, Varo explained in her notes as a reference to Freud, Jung, and Alfred Adler.[50] She daintily holds the end of a long white beard dangling a small egg-shaped male head over a well. She carries a basketful of threads, a clock, and a small hand mirror that symbolize her remaining psychological baggage. Varo's observations of her own painting written to explain its content emphasize the ironic nature of the psychoanalytic cure. The figure deposits the head because it is the "correct thing to do when leaving the psychoanalyst."[51] The humor in the painting, as well as in Varo's short description, lies in its hypercorrectness. The speculation surrounding the possible autobiographical nature of the painting also exacerbates the sarcastic wit. Kaplan suggests that perhaps the painting alludes to Varo's own visits to psychoanalysts although she admits in her biography on Varo that it is undocumented if Varo ever did undergo therapy.[52] It seems that Varo's interest in alchemy and the occult, and her claim that she was "hopelessly superstitious" support a general mistrust on the artist's part of the psychoanalytic process, or any institutionalized form of therapy. Varo criticizes the idea of the process of transference in her commentary when she suggests that there exists a certain "correct" reaction upon leaving the therapist's office. Her sarcastic tone implies that there conversely exists an incorrect behavior as well, leaving the reader to imagine the spectacle. The issue of correctness as a formality foregrounds the action of the painting noted in the figure's comically exaggerated psychoanalytic success rendered in the literal disposal of neurosis symbolized in the dangling head of the father. Varo alludes to the Freudian construction of the Oedipal complex, that is, the metaphorical destruction of the father figure. By literally painting the small disposable head of a man, Varo satirizes the notion of a metaphorical killing of the father and represents the idea here rather flippantly. Therefore, not only does Varo debunk the idea of a correct process of mental healing, but also she trivializes the very nature of that process by representing the impossible: a physical and literal dismissal of the Father, Order, and in Lacanian terms the official entrance into culture: verbal Language.[53]

Rodoreda exposes her protagonist's irreverence toward the structured patriarchy through laughter. Critics have read the end of *El carrer de les camèlies* as a return to nothingness and the revelation of skewed identity and origins. Kathleen Glenn compares Rodoreda's novel to the traditional picaresque genre and specifically to *Lazarillo de Tormes*.[54] She notes that Rodoreda's protagonist is from humble origins and makes her way in the world through illegal means, like Lazarillo. However, Glenn states that despite Cecília's eventual financial stability "Cecília . . . remains an alienated and lonely outsider, and her status as "the other woman" reinforces the sensation of alterity . . . she is still in essence a foundling, a love child who is loveless, a woman of no significance."[55] Although Glenn does point out that the first-person narration includes commentary revealing self-doubt, confusion, and "partial or total lack of comprehension,"[56] at the end of the novel Cecília comes to terms with her nonstatus by laughing at the system that imposes names and values on people. She not only overcomes her obsession with her origins but also demands from an outside position as the "other woman" (Other to the sign of the Father) that she regain her past.

Kristeva discusses the nature of time and its relation to the father. She distinguishes between an ordered time, effectively prefabricated by the father and seen as socially structured time and speech, and that which exists outside of time.

> There is no time without speech. Therefore, there is no time without the father. That, incidentally, is what the Father is: sign and time. It is understandable, then, that what the father doesn't say about the un-

conscious, what sign and time repress in the drives, appears as their *truth* (if there is no 'absolute', what is truth, if not the unspoken of the spoken?) and that this truth can be imagined only as a *woman*.[57]

Read through Kristeva's filter, Cecília's desperate search for her literal father expands into a metaphorical longing to pertain to society as demarcated by time and language. Her rejection of fathered identity and the constraints of family lineage, also placed within the confines of time according to Kristeva, will allow Cecília to overcome her sense of namelessness. The final chapter of the novel reveals how she defies ordered speech through laughter. The repressed drives of the semiotic lost in the speech and sign of the Father emerge in the wordlessness of laughter and its multiple possibilities of meaning, or perhaps in its dismissal of meaning.

Cecília's story begins when she is abandoned by a nameless "shadow" on the street of the novel's title. She is found with the name Cecília Ce scrawled on a scrap of paper pinned to her bib. The kind neighbors decide to take her in and raise her as their own. From early childhood, Cecília obsesses about her real father, the one who must have given her the name. She repeatedly escapes from her adoptive parents' house in search of her father, convinced that she will recognize him when she sees him. At a young age she runs away from home permanently with Eusebi, a neighborhood boy, and they live in a slum district on the edge of town. Her life is intolerable as she views the world through a crack in the makeshift walls. Eusebi's violent, erratic behavior seems to set a standard for Cecília's relationships with men. She is repeatedly enclosed, marginalized, and abused at the hands of violent, wealthy men. Her story is a roller coaster ride of physical and emotional abuse, various pregnancies and abortions, fear, and confusion. Her only hope of escape is a pathetic and persistent desire to attend the opera at the Liceu Opera House in Barcelona and thus belong to the upper class. Undoubtedly, the story paints a grim picture of the reality of a single woman born without a family and left to fate's devices. But, the final chapter of the novel reveals a surprisingly optimistic turn of events.

The final chapter functions as a microcosm of the novel, for it incorporates a search, disappointment, and revelation within its own contained structure. Just as the novel traces Cecília's search for a father figure, the final chapter reveals that this father figure exists only as a fabrication in her mind, imposed by the patriarchal society in which she cannot function as an individual. Cecília searches all over Barcelona to find the gardener who worked at the house where she grew up, hoping that he will know something about the mysterious identity of her father. She unexpectedly meets the old watchman who used to work at her adoptive parents' house who informs her that the gardener died some time ago. The watchman, a compounded proxy father figure who stands in for the gardener and then again for her real father, reveals to the young girl that her identity, rooted in a sense of origin, must be recognized instead of found. Cecília finally embraces her lack of identity as a type of personal freedom and through the medicinal power of laughter she regains her youth and innocence. Rodoreda brings the narrative full circle by ending the novel on the same street where the abandoned baby Cecília first appeared. This completion of a metaphorical life cycle brings Cecília back to her childhood through the memories of the watchman.

The watchman's stories tell of the young child's infancy, and his memories of her sleeping in her cradle encapsulate the lives and deaths of all those adults influential in her young life. The watchman jumps from entertaining memories of the baby Cecília to pondering the permanence of death defied by the souls that escape from the cemetery. The cradle to the grave allegory of this digression alludes to the timeless metaphor of the journey through life. Cecília makes sense of her own life only when another narrator reconstructs the events for her. The narrative technique of introducing a character that possesses memories of her life that Cecília does not poses questions about the nature of self-knowledge and consequent identity. Rodoreda effectively restructures Cecília's childhood through the words of the watchman that exist outside of chronological time as well as beyond the concept of familial inheritance. He disregards her desperate search for a father, filling the vacuum instead with his memories that Cecília appropriates as her own. Ironically, during the course of their conversation, it becomes clear the watchman found the baby Cecília abandoned on the street. He tells the story of her metaphorical birth, finally giving her the information she needs to construct a sense of beginning that has eluded her before. The baby's cry becomes an important identifying mark of autonomy just as laughter does for the adult Cecília. These nonverbal expressions are the bookends of Cecília's story as

Rodoreda presents it to the reader. Her entrance into society as an infant and then later at the end of the novel as a marginalized yet liberated woman are distinctly expressed through chaotic, nonordered, nonsymbolic forms of expression.

When the watchman first found the baby Cecília he thought she was just a pile of stolen goods that a robber had left behind. Only when he heard her cry did he realize that she was indeed an infant. She explains in her reported speech that what he really wanted to do was catch the thief rather than pick up the stolen goods but "m'havia sentit i havia vist el gos i havia corregut per espantar-lo perquè no em fes mal"[58] [he had heard me and had seen the dog and he ran to scare it away so that it wouldn't hurt me]. The infant's cry parallels Natàlia's cry at the end of La plaça del Diamant which she describes as "un crit d'infern . . . era la meva joventut que fugia amb un crit" (188) [a hellish scream . . . my youth escaped with that scream]. In both cases, female characters, marginalized from the symbolic laws of language, give voice to their existence and identity through primal screams. Rodoreda makes a poignant narrative choice in that her protagonists make their presence known, to others or to themselves, outside of the linguistic boundaries that label, constrain, and muffle their true identity. Thus, the cry from the infant and the scream from a grown woman serve the same purpose: to give form to the unknown, the unspeakable, that part of them that lies outside of symbolic structure.

Cecília's life becomes symbolized in the last chapter in another memory sparked by the watchman's tales. She remembers a pet bird that killed itself trying to get out of a cage and she admits that "amb allò de l'ocell havia descobert que tot es moria . . . volia que em posessin un vestit negre i preguntava si quan enterraven les persones també els enterraven el cap" (203) [with the bird episode I realized that everything dies . . . I wanted them to dress me in black and I asked if when they bury people do they also bury their heads]. The bird becomes a symbol of death and projects her fear of being buried alive, of not being able to see because her eyes are covered with dirt. The images of restraint, entrapment, and fear come to the surface of the text and emerge in Cecília's consciousness through the reconstruction of the past. By acknowledging her deeply rooted fear of death and abandonment, Cecília is able to overcome her lack of identity. She symbolically replaces the caged bird metaphor with another that mocks her youthful fearfulness.

The turning point in the chapter involves an inversion of the caged bird metaphor. Images of the jailed bird, buried human corpses, and the abandoned Cecília suggest an enclosed, inescapable reality. However, Cecília offers to buy the watchman a gift, presumably for his willingness to discuss and shed light on her obscure origins. When he rejects the idea of a cockatoo because it gives the evil eye, she makes a joke: "Vaig dir rient, sí, li compraré una cacatua i cada vegada que vindré a fer-li companyia la farem enrabiar perquè renegui, i després li farem beure til.la. Es va posar a riure de gust" (206) [I added, laughing, that I would buy him a cockatoo and each time that I came to pay him a visit we would make it furious so that it would curse us and then we'd give it some tea to drink. He broke out laughing with delight]. The bird image has changed from one of entrapment and violence to a humorous, nonsensical image provoking laughter. At this point in the chapter and for the short duration of the novel, every consequent exchange is met with laughter. The watchman offers Cecília a rosebush, much like the one her adoptive father bought for her in the first chapter of the novel. She responds positively, curls up in her chair assuming the position of a young girl with her feet up, elbows on her knees and her face in her hands. At this point she observes her surroundings and notes: "Tot era més gran i jo més petita" (207) [Everything was bigger and I was smaller]. After she again mentions the cockatoo, the watchman begins to laugh heartily and Cecília claims: "Jo també vaig riure i era com si m'anés tornant petita" (207) [I also laughed and it was as if I had become smaller]. Laughter acts as a bridge between the two characters as well as reconnecting Cecília to her youth. Laughter as a subversive means of communication seems to minimize the desperation of her futile search for a father figure. Once she has gained an awareness of her past through the memories of the watchman and recognizes that her origins have little to do with any one person, namely a father, she crosses the linguistic boundary that has held her down and silenced her throughout her life. Perhaps the laughter marks a revelation in the novel because it is the first time the reader has access to this joyful facet of the protagonist's personality. Instead of writing a tragic ending to her tragic life, Rodoreda has inverted our expectations as readers and gives Cecília a voice.

Her newly found voice also connects the protagonist to her past. Once again the watchman serves to reinstate precious memories that the infant Cecília could not possibly retain. He tells Cecília about the time when her adoptive parents invited him in to see how the young toddler had bunched up all the covers and grasped on to a pillow. Her adoptive mother remarks: "¡pobre marit el dia que en tingui!" (208) [poor husband, the day she has one!] and they all laugh. Then the group of adults leaves the sleeping child: "Van sortir a fora morint-se de riure" (208) [they left in side-splitting laughter]. Thus the adult's laughter prefigures Cecília's own wild adult laughter while sharing stories with the watchman. The recuperation of her lost youth and precarious identity seems finalized when the watchman explains how he found the baby Cecília and he swung her in his arms for a while, whispered her name, and the baby laughed (209). The cyclical nature of the novel unfolds with this final image of the watchman/"father" remembering rocking the baby Cecília in his arms. This image suggests that the shadowy father figure that plagued Cecília has been transformed from pain and fear to acceptance and laughter. Her unfortunate circumstances in life have not stripped her of the power to reconcile with her past. She admits earlier in the chapter her difficulty in answering the watchman's question about her life: "Vaig estar a punt de dir-li que l'havia passada buscant coses perdudes i enterrant enamoraments, però no vaig dir res com si no l'hagués sentit . . ." (206) [I was about to tell him that I had spent my life looking for lost things and burying loves, but I didn't answer, as if I hadn't heard him]. As she defines her life as a fruitless search for "lost things" and realizes that it has only brought her misfortune, she moves away from the feelings of lack and to a more fulfilling self-image.

The various moments of laughter in the final pages of the novel suggest a turning point in Cecília's life. She expresses herself freely through laughter as she embraces positive images of her childhood and infancy and discards the consuming idea of namelessness and isolation generated by the desire to obtain the correct language and consequent admission into male society. Cecília has always lived outside of social law, physically on the margins of society in the slums, and emotionally as a prostitute, floating from man to man searching for order and meaning in her life. The laughter breaks the walls that surround her and crumbles the serious, desperate search for the language of the father that will allow her entry into the symbolically controlled discourse of culture.

Rodoreda's use of laughter, just like Varo's use of humor, deconstructs patriarchal notions of entrance and exclusion into society posited by general psychoanalytic ideology. Both women uncover the potential to subvert through laughter. Neither woman seeks to destroy the existing paradigm, as Pollock suggests, but each casts a light on the exclusionary tactics of certain accepted patriarchal systems. However, Cecília's search for an adequate form of expression parallels Rodoreda's own search for a way in which to express herself artistically during the turbulent and often lonely years of her exile that led her to painting.

WOMEN'S PORTRAITURE: VISUAL AND VERBAL FORMULATIONS OF IDENTITY

Rodoreda's extensive body of artwork offers revealing insight into her literary works as well as into her struggle with isolation while living exiled in Geneva during the 1940s and early 1950s when she produced all of her paintings and not one piece of literature. It is understandable that Rodoreda would search for ways to express her solitude in exile through means other than words. María Lagos-Pope observes: "For the creative artist exile is an especially traumatic experience, not just because of the physical displacement from the native land but because his or her professional tools are inextricably related to the cultural and linguistic realities of his/her country of origin."[59] Rodoreda wrote all of her letters, diaries, and literary works in Catalan. During the years of Franco's reign in Spain (1939–75) the Catalan language was banned for public use. All public manifestations of the language were considered illegal, including theater productions and of course the publication of Catalan literature. For Rodoreda, the thought of writing in Catalan, even though she was physically safe from the consequences in exile, posed not only a legal problem but also an identity crisis. She had been stripped of her literary identity and perhaps felt less skilled writing in Castilian and, of course, how could she publish works written in a forbidden tongue? Bearing in mind these obstacles, painting offers a logical and liberating alternative to writing as a less linguistically specific form of expression. David Rosenthal explains Rodoreda's aversion to writing as she herself expressed it in an interview with the magazine *Serra d'or*:

I couldn't have written a novel if they'd beaten it out of me. I was too disconnected from everything, or maybe too terribly bound up with everything, though that might sound like a paradox. In general, literature made me feel like vomiting.[60]

Writing for Rodoreda during these years was a source of anguish, a glaring reminder of what she had lost with the fall of the Second Republic into the hands of Franco's dictatorship. Rodoreda's portraits of women compared with those of Remedios Varo offer insight into the conflicting ideas of motherhood and isolation present in both artists' work.

Rodoreda's human figures appear as disproportional, geometric shapes that pay tribute to the painters she herself loved, who are notably all men: Pablo Picasso, Joan Miró, and Paul Klee. Oversized heads occupy the entire space of the canvas and sit on tiny, trunk-like, armless bodies. Almond-shaped eyes opened wide stare straight ahead as if frightened or startled, confronting the viewer with an unsettling gaze. The likeness to Picasso's female figures in his celebrated painting *Les Demoiselles d'Avignon* (1907) is evident in the African masklike facial structures as well as in the distorted human features that challenge traditional notions of angle and perspective.

An untitled watercolor from the Fundació Mercè Rodoreda painted sometime during the 1940s or 1950s is a confrontational representation of woman. The naïve composition and distorted masklike expression are accentuated by Rodoreda's trademark: wide-set eyes staring out confronting the viewer. Rodoreda suggests hair with three lines projecting from either side of the figure's head, gently curved yellow lines on the right side and less tamed purple lines flipping up on the left. She wears a boldly patterned blouse with puffy sleeves that seem to grow directly from her body. The dark zigzag pattern of the blouse sleeves contrasts sharply with the curvy lines of her hair. Perhaps this watercolor is an intimate self-portrait, revealing two opposite sides of her personality: the strict and ordered right side and the carefree, unruly left. The watercolor echoes an ekphrastic passage, a written description of the plastic arts, in Rodoreda's short story *Paràlisi [Paralysis]*. The protagonist/painter describes verbally her own painting of a woman: "mitja cara ratllada amb ratlles fines"[61] [half of the face striped with fine lines]. Maryellen Bieder describes this image that could very well be

M. Rodoreda. Untitled watercolor c. 1953.

a literary incarnation of Rodoreda's watercolor with the contrasting sides of the woman emphasized by her controlled hair on one side and the untamed hair on the other as "la mitad controlada y visible de la mujer es la mitad que reconoce el mundo; la otra mitad, . . . permanece invisible y desconocida"[62] [the controlled and visible half of the woman is the half that the world recognizes; the other half . . . remains invisible and unknown]. Rodoreda's watercolor and her written description reflect the dual personality of a complex, multilayered individual.

The watercolor has the feel of a classic portrait as the stoic character gazes directly out at the viewer. Yet this woman looks as if she expects something in return. Her aggressive eyes and partially opened mouth suggest that she is engaged in some form of conversation, perhaps caught in midsentence.

The framing of the figure resulting from Rodoreda's use of space and structure suggests an image reflected in a mirror. The idea of the canvas as a mirror is a common trope in the analysis of women's self-portraits such as those by the Mexican painter Frida Kahlo and Remedios Varo. Women painting women disrupt the traditional objectification of the female body, or what is called the male gaze, which refers to the subject position that traditionally placed men in the active role of seeing and therefore male artists were able to recreate through painting their own version of reality.[63] A woman artist who places herself outside the prescribed objectified role as model and instead seeks to recreate her worldvision must confront the renegotiation of the traditional painter and painted, the imposed male/female opposition. Therefore, many women artists including Rodoreda painted self-portraits in order to directly address the problematic position of female artists. Whitney Chadwick discusses the personal nature of women's painting within the surrealist movement: "alienated both from conventional social roles as women and from Surrealism's cultivation of woman as the femme-enfant they [women painters] were forced to derive images from personal experience rather than collective goals."[64] The self-portrait is a way for women to confront their identity through pictorial representation of their own experience, instead of universal life experience which was traditionally male and relegated woman to the objectified position.

Rodoreda's portrait of a woman, which can be considered a kind of emotional self-portrait since it is rather abstract and not a realistic rendition of her features, breaks Chadwick's mold in several ways. Rodoreda painted in the 1940s and 1950s and therefore had a short history of women painters to draw from, most notably the surrealists, but her works in general move away from the individual concrete experience of a particular woman. Unlike the autobiographical paintings by Kahlo, *The Two Fridas* (1939) or her shocking, brutal version of miscarriage in *Henry Ford Hospital* (1933), Rodoreda moves toward more universal representations of inner chaos and turmoil. The mirror image of the woman in the water-color represents a type of Everywoman, her powerful presence pays tribute not only to Rodoreda's own inner strength facing exile from Catalunya and life on foreign soil but also to the strength of the human spirit. Rodoreda creates abstract, depersonalized figures be-cause she is not concerned with telling her personal story but rather the story of female suffering, fear, and loss. Physical render-ing of inner fear, instead of the outward manifestations we find in Kahlo's work, exposes human, not personal, tragedy that allows the viewer who identifies with that fear to appropriate the emotion and make it her own.

Remedios Varo's use of the self-portrait aligns her style with that of Kahlo but only in the sense that Varo paints her own features recognizably in her figures. Varo tends not to play out personal strife on the canvas but rather portrays herself in various roles in surreal dreamscapes. Hayden Herrera reports in her biography of Kahlo that Breton's patronizing demarcation of Mexico as the sur-realist country par excellence deeply offended Kahlo, who repeat-edly said about the European surrealists: "they make me vomit. They are so damn 'intellectual' and rotten that I can't stand them anymore."[65] It seems evident in the repetitious themes found in her painting that Kahlo painted her own private and painful reality without any of the surrealist intentions of escape or universal epis-temological inquiry. Varo on the other hand incorporated themes of exploration, scientific discovery, and physical mutations, all rep-resenting experimentation in alchemy and metamorphosis as ways of intellectualizing the human experience. Her fascination with the creative process exemplifies her scientific curiosity and for the most part eludes themes of motherhood and childrearing typically associated with female creation.

In *Creation of the Birds* from 1958, a female figure resembling Varo sits peacefully at a table where she creates birds by refracting light with a magnifying glass. The figure is part owl and part woman, suggesting a harmonic convergence of creative or repro-ductive power and intelligence. The owl is mythologically linked to Minerva or Athena, the goddess of wisdom, and therefore is known as the wisest of the birds in popular culture. Varo's depiction of the

R. Varo. *Creation of the Birds* 1958.

female/owl creator is nurturing while scientific but void of the physical horror of birth found in Kahlo's work.

Celestial Pablum painted in the same year, is the only direct representation and overt criticism of motherhood found in Varo's body of work. A depressed, slumped woman confined to a tiny room in a tower listlessly feeds the waning moon spoonfuls of stardust. The moon itself looks unhappy and is locked up in a small cage, heightening the sense of entrapment in the painting. Chadwick interprets the painting as exposing the fear latent in childrearing. She describes the image as unique in its powerful portrayal of conflicts inherent in maternity: the giving over of the sexual being to the production of milk and the nurturing of the infant, the dramatic physical changes initiated by pregnancy and lactation, the mother's exhaustion and feared loss of autonomy.[66]

While Varo's painting does suggest the exhaustion involved in caring for an infant, the fear caused by ignorance surrounding motherhood is perhaps best expressed in Rodoreda's deformed, overwhelmed female figures in several of her drawings.

R. Varo. *Celestial Pablum* 1958.

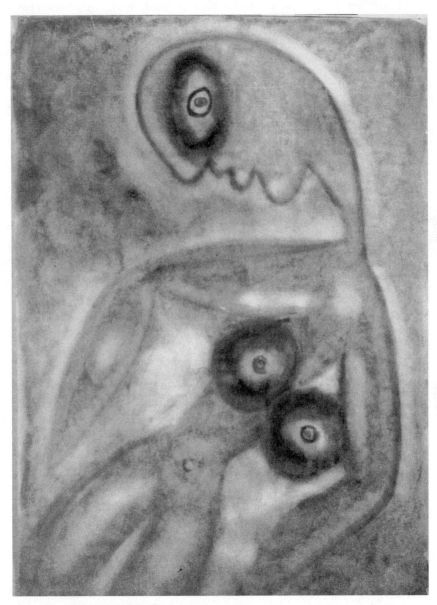

M. Rodoreda. Untitled nude drawing c. 1950.

One of her drawings speaks for the darker side of the artist's psyche concerning femininity and the oppressive demands of motherhood. The untitled, undated drawing from the forties or fifties depicts a female human figure falling precariously to one side. The limp figure lacks control over her movements and her limbs are undefined shapes only suggesting arms and legs. Her unstable position becomes more alarming when the viewer notices that she has no hands to break her fall; her arms simply taper off into points. Her bald head is pitched forward unnaturally over her body as if her neck were broken. The figure seems thrown off balance by the two large and darkened spheres representing breasts that don't fit onto her thin body but instead sit lopsided, connected to each other, but not to the figure. One visible eye is wide open, staring out from the canvas enclosed in a dark oval that echoes the dark circles around the breasts. Rodoreda defines texture in her drawing by smudging lines, erasing pencil shading to leave bright white streaks and by contrasting dark lines of the figure against a cloudy gray background.

The unsettling lack of balance in the drawing disturbs traditional notions of composition and line. The tilted figure is helpless and if she is falling she cannot save herself, for her body seems out of control and her missing hands add to her awkwardness. However, the most noticeable impediments are the disproportionate, darkly circled breasts. It seems as if their weight or faulty positioning causes the figure to struggle with her balance. Symbolically the breasts represent maternity, and in this case an overwhelming, insurmountable responsibility. The enlarged breasts in the drawing also function metonymically as feminine sexuality. They are spatially misplaced in the drawing and therefore cause danger to the figure just as misunderstood feminine sexuality poses a threat to women in society. We already have examined the shocking and unpleasant experience of Natàlia's wedding night and the birth of her first child in *La plaça del Diamant*. The drawing of the woman figure falling out of control is a parallel symbol to Natàlia's lack of dominion over her sexual self, creating a dialogue in which Rodoreda addresses the issue of oppressed, misunderstood feminine sexuality.

The distorted female bodies that represent a psychological discomfort with the roles of motherhood and woman are not the only connections between Rodoreda's artwork and her literary production. The importance of visual images in both *La plaça del Diamant* and *El carrer de les camèlies* becomes apparent as the protagonists of each novel observe and remember very specific paintings at key moments in the narrative. Both novels were published after Rodoreda's most productive period as an artist, in 1962 and 1966 respectively. The protagonists of the novels are both drawn to paintings and seem to identify their particular situations with painted scenes. Far more than mere coincidence, the presence of paintings as catalysts for self-realization in Rodoreda's novels stems from her own success of self-expression through the visual arts.

In *La plaça del Diamant* the protagonist, Natàlia, observes a strange and disturbing painting in Senyora Enriqueta's house:

> . . . figurava tot de llagostes amb corona d'or, cara d'home i cabells de dona, i tota l'herba al voltant de les llagostes, que sortien d'un pou, era cremada, i el mar al fons, i el cel per sobre, eren de color de sang de bou i les llagostes duien cuirassa de ferro i mataven a cops de cua. A fora plovia. (38)

> [. . . there were some lobsters with a golden crown, human face and a woman's hair and all of the grass surrounding the lobsters, who emerged from a well, was burnt, and the sea in the background and the sky above were the color of ox blood and the lobsters wore iron armor and killed with blows of their tails. Outside it rained.]

The surreal painting of lobsters emerging from a well into a blood-red war zone appears at various points in the novel as a reference to Natàlia's unconscious mind. The abrupt shift from the detailed description of the painting to the statement "outside it was raining" marks the significance of two separate spatial realities: that of the painting, and the external represented by the weather. While the painting occupies and defines the space inside Enriqueta's house and inside Natàlia's mind, the external world continues on uninterrupted and oblivious to human emotion and suffering.

During Natàlia's wedding to Quimet, the lobster painting reappears in the text as a symbol of violence. The wedding sermon focuses on how Eve was made from one of Adam's ribs and emphasizes how Adam had to educate Eve not to destroy the flowers in Paradise because "Adam, que era el pare de tots els homes, només volia el bé" (46) [Adam, who was the father of all men, only wanted what was good]. After the sermon Natàlia wonders how the priest would react to the lobsters in the painting, "amb el cap tan

barrejat, que mataven a cops de cua . . ." (46) [with that complicated head that killed with blows of its tail . . .]. Neus Carbonell
has suggested that the longhaired lobsters represent for Natàlia a
form of androgynous utopia and that the protagonist's evolution in
the novel moves toward "a new Symbolic Order where sexual di-
chotomies do not occur, and the suffering inflicted by them is also
extinguished."[67] However, in the sequence of events in the text the
image of the painting appears immediately after the priest's subtly
violent rendition of female submission to man. The physical violence of taking one of Adam's ribs in order to create woman, of Eve
blowing off the petals and thus destroying a flower and Adam verbally reprimanding her because she had hurt the flower conjure up
related images of violence for Natàlia. The first thing she thinks of
is the lobster painting and she wonders what the priest would say if
he could see the violence of the lobsters killing each other. Therefore, the painting is perhaps more directly related to the text and
completes the chain of violent images on Natàlia's wedding day that
eventually will define her sexuality, motherhood, and social reality.

The painting also alludes to the violence of the Spanish civil war.
Hunger, the death of Natàlia's first husband, and her own thoughts
of suicide stem directly from the oppressive conditions of wartime
Barcelona. The warring lobsters, which combine human and animal characteristics, can be considered an allegory of the civil war.[68]
The surreal juxtaposition of incongruous objects, such as lobsters
emerging from a well, or their long hair, seems to personify the ab-
surdity and incomprehensibility of the war. The recurring vision of
the disturbing painting expresses the violence that Natàlia cannot
imagine, much less verbalize. She relates to the painting as an expression of the unspeakable: the illogical death and horror of the
Spanish civil war. In a similar way, Rodoreda herself found that she
could express the isolation and rupture caused by the Spanish civil
war through pictorial images that were perhaps less difficult to create than stories at that time of her life. The visual images can symbolically allude to various personal experiences without the painful
recreation of minute details.

In another episode from the novel, Natàlia takes her two young
children to Enriqueta's house for safekeeping while she goes to
work. As soon as they arrive, "el nen, de seguida, es va enfilar a
mirar les llagostes" [the boy, immediately, situated himself to look
at the lobsters] and after he is called away "el nen tornava a ser a

dalt de la cadira, encastat a les llagostes. Plovisquejava" (91) [he once again climbed up on the chair, glued to the lobsters. It was drizzling]. Again, the contrast of the inner world of the house dominated by the painting and the outer world is highlighted by the sudden shift in narration from the child staring at the painting to the abrupt weather report. While the lobster picture plagues the inner, emotional realm with images of violence and death, the world outside continues to ignore the family's trauma.

Later in the novel, when the events of the war are heating up and Quimet has left to fight at the front, Natàlia returns one day to Enriqueta's house to pick up her children and she finds them staring at the painting. Their interest has become an obsession, for she exclaims: "Els treballs que vaig tenir per treure'ls d'allà" (130) [What a chore it was to tear them away]. In the next chapter, she is forced by circumstance to take Antoni, her son, to a youth colony for starving children. One of the emotional low points of the novel, this chapter describes the bombing of Barcelona and the hopelessness of a single woman trying to survive the war. Antoni's prior fascination with the violent lobster painting has become his own reality as he falls victim to the harsh circumstances of war depicted allegorically in the painting. The apocalyptic scene of the lobsters attracts the young boy's attention but ironically the iconography narrates his own shattered familial situation.

Rodoreda's protagonist, Cecília Ce, from *El carrer de les camèlies,* also sees her own morbid situation represented symbolically in a painting. The curious scene that occurs at the low point of Cecília's life involves a portrait of a woman. Cecília is living with Eladi, who forces her to drink cognac in excess, eat, sleep, and parade around the house naked, yet refuses to touch her for fear she will "tarnish" (153). One day when she has been left alone in the house, Cecília decides to search for her suitcases and clothes and happens upon a portrait.

> Em vaig quedar sense respirar de tan misteriós que vaig trobar-lo. Era una noia de cabells foscos, tallats curts, partits per una clenxa, amb un serrell que li tapava tot el front. Tenia els braços plegats damunt d'una taula, descansava la cara en els braços, i amb els llavis una mica enfora mossegava un collaret de perles. El que fascinava eren els ulls, que miraven fixament amb la nina una mica enlaire i a sota d'aquelles ulls n'hi tenia dos més d'iguals i no es podia acabar de saber si mirava amb els de dalt o amb els de baix o amb tots quatre alhora. (145–46)

[It took my breath away there was so much mystery in it. It was of a girl with dark, short, parted hair, with bangs that covered her forehead. She had her arms crossed on a table, she rested her face on her arms and with her pouting lips she chewed on a pearl necklace. The fascinating thing were her eyes that stared with the pupil on the top part of the eyeball, and below those eyes were another two exactly the same yet it was impossible to tell if she was looking with the ones on top or the ones on the bottom, or maybe with all four at the same time.]

The reader cannot be sure that the four-eyed woman is not just a hallucination due to Cecília's demoralized state of constant inebriation, yet the fact that her breath is taken away by the pouting four-eyed woman in the painting connects this scene to Rodoreda's own artistic production. Once again the idea of a painting acting as a mirror and reflecting a horrific and undesirable reality, as seen in her own artistic representations of women as well as in *La plaça del Diamant*, links her artistic compositions to her literary production. Cecília pauses in front of the portrait confused by the gaze of the woman. She can't tell where she is looking just as she herself lives in a disorienting, somewhat surreal circumstance. The portrait reflects Cecília's own directionless life as she identifies with the woman's directionless gaze.

Aside from symbolic interpretations of the portrait, the recurring use of painting that we have seen in two of Rodoreda's novels heightens certain narrative moments by creating images allegorical to the character's experience. Thus, the reader must decipher the inclusion of the visual into the written and in doing so we discover the impact and authority that a painting has in the narrative and how Rodoreda crosses narrative boundaries. Margaret Persin explains this idea as reading the writer's own analytical process of representation: "The reader of the literary text must read and interpret the reading process of the writer, who, in turn reads and interprets a visual text."[69] By describing an image with words, Rodoreda forces the reader to recreate not only the images of the narrative but also the extratextual image of the painting. That is to say, the painting exists as a work of art outside of the text, separate from the events that shape the character's lives and therefore as a timeless artifact attains a certain authority within the text. This leap from textual narrative to visual recreation disrupts traditional linear storytelling and introduces an association between words and images that enhances the symbolic value of the text. As readers, we must be willing to *see* the portrait as Cecília sees it and then evaluate not only her reactions to it but our own reactions as well.

One of the other pencil-and-charcoal drawings reveals yet another side of Rodoreda's artistic talent and affirms her dedication to issues of female identity. Another drawing of a female figure, again without a date but executed sometime during the forties or fifties, stares with wide eyes at the viewer. However, her elongated body stretches the length of the canvas and, in contrast to the other works mentioned, her head is quite small, only occupying the very top portion of the picture. The mood of this drawing contrasts with the aggressive mirror image of the first watercolor discussed and bears none of the violent sexual imagery of the other drawing. The figure is thin-waisted, wide-hipped yet dainty and holds her hands up defensively to her chest with her fingers spread apart. She wears a patterned striped skirt that echoes the pattern of her braided hair. The attention to detail on clothing and hair, not unlike that of the watercolor, seems to indicate the socially imposed rules of female adornment. However, this drawing fits neatly into the trio presented as it links the works together through erotic female imagery. The clothed figure cradles two large round breasts in her arms. Similar to the other drawing of the unbalanced anatomy, this woman also seems to struggle with body parts that do not seem to be her own. This is another attempt on Rodoreda's part to reveal symbolically the troublesome female and maternal role that she herself refused to play. She had left her only son and husband behind in Barcelona never to remarry, and her long-term relationship with the married Armand Obiols was often frowned upon by members of her own supposedly liberal group of friends. Therefore, the pictorial image of an adorned woman struggling with her feminine identity suggests the conflicting emotions Rodoreda may have felt about her own circumstance.

Another important aspect of Rodoreda's drawing is the connection it provides to other artists of her time. Imitation of style suggests that Rodoreda studied other painters, was aware of current trends, and consciously worked toward perfecting her own style. Rodoreda's drawing of the tall female figure adorned with striped clothes holding her hands up to her chest bears a striking resemblance to a virtually unknown clay sculpture by Pablo Picasso. One of Picasso's lesser-known clay pieces is entitled "Woman With a

M. Rodoreda. Untitled drawing of woman c. 1950.

Mantilla" from around 1949.[70] The painted clay statuette wears a similar designed dress; her elongated body widens at the hips as does the figure in Rodoreda's drawing. Both the drawing and the clay statue place the woman's folded arms, hands spread open, framing large, uncovered breasts. The most notable distinction, however, is the calm, controlled facial expression radiating authority on Picasso's figure compared with the startled look of surprise that Rodoreda gives her drawing. Nevertheless, it is doubtful that Rodoreda actually saw this statue because by 1954 she was living in Geneva and Picasso pursued clay-work in southern France. Also, since clay wasn't his primary medium, the pieces may not have been shown or circulated in a public forum. In any case, the similarity reveals Rodoreda's attention to detail, line, and form. Her love of Picasso's work and its influence on her own style is a well-known and evident fact. The clay figure bears the stamp of Picasso's signature style in the voluptuous curves and distorted proportions of the female body. However, Rodoreda challenges representations of the female body that elicit erotic pleasure or repulsion according to the male gaze. Her drawings strike a much more profound psychological chord and emphasize the unsettling fissure between being a woman artist and dealing with the inherent misogyny inscribed into images that manipulate and distort the female body.

As a writer whose language suffered from political prohibition, Rodoreda found herself in exile unable to use the tools of her trade. While the theme of exile has been studied in many of Rodoreda's literary works, the solitary images found so often in her art also speak out on the topic and deserve analysis. Rodoreda's most memorable literary characters struggle with isolation and imposed patriarchal modes of femininity. Visual representations of the literary found in her art can help understand the point of view of the writer. Just as Federico García Lorca's drawings that accompany the book of poems *El poeta en Nueva York* (1929–30) enrich and broaden our understanding of that complex work, Rodoreda's art may serve a similar function in redefining restrictive boundaries that separate the visual and the verbal.

ALCHEMY, ABJECTION AND THE POWERS OF METAMORPHOSIS

In the gap between visual and verbal the unique viewpoint of the feminine voice finds expression. Perhaps this dual form of expression led Rodoreda to embrace her inner exile and create overriding metaphors that link the two art forms. The visual/verbal dialogue places the artist/writer outside of demarcated disciplinary lines. In a way the individual must exile herself from these categories in order to successfully express herself. To try to bridge the gap between visual and verbal elements of literature and art involves overcoming the academic demarcations of art types. Breaking the rigid boundaries of narration, iconography, metaphor, and symbol frees the reader or viewer to explore various modes of innovative interpretation and comparison. In other words, the systematic need of institutionalized art appreciation to separate and categorize not only styles but also types of art lessens the possibilities of comparative analysis. Interdisciplinary approaches to painting, drawing, literature, and music enrich the social concept of art and its importance to modern society. In an attempt to contribute to an artistic discourse not limited to pictorial images or written descriptions, one final question will be considered: how can metamorphosis be metatextually linked to both the painting and writing of Varo and Rodoreda? Both women worked with the themes of feminine autonomy, sexuality, and motherhood, and metamorphosis provides a way to further explore possible feminist identities and combat the silence of enforced artistic exile.

In two short stories by Rodoreda, "La meva Cristina" [My Christina] and "La salamandra" [The Salamander] as well as in several paintings by Varo, the transformative qualities of physical development imply spiritual growth and movement toward self-understanding. This movement is in effect a proactive, self-imposed exile from the constraints of the female body, a rebellion against the highly eroticized, publicized space. Ana Rueda points out the equalizing effect of the transformative process: "Metamorphosis has erased all demarcations between animal and human, personal and eternal, past and present, here and there, which cease to exist as distinct categories."[71] While this totalizing force blurs normative visions of reality, in Rodoreda's stories the process of metamorphosis harmonizes conflicting societal notions of woman. Both female figures, the whale in "La meva Cristina" and the salamander in "La salamandra," challenge static notions of femininity and motherhood prevalent in the societies that systematically ostracize them. Likewise, the focus on metamorphosis in Varo's artwork metaphorically champions the development and change of women's roles in traditional patriarchy. Varo insisted on the transformative powers of alchemy, an alternative science based on the physical mutations of substances representing spiritual growth. Her paintings are populated with allusions to fantastical physical changes with alchemy as the catalyst. Kaplan notes in Varo's biography that she and her friend Leonora Carrington often concocted bizarre home remedies and even jotted down humorous "recipes" to provoke erotic dreams. Kaplan states:

> They (Varo and Carrington) had both long been interested in the occult, stimulated by the Surrealist belief in "occultation of the Marvelous" and by wide reading in witchcraft, alchemy, sorcery, Tarot and magic. They found Mexico a fertile atmosphere where magic was part of daily reality: traveling herb salesmen would set up on street corners with displays of seeds, insects, chameleons, special candles, seashells, and neatly wrapped parcels with such mysterious labels as "Sexual Weakness"—all used for the practice of witchcraft by the *curanderas, brujas* and *espiritualistas*. . . .[72]

The fusion of the empowered female as the creator of life and the exploratory "mad" scientist presents a unique portrait of the woman artist. Whitney Chadwick addresses the power of the female friendship when she cites that experimentation with alchemy was a way for women to "sever their work from male creative models and collaborate in developing a new pictorial language that spoke directly to their needs as women."[73] While both women cross established cultural boundaries of reason versus emotion, the newly created female subject embodies a fusion of traditionally masculine and feminine socially diagnosed qualities. The sailor in "La meva Cristina" who ingests the flesh of the female whale symbolically embodies this unique hybrid. An analysis of Rodoreda's two stories and of several of Varo's paintings will rely on ideas of alchemy and abjection, which serve as the basis to a discussion of metamorphosis in their works. The idea of alchemy as an alternative science engendering physical (chemical) and spiritual change and abjection as a transformative process of life and death help uncover the meaning of metamorphosis in Rodoreda's and Varo's work.

Paul Kugler discusses the role of alchemy as a transformative science both literally and metaphorically. Kugler claims that language and not the ego places demands on human beings: it is "language who calls us for literary exaltation, that insists that we speak."[74] His focus is on the psychoanalytic process of deconstructing phonetic associations between symbols (words) and emphasizing the speakers' random assigning of emotional values to sounds rather than to words' standardized meanings.[75] To clarify his ideas he turns to the practice of alchemy:

> The early alchemists were deeply involved on a literal level with the process of transference. They developed the art of freeing that part of their soul which was "asleep" and imprisoned in matter. The alchemical transmutation, the *magnum opus,* involved liberating those meaningful aspects of the personality that were unconsciously concretized through projection in the material world.[76]

The alchemist transforms a material or *prima materia* into an unrelated yet recognizable form and thus instills the physically altered material with symbolic significance of release. Precisely this interest in transformation and release emerges as a central theme in the later work of Rodoreda and Varo. The restrictions of the material body and tangentially the material symbolic world (language) drive both women to experiment with the implication of actual physical reconstructions of life. As Kugler states: "the transformation of the literal into the metaphorical is the essence of dream interpretation."[77] Alchemy and metamorphosis, growing out of the surrealists' dedication to Freud and dream interpretation, become reconstructed in these women's work as rebellious acts of subversion. Because the female body, a sacred erotic artistic space for men, is transformed by women into nongendered shapes and forms, namely animals and insects, the space becomes freed from monolithic sexual interpretation. A woman's body becomes disassociated with her sexual organs through metamorphosis, opening up the artistic space to allow for other types of representation and consequent interpretation. In regard to phonetic language associations as well as the transformative power of alchemy, Kugler concludes that "this process involves freeing the soul (the meaning concept) from its imprisonment in matter (the literal object of reference) . . . Matter is transformed into imagination."[78]

In "La salamandra," published in 1969, Rodoreda incorporates myth, legend, and fantasy to tell the story of a young woman suspected of witchcraft who is burned at the stake and physically transformed into a salamander. An omniscient first-person narrator who maintains her capacity of observation throughout her transformation tells the story. Elizabeth Rhodes defends Rodoreda's interest in feminist issues. She concludes that even though Rodoreda's women characters don't rebel, they are constantly aware of the injustice and continually commenting on the problematic situation for women in society.[79] However, the metamorphosis of Rodoreda's characters does in fact act as a textual rebellion against the eroticized space of the female body appropriated by male desire. It locates the notion of female in a metaphysical juncture uniting the woman and the salamander through a consistent narrative voice. Mercè Clarasó points out: "within the terms of the story itself we are not authorised to consider the salamander any less real than the woman it has replaced."[80] The consistent narrative voice metaphorically speaks strongly through a physical change that allows her to reevaluate her role in society when faced with adversity, not only as a woman and later as a salamander but also in both cases as a female outcast.

Ana Rueda and Janet Pérez note the differences between Rodoreda's short story and Nathaniel Hawthorne's celebrated novel of 1850, *The Scarlet Letter*. Most notably the shift in perspective of Rodoreda's story, where "the adulterous man is known and goes scot-free,"[81] inscribes the woman's desire with a more ambiguous social commentary than Hawthorne's highly moralistic tale of Hester Prynne. A woman's sexuality doesn't condemn her in Rodoreda's story, but her marginalization disempowers her and exiles her from society. Rueda points out that in Hawthorne's novel "the unmistakable moral intention of the story is never put in question."[82] The moral ambiguity of the salamander character resides in her lack of conviction concerning her own actions. She exhibits a "mixture of resignation and unawareness" clearly lacking a feminist consciousness or sense of injustice.[83] Once changed into a salamander, the narrator maintains her socialized submissive voice, never rebelling against her form, her adulterous lover, or her twisted fate. Therefore, Rodoreda's lack of moralizing refuses to pinpoint or accuse a sector of society for the woman/salamander's plight, but she does address the "double standard of morality" which allows men extramarital relationships and condemns

women for the same activity.⁸⁴ Once again Rodoreda has left moralizing, filling in information gaps, and synthesizing up to the reader.

The story begins under a weeping willow where the protagonist
is forced into a sexual relationship with an unnamed man. Through
the language used to describe their first encounter, Rodoreda fore-
shadows the transformation of the woman into a small animal.
While the protagonist looks into the mirror of the pond she claims:
"vaig veure la cara d'ell al costat de la meva com si des de l'altra
banda dues ombres m'estiguessin mirant"⁸⁵ [I saw his face next to
mine as if from the other side two shadows were watching me]. The
two shadows indicate the dual nature of the protagonist and of the
role the man will play in her transformation. The pond functioning
as a mirror not only reveals the dual nature of the characters that
will be developed in the story, but also indicates that she will one
day live on "the other side" of the pond, that is beneath its glassy
façade. This double vision at the outset of the story suggests a double reality or the possibility of various interpretations of the acts
that follow. This narrative technique contributes to what Rueda describes as the "contradictory textual signals that resist categorical
evaluation and undermine their (the readers') confidence in inter-
preting."⁸⁶ The reader then immediately expects duality to play a
major part in the telling of the story and therefore can make the
leap of faith necessary to fuse the narration of the woman with the
voice of the salamander. The verbs used to describe her reaction
to the man indicate pursuit and entrapment and also foretell the
woman's future predicament as an animal:

> I perquè no semblés que estava espantada, em vaig alçar sense dir res
> . . . però tot d'una em va venir por i vaig arrencar a córrer i quan em
> vaig adonar que m'aconseguia em vaig quedar sota del salze, d'esquena
> a la soca, i ell es va plantar al meu davant amb els braços estesos a
> banda i banda perquè no pogués fugir." (237)

> [So that I didn't seem afraid, I got up without saying a thing . . . but
> suddenly I got scared and I ran away and when I realized that he was
> following me and that he was catching up to me, I stopped underneath
> the willow with my back to the trunk and he stopped right in front of
> me with his arms open wide so that I couldn't escape.]

While the woman is unable to escape from the man physically or
emotionally and becomes his mistress, once she has been trans-

formed into a salamander she instinctually and ironically masters this aspect of survival and repeatedly escapes from dangerous, even life-threatening situations. However, while still a human being, the protagonist and the man are caught making love in the forest by his wife, who immediately places blame on the young woman, calling her a witch. The wife incites the hatred of the entire town that collectively and namelessly torments the young woman by hanging dead animal heads on her porch and she is eventually dragged off by the angry mob to the town square to be burned. The metamorphosis that the protagonist undergoes during the burning acts as a central axis of the story for it is both a death and a rebirth. Rhodes has noted that the thirteen paragraphs of the story "culminate in paragraph seven, precisely the one in which the burning protagonist actually becomes the salamander."[87] This exact positioning of the crucial action is intended to divide the narrative into two halves, or two lives. The woman notices her body transforming yet she is not frightened by the transformation: "I em vaig posar a caminar per damunt de les brases, molt a poc a poc, perquè la cua em pesava" (240) [I began to walk over the coals very slowly because the tail weighed me down]. As the turning point of the story, the woman's transformation is a physical manifestation of her marginalized position in the town that can be seen as a microcosm of society. She notices while she is burning that "cada home, cada dona i cada criatura era com una ombra feliç, perquè jo cremava"(240) [every man, woman and child was like a happy shadow because I was burning]. The unwarranted happiness of the townspeople emotionally places the protagonist outside of the communally conceived social unit as "un torrent d'aigua vermella," or the torrential red water that suggests the flames of the fire, separates her from the crowd. Her otherness becomes both physically and emotionally exaggerated with the metamorphosis, yet she continues to exist on the margins of society and maintain a presence there.

Her analytical abilities sharpen ironically with the devolution of her bodily form. *Boutell's Heraldry* defines the salamander as "generally represented as a lizard-like creature amid flames" likening the image to that of the burnt phoenix rising from the ashes symbolic of everlasting life.[88] The woman/salamander slithers away from the fire, not in spiritual triumph but rather completely transformed into a swampbound creature that lives in limbo; half on land and half in water.

The external world has not changed for the salamander, for she goes to the same weeping willow that opened the story and then decides to go into town. She returns to her own house that has been burned to the ground. She then goes to the home of her former lover and she watches from under the bed as he and his wife go about their nightly rituals before going to sleep. Suddenly the narration shifts from the exterior description to the interior chaos of the protagonist/salamander. The ordered life of her lover and his wife, exemplified in their marriage, their home, and daily routines, heightens the protagonist's sense of displacement and confusion. Her presence in the world seems to conflict with her physical self: "vaig començar a resar per mi perquè a dintre meu, tot i que no era morta, no hi havia res que fos viu del tot, i resava fort" (241–42) [I began to pray for myself, in my own mind, even though I wasn't dead I wasn't totally alive either, I prayed with all my might]. Therefore, her own transformation has served to heighten her ontological quandary from which she suffered initially as the "other" woman, the witch, the outcast. The double shadow from the beginning of the story has become emblematic of her own existence. She hears her previous life echoed in the words of the man who once told her "La meva dona ets tu; només tu" (238) [you, only you, are my wife]. In a warped repetition of the opening scene, the salamander/ woman hides under the bed and as she hears her lover and his wife she remarks: "Tot era igual. Només tu, deia ell" (242) [Everything was the same, "only you," he was saying].

In an act of defiance that breaks with normative behavior of the mistress, the salamander scurries up into the bed. Her presence in the bed with the man and his wife allows her to appropriate the sacred space of matrimony. However, the man moves a bit and "la cama em feia pes al damunt. No em podia moure. Vaig respirar fort perquè m'ofegava i li vaig fregar la galta per la cama, amb molt de compte que no es despertés" (242) [his leg weighed down on top of me. I couldn't move. I breathed deeply because he was suffocating me and I stroked my cheek along his leg, very carefully as not to wake him]. Even as the man squashes her, she tenderly rubs her salamander cheek on his leg. She is fully aware of her position as the outsider and accepts the pain for a fleeting moment of pleasure.

The next morning she is discovered by the man's wife who chases her out of the house swatting at her with a broom, ironically the symbol of the fleeing witch. The salamander is caught in the barn, tortured by some boys who throw rocks at her, and eventually takes refuge in the pond to nurse her hand dangling from a mere tendon. Three playful eels come along and bite off her wounded hand. As she watches the eels play with her hand as if it were a toy she remembers specific images from her spying post underneath the bed: "les cames penjades al costat del llit; . . . jo em veia sota de la creu feta d'ombra, damunt d'un foc de colors" (243) [legs hanging from the bed . . . I saw myself under the shadowy cross, on top of a colorful fire] and she concludes: "jo era a totes dues bandes: entre el llot, amb les anguiles, i una mica en aquell món de no sé on . . ." (243) [I was on both sides; in the swamp with the eels and a little bit in that world of I don't know where]. Once again the physical mutation implied by losing her hand brings the salamander/woman to a seemingly new level of understanding regarding her circumstance. Perhaps the salamander who takes refuge in the pond after living like a fish out of water can act as a metaphor for Rodoreda's own experience in exile.

As discussed, her emotional distress experienced in the solitude of living in exile halted her literary production. Perhaps the salamander's severed hand mirrors Rodoreda's own inability to write. Also her relationship with a married man, Armand Obiols, caused her years of unhappiness. In a letter to her friend Anna Murià dated 17 March 1947, Rodoreda wrote: "L'Obiols m'ha dit categòricament que vol tornar a casa seva. Jo no tinc una rival, Anna, el que veritablement tinc és un *enemic*. I l'enemic és l'home que estimo."[89] [Obiols has told me definitively that he wants to return home. I don't have a rival, Anna, what I really have is an enemy. And the enemy is the man I love]. Regardless of biographical coincidences, the metamorphosis in "La salamandra" taps into much more universal themes of emotional exile and displacement. Rueda notes: "Religion, politics, institutions and social laws are exposed, under the power of metamorphosis, as arbitrary and unessential discriminations."[90] Metamorphosis challenges prejudice and redirects upheld notions of ethics and morality. Adultery and witchcraft lose their polemical scandalous association in Rodoreda's story and become a backdrop for the physical and emotional journey of a being. Moral codes are broken, disallowing a finite reading of the story. The development of the narrative resides in the challenge of change and the ways an outsider or marginalized being looks in at the world trying to rationalize her lesser form of existence. Rodoreda avoids moral positioning on adultery, witchcraft, and capital punishment, pushing to the fringes of the text the righteous prose-lytizing often characteristic of these issues. Her focus is much more metaphysical, ontological, and philosophical.

In another story of metamorphosis, "La meva Cristina" [My Christina], Rodoreda employs a similar technique of ambiguous moralizing in order to subvert traditionally sacred ethical symbols. Throughout the narrative, Rodoreda reinvents the traditional symbolic importance of the story's biblical predecessor. The plot involves a shipwrecked sailor who is swallowed by a whale. While the sailor initially is grateful to the whale for saving his life, he suffers from hunger and thirst. Rodoreda's narrative contains deviant symbolism that strips her story of allegorical purposes compared to the biblical blueprint, the narrative of the great fish from the Book of Jonah.

When the sailor spies a green coast through the whale's partially opened mouth, he begins to pray and escapes through the meshy opening: "les barnilles s'havien obert com la porta d'una resclosa i jo vaig anar-me'n cap a la mar de Déu"[91] [the bars had opened like the door of a prison cell and I went toward the sea of God]. Up to this point, the whale functions in tandem with the sacred sanctuary of the great fish in the Bible story: the animal threatens man's trusting relationship with God and society while providing a meditative opportunity for redemption. But Rodoreda's whale swallows up the sailor again immediately after his escape, quickly destroying his sense of freedom and punishing him to the fleshy jail once more. Traditionally in Christian art the whale is equated with evil, which aligns Rodoreda's whale with the ostracized salamander/witch from her other short story. George Ferguson explains: "the whale's open mouth was often depicted to represent the open gates of Hell,"[92] thus the whale damns the sailor to an infernal existence.

Suddenly the whale is no longer a temple of the Father similar to where Jonah prays to God for deliverance in the Bible. But the whale, named Cristina by the sailor after his sunken ship and thus randomly gendered as female, "adheres to the myth of 'the Terrible Mother'" who, overprotective of her child, swallows him again into the isolation of her empty metaphorical womb.[93] However, the whale, in this case personified as the incarnation of the virgin saint Christina the Astonishing, serves as a vehicle through which the sailor in turn becomes feminized, not reborn in accordance with a maternal myth, but transformed into the abhorrent, rejected female. Thus the textual metamorphosis of the symbolic biblical great fish that Rodoreda employs strips the whale of symbolic reference to salvation and replaces it with a universal female. In this sense the textual symbolic slippage demands that the reader reconsider not only the moral implications of the biblical allegory but also the very nature of symbol and allegory.

The sailor recalls that when Cristina recaptures him, "va començar el mal viure" (254) [the hard life began] and he begins to torture the whale with a large knife, cutting up sections of the roof of her mouth to eat. What is not clear in the narrative is whether the sailor eats Cristina out of anger or for pure survival, for he claims: "me la menjava ben mastegada com havia fet amb la del mariner" (254) [I ate it up, chewing thoroughly, like I had done with the sailor] referring to a dead sailor that served as his food source when he initially arrived inside the whale. Rueda notes: the "story violates several cultural taboos, from the torture of the whale-mother and cannibalism to the repudiation of family law."[94] Saint Christina underwent similar torture. Her tormentors "had her body torn by iron hooks" and "her tongue was cut out"[95] just as the sailor jabs and slashes at Cristina's flesh with a ladle, "vaig tornar a clavar el cassonet" (253) [I struck again with the ladle], and cuts out a part of her tongue, "li vaig escapçar un gra de la llengua" (254) [I cut out a bud from her tongue]. The similarities between the saint's plight and the whale's suggest that Rodoreda drew on her Catholic education and combined that knowledge with the irreverence of the avant-garde to characterize a suffering female in a surreal rendition of a saint's martyrdom.

One of Saint Christina's miraculous feats was to "remain for a long time under the waters of the Meuse; indeed frequently she stayed there for six or more days at a time."[96] Rodoreda's sailor observes that the whale "La Cristina va enfonsar-se. Vam estar molta estona dintre l'aigua"(253) [Cristina went under and we spent long periods of time beneath the sea] and later she dies a martyr, having given her life and flesh to the sailor: "en aquella roca va morir, tota marcada per dintre" (255) [she died on that rock, all cut up inside].

The whale as virgin martyr Christina gives character, gender, and destiny to an otherwise figurative symbol. In the collected lives of the saints written in 1761, the "Vida de santa Christina, virgen y martyr" tells of her suffering at the hands of the ultimate patriarch

symbolized in her father. The seeds of Rodoreda's female characterization of the whale seem planted in the violent act of silencing:
"cortáronle la lengua, y fin ella hablaba, y fe entendía mejor"[97]
[they cut out her tongue and she spoke no more and better understood her faith]. Rodoreda then figured the whale not as a maternal
body or universal womb, but as the metaphorical space of bodily
violence that attests to a certain textual violence in the restructuring of myth. The whale must be feminine, for it is this very aspect
of her that the sailor ingests and consequently externalizes in the
pearl crust he wears. His association with the female has become
both an internal and external metamorphosis rendering him completely marginalized once he returns to dominant culture.

The parallels drawn between the sailor and the whale unite them
symbolically; the human feelings of emptiness become the physical
hollow of Cristina's mouth: "jo era com el buit de la galta de la Cristina" (255) [I was as empty as the cheek in Cristina's mouth].
Through his rebellious acts of cultural subversion, the sailor actually becomes like the whale. He ingests her meat, an act that leaves
him unable to eat once he returns to society for he claims: "tenia
el dintre com una nafra viva, rosegat i podrit per tota la carn ma-
lalta que havia menjat de la meva Cristina" (255) [my insides were
open wounds, chewed and rotted by all the bad meat that I had
eaten from Cristina]. His insides have mutated into the same sickly
state as the environment inside the whale; he has literally become
transformed internally through his disregard for the holy body. The
literal disfigurement of his entrails symbolically reveals an emotional or spiritual change as well. Just as the woman's physical
change into a salamander served as a catalyst to her emotional
growth, the sailor also experiences a physical change that matures
him spiritually.

The sailor undergoes an external metamorphosis while inside
the whale that functions as another form of appropriation of the
female whale's body. Carme Arnau affirms that metamorphosis in
Rodoreda's short stories frequently serves as a visible sign of marginalization and that the total sum of Rodoreda's characterizations
culminate in the formulation of an androgynous being: the feminized man and the masculine woman.[98] Arnau's observations support a recontextualized reading of the narrative symbols in
Rodoreda's story including the sailor's drastic internal and physical
transformation.

After years of living inside of the whale, the sailor declares: "A l'últim em vaig cansar" [finally I grew tired] and he curls up in a hollowed-out corner of her mouth to sleep or perhaps to die. Cristina soothes the worn sailor by covering him with layers of mucus that eventually form a pearly shell covering his entire body. The eventual expulsion of the irritant pearl/sailor from the whale's body doubly emphasizes his nonstate, for he is unwelcome inside the whale as well as outside in society. In order to save herself from the sailor's destructive behavior toward her, Cristina covers him with saliva creating the pearl that her system instinctually rejects. The sailor's unpleasant physical appearance prohibits his integration into society; he is nameless and placeless in either system.[99] When the sailor is finally free to leave the whale he describes the world as "el món dels llimbs" (255) [a world in limbo]. He is singled out by members of society for his external appearance and labeled "the pearl man." In a hospital the nuns try to crack open the shell revealing tender skin underneath, but the excruciating pain forces them to leave a section of shell on the man's face. This reminder of Cristina, which he describes as "tan ben enganxada, tan ben casada amb la meva carn" (256) [tightly stuck, so firmly married to my skin] will mark him forever as an outsider. The final words of the story that present the sarcasm of the town officials who mock the sailor's attempts to become a citizen confirm his position as eternally marginalized: "em va treure a fora, i anava dient: demà, demà- com una cançó" (257) [He threw me out while saying, tomorrow, tomorrow as if it were a song]. The sailor's unending quest for identity along with his constant reminder of Cristina, the crust of pearl "married" to his face, reveal the underlying desire and repulsion of the abject.

Kristeva's ideas surrounding the abject and abjection can be useful in understanding metamorphosis as an ongoing experience, reaching far beyond the limits of the physical. If we consider metamorphosis in Rodoreda's narratives as a form of rejection of an abhorrent object or place, the burning body of the woman who turns into a salamander or the decaying flesh of the whale, then metamorphosis facilitates the rejection of the improper and unclean, guaranteeing survival and life itself. Kelly Oliver explains that "the abject is what threatens identity"[100] assuming that identity exists apart from the abject but as Kristeva explains it, it also locates the unstable subject in a specific realm opposite to the Other. She in-

sists that the abject does not take form in an object, but is the sensation of a border, a tenuous position of constant flux between want,
repulsion, and death, just as the sailor's survival technique depends
upon consuming the whale's flesh. Kristeva states: "Food loathing
is perhaps the most elementary and most archaic form of abjection."[101] Inside the whale, the sailor becomes covered to his shoulders in "una glopada d'aigua amb un baf de peix mal paït" (251) [a
stream of water that stank like vomited fish] which is the regurgi-
tated whale's food source. While he is disgusted by the stink of rotting carcasses, he will want and consume the very flesh nourished
by the vomited fish. He is not separating himself from the abject
out of fear but constantly moving into that very realm that repulses
him, embracing it as part of him. After he has left his whale-home
and ventures out into society, he associates himself with her rotting
corpse, comparing his insides to hers as "rosegat i podrit" [chewed
up and rotten]. The connection between abjection and rebirth appears in Kristeva's essay repeatedly. Her affirmation "I give birth to
myself amid the violence of sobs, of vomit" signifies the process of
expurgation, the defilement that also purifies.[102]

The privileging of spiritual transformation in the story becomes
clear through the failed efforts of a chronological recording of the
sailor's mutation from human to pearl. His efforts to demarcate the
passage of time by slashing lines in Cristina's mouth only serve to
accentuate his hysteria and contribute to the mutilation of the
whale. Time becomes his enemy as each passing day gives form to
his entrapment and helplessness. His efforts give way to oblivion as
he retreats into a corner to die, yet this oblivion allows him to be
metaphorically reborn in another form, estranged and forever separate from his previous self. As Kristeva explains, "The time of abjection is double: a time of oblivion and thunder, of veiled infinity and
the moment when revelation bursts forth."[103] She later affirms that
abjection "is an alchemy that transforms death drive in a start of
life, of new significance."[104] Kristeva locates the magical source of
transformation within the abject, revealing the importance of alchemy not only to metamorphosis but also to the renewal of multiple identities. The mystical transformations of woman to
salamander and man to pearl link the physical metamorphosis,
through alchemy and abjection, to revelation. At the same time the
cultural relevance of Rodoreda's textual reconstruction of the
whale symbol from mediating sanctuary into female saint and mar-

tyr calls into question the permanence of symbols embedded in a collective social consciousness, generating explicit reformulations of literary conventions.

The revelation of character or subject position through metamorphosis emerges repeatedly in visual images of Remedios Varo's work. However, Varo avoids the violence of Rodoreda's physical metamorphosis and instead proposes a more cerebral, scientific interpretation of mutation. This aspect of her work is evident not only in the subject matter but also in her meticulous, detailed brushwork. Janet Kaplan notes that Varo's painting can be likened to "a medieval Book of Hours in its smallness of scale, minuteness of detail and luminosity of surface."[105] Kaplan explains that a Book of Hours was a small book of images inspiring hope and harmony to be carried around and used in daily prayer and meditation. Varo's work also seems to inspire deep contemplation as she combines skillfully and seamlessly randomly related concepts such as surrealism, science, fantasy, alchemy, metamorphosis, philosophy, and chaos.

Revelation or the Clockmaker from 1955 combines several of the aforementioned interrelated concepts while it stands as the best example of Varo's interest in the connections between verbal and visual expression within her own work. In a humorous letter created by Varo directed to "a scientist" dated 1959, Varo describes a fictional experiment gone wrong:

> alguien que ha pasado por la calle delante de la ventana ha proyectado su sombra sobre la mesa de experimentación y sobre las sustancias que yo tenía allí en emulsión; estas sustancias se han separado, dejando una minúscula y pequeña partícula brillante; una especia de perla, que ha salido por la ventana como una flecha, elevándose en el espacio y desapareciendo de mi vista rápidamente.[106]

> [somebody passing by on the street in front of my window projected his shadow over the experiment table where I had some specimens in solution; these specimens separated, leaving behind a minuscule, tiny brilliant particle; a type of pearl, that flew out of the window like an arrow, elevating itself in space and disappearing rapidly from my sight.]

In her letter she asks for the scientist's advice for she has released a substance that will destroy the earth's atmosphere in sixty-two years. She explains that obviously "no tenemos por qué inquie-

R. Varo. *Revelation or The Clockmaker* **1955.**

tarnos personalmente, pero hay que pensar en nuestros sobrinos y descendientes"[107] [we have no reason to worry personally but we must think of our nieces and nephews and our descendants]. Of course, the presence of some kind of pearl links the image to Rodoreda's pearl-encased sailor. The pearl becomes an intertextual symbol of metamorphosis representing the solidity and permanence of a material created from sand, mucus, and water. Also the beauty and perfection of a round white pearl becomes subverted in both cases at hand; Rodoreda's sailor is a monstrous outcast, and Varo's flying pearl will destroy the earth.

Varo's narrative reflects the iconography of her painting of 1955. A young man (who resembles Varo herself) sits at a table littered with clock mechanisms as a sphere of transparent white energy enters through an open window. The young scientist looks startled and knocks several pieces of clockwork off his table. The small room where he works seems oppressive due to the sagging cloth ceiling held up by the pointed tops of eight grandfather clocks. These large clocks tell the same time but represent different eras in the development of human history for inside the cabinet of each clock is a figure in period dress. Varo wrote a short description on the back of a photograph of the painting sent to her brother and she offers more information than is apparent in the painting itself. "A su alrededor hay cantidad de relojes que marcan todos la misma hora, pero dentro de cada uno hay *el mismo personaje* en muy diferentes épocas . . . Cada reloj tiene una ventana con rejas, como en una cárcel"[108] [around him are a number of clocks that all tell the same time, but inside of each one is *the same person* in very different time periods . . . Each clock has a window with bars, like a jail cell]. Only with the artist's words does the viewer understand the link between the main figure and the smaller, indistinguishable figures in the clocks. This short description written by Varo adds valuable contextual information unavailable in the painting. Varo seeks to defy the passage of time and cheat death by replicating the central figure in all of the clocks. Here her beliefs in reincarnation and the survival of the spiritual side of human life dominate the mechanical elements of the painting. The mystical whirling spiral that enters the room and the clocks themselves hover over the tableful of gadgets. Kaplan describes this painting as an homage to science when she claims: "Varo here celebrates science at its best, as a creative discipline open to the Marvelous."[109] On the other hand, the structure and spatial relationships in the painting seem to favor the marvelous and Varo's own words add a voice of creative authority in an afterthought on the permanence of the human spirit that overshadows the mechanical. Undoubtedly, Varo valued science, engineering, chemistry, and discovery, yet her instinct is to recontextualize the laboratory and the scientist. Her paintings in this sense develop the idea fomented by the surrealists that celebrates science but emphasizes the imagination.[110]

In *Discovery of a Mutant Geologist* from 1961, Varo again incorporates metamorphosis and discovery. The painting deals with a barren landscape in which several levels of discovery take place. The geologist who sprouts large insect wings and a small raccoon's tail peers through a telescope at a single gigantic flower growing out of the dirt. This figure with his insect wings harkens back to Varo's earlier painting *Double Agent* where the androgynous figure stands still with a large bee on its back. Varo's travels to Venezuela in the fifties inspired her keen observation of insect life and detailed rendition of discovery and exploration. In this imaginative scene, the

R. Varo. *Discovery of a Mutant Geologist* 1961.

person and insect have become one. The wings suggest movement and flight facilitating the geologist's search for new plant life. The wings on the figure liberate him from the overwhelming sense of entrapment or abandonment as does the expansive brown sky peeking above the jagged rock in the background. He is free to simply fly away at any time. The internal spaces, small rooms, low ceilings, and heavy overhanging foliage characteristic of Varo's later paintings have been replaced here with an open if unattractive space.

The levels of discovery within this painting are written directly into the title: *Discovery of a Mutant Geologist*. Initially it may seem that the title refers to the flower as that which the geologist discovered. But, the title suggests that we, the viewers, may have discovered a mutant geologist who just happens to be looking at a flower. Therefore, we are the scientists who spy a creature and label him as a discovery. The figure's intent gaze on the flower reproduces our gaze directed toward the painting itself. Thus, the actual work of art becomes a meta-image, as if it were a found text with meaning independent from the apparent images. The viewer watches the mutant geologist watch the mutant flower and each step into the space and context of the painting activates the viewer's imagination in her willingness to participate in the triple gaze. Varo tricks the viewer into "discovering" the mutant geologist through the subtle humor of the title's word game and in doing so she disrupts our comfortable position as the silent and invisible viewer of art. We have discovered the geologist who in turn stands motionless yet physically transformed as he watches the flower: we also stand motionless and in some internal way are transformed as we watch him.

The last painting that shows overt physical metamorphosis is *Mimesis* from 1960. "Although presented with humor (as chair and table legs play footsie), *Mimesis* conveys desperation."[111] The desperation lies in the completion of the transformation of the central figure into a static piece of furniture. Her skin takes on the pattern of the chair she sits in and her hands and feet become chair arms and legs. However, the humor in this painting goes beyond the lively antics of the furniture. The implied linguistic irony of chair arms and legs becomes literal in Varo's rendition of boredom. Her fascination with alchemy and the physical properties of the *prima materia* that holds the symbolic transformation of the soul comes

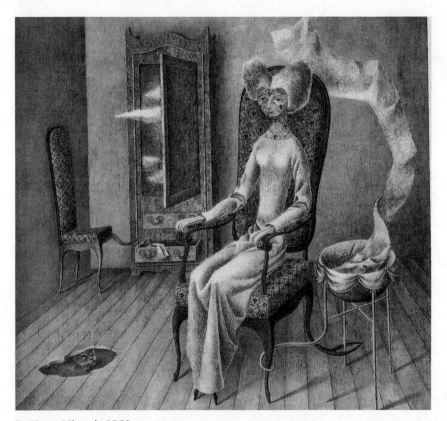

R. Varo. *Mimesis* **1960.**

alive in this painting. The transference of playfulness from the
human being to the furniture displaces the erotic nature of the female body onto the uncharted territory of erotic furniture.

As mentioned before, the de-eroticization of the female body recasts erotic nature in other beings such as animals or insects and
in this case a fantastical world of animated wood. Deborah Haynes
has written about the gender ambiguity in Varo's work as a masking
effect. Haynes concludes that the "representation of a gender-am-
biguous subject . . . allowed her [Varo] to resist supposedly natural
cultural stereotypes about female identity and to show these sexual
stereotypes as constructions."[112] In *Mimesis*, Varo achieves this
same end not through a masquerade but rather the physical metamorphosis of the female body.

The woman sits in sharp contrast to her surroundings, which
propose an inversion of objective reality. Just as we, the viewers,

observe the mutant geologist, here the human form is observed by a small cat from underneath the floorboards as well as by the viewer. The main difference in this particular image of metamorphosis from the others discussed is that the consciousness of the woman comes into question. Perhaps the image is more accurately read as a transference of consciousness to inanimate objects and to the startled cat who Varo herself describes as suffering from "susto y asombro al regreso, cuando ve la transformación"[113] [fright and amazement upon returning, when he sees the transformation]. The cat acting as a pictorial viewer representing the universal topos of the outsider's gaze reacts in a surprisingly human way. Gunther Gerszo depicted Varo in a painting entitled *The Days of Gabino Barreda Street* (1944) as a feline figure surrounded by cats. Gerszo's painting commemorates the first house that Varo and Benjamin Péret bought in Mexico and the camaraderie that many exiled European artists found there.[114] Also, many of Varo's female characters have wide-set oval-shaped eyes and pointed faces suggesting a feline personification. Beatriz Varo recalls her aunt Remedios's special fondness for cats as she took in many strays from the street.[115] Therefore, the cat peeking from beneath the floorboards in *Mimesis* could be a representation of the objective gaze of the artist herself. Varo subverts the subjective and objective gaze in the same way here as in her painting *Discovery of a Mutant Geologist*. The main focal point of *Mimesis* seems to be the transformation of the female figure. Yet as the viewer becomes more involved with the relationships established in the painting, we realize that the lively furniture and the conscientious cat demand our attention. Our role as a viewer of art goes through many changes and finally the cat's surprised reaction becomes our own, thus we formulate part of the visual composition. Artist, subject, object, and viewer become indiscernible categories as the painting leads us to question who is being watched or discovered. The woman in the chair represents a tangible example of metamorphosis while the relationships within the painting reflect the metamorphosis of rigid subject positions such as artist and viewer.

Metamorphosis breaks with objective reality in the context of the painting because of the presence of the astonished cat, who reacts as if he were human, the personification of the furniture, and the dehumanization of the woman. Geraldine Nichols explains that the enterprise of the fantasy writer (or in this case, Varo the painter) is to "explore and deconstruct the limiting categories of gender distinction."[116] Citing Rosemary Jackson, she continues to describe the effects of fantasy writing on gender: "Gender differences of male and female are subverted and generic differences between animal, vegetable and mineral are blurred in fantasy's attempt to 'turn over' 'normal' perceptions and undermine 'realistic' ways of seeing."[117] Theories of fantasy in literature translate directly to the visual images created by Varo. The blurring of boundaries between male/female and animal/human calls into question traditional ways of understanding the world in which we live.

Rodoreda and Varo emerged out of a dominantly patriarchal intellectual society destroyed by the Spanish civil war, taking with them several fundamental ideas of surrealism. Metamorphosis and its link to the fantastic are prevalent in surrealist painting and writing. Their work serves as a catalyst for a reconsideration of what the Surrealist movement meant to artists living in Europe and in exile. Breton and his manifestos inspired exploration and revelation that these women transcribed into feminine identity issues apparent in their art and literature. Breton's view propagated certain misogynist expectations, but the study of women's art and literature produced at the same time demands an analytical reorientation concerning the true nature of surrealism. As witnesses to the rise and fall of the Catalan avant-garde, Rodoreda and Varo both developed alternative visions of reality necessitated by the upheaval of their own personal and regional histories and partly due to the binding laws of surrealism that limited their creative identity. These two women generate multiple sites of discourse including their interest and work in both the visual and verbal arts. They extend the possibilities of surrealism and pay tribute to the revolutionary and visionary changes of the movement by continuing the search for a female autonomous identity. Rodoreda and Varo never completely liberated themselves from dominant male influence as both women were attached emotionally and financially to men and to patriarchal artistic laws for their entire careers. However, their discourse involving social exile, feminine role-playing, and physical and emotional growth invents an artistic space from which the next generation of writers and artists will create and eventually establish an autonomous polysemantic artistic female identity.

The specific acts of subversion found in Rodoreda's and Varo's artistic project can be considered as political, social, and artistic.

Robert Belton points out that the surrealist men formulated a strictly encoded set of expectations for the consumption of art that is partly explained in Breton's manifestos. Belton explains that the surrealist men "were all partly formed by conventions and cultural fashions that were wide spread in both bourgeois society and its antitheses."[118] It is precisely these shared convictions and cultural formation that excluded women from the surrealist group.

Instead of sharing the male-dominated horizon of expectations, Rodoreda and Varo, as examples of women working within the movement as opposed to others like painter Léonor Fini or Frida Kahlo who rejected the "old boys' club" from the outset, had to establish a separate agenda employing other types of subversive acts outside of the surrealist code.[119] As opposed to acts of shock and sexual perversion that male surrealists inscribed in a working system of iconography and literature that was sure to rattle the middle to upper-class art-consuming public, women surrealists opted for a more intellectual and spiritual margin from which to counter dominant discourse. Rodoreda's use of textual subversion and Varo's female figures fleeing toward autonomy are two ways in which these women oppose male domination of female identity.

The crucial difference between the male surrealists' agenda and the women's lies in this question of female identity. Male surrealists sought to shock bourgeois attitudes toward feminine decorum by violently recapitulating female sexuality as monstrous and dangerous. The threat of sexuality was enticing because ultimately in society women as bodies could always be tamed into submission, therefore the exchange between violent women and violence toward women created a dialogue between the artist and a patriarchal society that easily recognized and accepted both terms of the equation.

On the other hand, women surrealists were forced to reject not only this dialogue of violent women and violence but also to reject the society that understood such symbolism in art. Women were not deconstructing a social ideal such as art or woman but were forced to deconstruct their very own culturally rendered selves. Thus the subversive acts such as silence, laughter, and metamorphosis cross from the symbolic into the semiotic. Language becomes ineffectual for feminist expression as it relies on a certain cultural horizon of expectations where the term *woman* means submission.

The individual exiled from the body as a material space where identity is located becomes a fundamental trait of both Rodoreda and Varo's work. Following author Franz Kafka's narrative lead and utilizing metamorphosis to explore alternative realities allow the visual and verbal texts to introduce various levels of existence, implying a fluctuation of subject positions. Women and men undergo physical transformations in Rodoreda and Varo's work, not mutilations or dismemberment as seen in numerous images of women in male surrealist art. Perhaps the physical manifestations of a misogynist artistic ideology fell so quickly out of favor and abstract expressionism took its place because of the reality of physical mutilation experienced in Spain during the civil war.

Catalunya, defeated politically and artistically, became an ironic realization of the surrealists' attraction to violence. For Rodoreda and Varo living in exile, the act of displacing change onto forms other than human bodies, or transforming the human body into an animal or mineral form, was perhaps a way to distance themselves from their own experience as vulnerable targets fleeing their homeland. Nevertheless, this process of exile provided them with a working vocabulary of marginalization that they had experienced in Catalunya before as women. With the defeat of the Second Republic the entire Catalan liberal nation fell to the margins of Spanish and European society. The women, who now experienced their regional and linguistic limitations in exile on par with the gender-based limitations imposed by European society in general, began to seriously reformulate both regional and artistic identities.

In Rodoreda's texts and Varo's paintings these reformulations of identity are the seeds of change that will be nurtured by following generations of writers and artists. As opposed to the male surrealists who sought to challenge societal assumptions regarding the individual's relationship to reality, the women surrealists reestablished their own relationship with art, language, and society. The disadvantage in separating artistic agendas along gender lines suggests what Pollock calls "the deadly paradox: to name what makes it interesting to study artists who are women is to condemn the artists to being less than artists: "women." "[120] Pollock resolves the paradox by pointing out the ability of art to cross all barriers of difference. Just as the question of regional identity that is located in the repression and eventual liberation of the Catalan language speaks for all marginalized regional spaces, women's artistic experimentations in identity open up a discourse on multiple subject positions that indeed breaks gender boundaries regardless of the biology of the artist.

Therefore, these acts of subversion amount to a radical feminism, or rethinking the term "woman." Therein lies the importance of Varo and Rodoreda's work. However, they were two privileged women who were granted access into the literary and artistic worlds through their associations with men, and Varo was economically supported by her third husband, Walter Gruen, which allowed her to leave commercial painting behind for her more expressive signature canvases. While neither woman was politically minded, both explore a feminist agenda in their work. Perhaps their lives seem superficially in line with the larger dominant discourse, yet both women confront certain ideologies and attack them from a female point of view. Rodoreda tries to redefine Christian myth and martyrdom at a time when Franco's Catholic fervor labeled all women as homemakers, wives, and mothers. By recognizing religion as a social force that limits women's participation in society, Rodoreda implicates herself as a cultural critic. Varo's alternate views of motherhood in the early fifties and sixties place her on the cusp of the radical rethinking of home and family published in Betty Friedan's *The Feminine Mystique* in 1963, the year of Varo's death. Placed in a historical context of overt Catholicism in Catalunya and the recognition of surrealism as decidedly Mexican by André Breton, Varo and Rodoreda affirm their artistic position of rebellion by directly challenging the progress of dominant discourse.

2

Familial Exile: Montserrat Roig's Rebellious Brand of Feminism

Las ciudades, como los países y las personas, si tienen algo que decirnos requieren un espacio de tiempo nada más; pasado éste, nos cansan. Sólo si el diálogo quedó interrumpido podemos desear volver a ellas. [Cities, like countries and people, if they have something to tell us require a small amount of time, nothing more; this past, they tire us. Only if the dialogue was interrupted do we desire to return to them.]

—Luis Cernuda, *Historial de un libro*

MONTSERRAT ROIG NEVER EXPERIENCED THE RUPTURE OF PHYSICAL exile as did both Mercè Rodoreda and Remedios Varo. However, Roig brings to her narrative a distinctly feminist view of social and political events that shape the way a young woman figures herself into the Catalan cultural dynamic. By approaching both political and literary history from a female perspective, Roig sees herself automatically sidelined from these traditions, in effect exiled from the prevalent national discourse on account of her gender. Uncovering the subaltern voice of women's perspective on patriarchal histories has been the project of feminist criticism for most of the twentieth century.[1] Roig openly claimed herself a feminist as Catherine Davies points out and her literary career focused on what she considered problematic convergences of being female and a writer.[2] Her texts question the validity of institutionalized culture from a radical viewpoint and include criticisms of such social and political constructions as socialism, feminism, marriage, love, and motherhood.

Roig, a woman struggling to become a professional writer in the male-dominated public sphere, experienced the displacement, isolation, and longing for wholeness in a literary sense that Rodoreda and Varo expressed in a very literal sense. Roig's works resound with the unjust pejorative status of women in society. She confronts the reductive role of women in political movements, in family dynamics, and in interpersonal relationships with men. However, her brand of feminism is not an anti-man stance, but rather a questioning of social constructs and a disclosure of female oppression. Roig, in fact, sees feminism itself as a social construct that falls victim to power stratification and therefore, just as all social/political labels, requires close analysis. Her dissection of love has been criticized as sentimental and not militant. Far from sentimental, Roig's intellectual exile from the most sacred social construction of family provides her with the distance from which to address various forms of love as social instruments and then to reinstate love into a feminist vocabulary.

Isolina Ballesteros concentrates on the rampant criticism of Roig's work by Spanish feminist Lydia Falcón, whose scathing remarks about contemporary peninsular fiction displace the literary value of the text onto political judgments of random association. Falcón writes: "Las protagonistas de la llamada novelística feminista ¿se lo creerán? son inmaduras, débiles, vacilantes, enamoradas del amor, engañadas por mozos algo egoístas" [The protagonists of the so-called feminist novel, if you can believe it, are immature, weak, indecisive, in love with love, tricked by somewhat pompous boys] and she claims:

> Las heroínas de nuestra narrativa femenina no tienen problemas económicos, casi nunca profesionales . . . no poseen maridos gruñones, golpeadores, borrachos, niños subnormales o molestos . . . ninguno de los personajes que constituyen el variopinto y asfixiante entorno familiar.[3]

> [Heroines of our feminine narrative don't have economic problems, almost never professional ones . . . they don't have griping, drunken husbands who beat them, bothersome or handicapped kids . . . none of the characters that make up the complex and asphyxiating family scene.]

Falcón seems to suggest that only a woman oppressed and victimized by her family can represent or describe feminine reality. However, Roig's early novels that comprise the trilogy *Ramona, adéu* [*Good-bye, Ramona*] (1972) *El temps de les cireres* [*Time of Cherries*] (1976), and *L'hora violeta* [*The Violet Hour*] (1980) reveal that this very idea of woman subjected to her family and defined by a male protagonist (the abusive husband or indifferent father) is itself a creation of the patriarchy, a mode of discourse to keep women down and stuck in the quagmire of victimization in the "asfixiante entorno familiar." Contrary to Falcón's claim, familial relationships comprise the core of Roig's narrative discourse, especially the relationships between female family members. Ballesteros suggests: "Roig's feminism should be understood as an individual struggle that does not turn woman into a merely ideological construction."[4] Nevertheless, the struggle presented in Roig's trilogy involves generations of women moving from the private domestic domain into the public, urban sphere of influence. Therefore, to label her representation of women's struggle as purely individual fails to capture the communal spirit and female solidarity formulated specifically in Roig's trilogy.

Ramón Buckley links Roig's feminism to that of Julia Kristeva. He sees both women's plight as symptomatic of feminism in the sixties: "Women could only be understood if they were to be considered from the 'outside', that is, from the male viewpoint,"[5] yet of course women had no other recourse than to express themselves in the code of the patriarchy and thus women became involved in the power struggle inspired by language. Buckley claims that only in Roig's last novel, *La veu melodiosa* [*The Melodious Voice*] (1987), does she finally recognize patriarchy as an ideology and that "patriarchy will always try to impose itself by conceptualizing reality."[6] Buckley claims: "She dies, I believe, at the verge of discovering her own voice as a novelist, beyond the dialectics of castration, which had so influenced her own early writing."[7] In light of Buckley's provocative statement that Roig hadn't yet found her "voice as a novelist" upon dying, I argue that Roig not only had a keenly formulated sense of her own literary voice from the outset of her writing career but that she explicitly outlines her intentions and project as a novelist in her first collection of short stories that serves as a springboard for her trilogy. In the trilogy Roig carefully delineates the detrimental effects that patriarchy, as ideology and institution, has on both men and women who try unsuccessfully to function in a familial system of learned behaviors and hierarchies.

In order for women to function within the established system of hierarchies, namely exclusionary patriarchal language as Buckley points out in his comparison between Roig and Kristeva, women writers must develop an alternative approach to language. Among

French feminists in the seventies this new form of expression emerged as *écriture féminine*. Kristeva, Luce Irigaray, and Hélène Cixous all formulated various theories around the idea of a nontraditional, distinctly feminine literary language. Susan Sellers points out two important characteristics of feminine writing. The first is the inscription into experience of nonsymbolic articulations as manifested, for example, in the maternal body in relation to "self and m/other." Secondly, feminine writing proposes a subject position that "refuses to appropriate or annihilate the other's difference" thus exercising alternative forms of relation, perception, and expression.[8] Both Kristeva and Irigaray develop the notion of a feminine writing through a semiotic rendering of the maternal body. Irigaray confronts Freudian sexual constructs and she writes of women as "castrated of words."[9] Her suggestion to insist "deliberately upon those *blanks* in discourse which recall the places of her exclusion"[10] explains Roig's own literary project involving the rereading and reinscription of a feminine voice that fills those voids implicit in the dominant culture. Julia Kristeva extends the idea of a feminine expression to that of feminine reading required to understand feminine writing: "Faced with this poetic language that defies knowledge, many of us are rather tempted to leave our shelter to deal with literature only by miming its meanderings, rather than by positing it as an object of knowledge."[11] Yet she suggests that a woman reader and critic is the "ultimate guarantee of sociality beyond the wreckage of the paternal symbolic function" and can push theoretical reason beyond "bio-physiological sociohistorical constraints."[12] These French theorists value the kind of writing that Roig pursues: not a denial of History but rather an unlimited expression of feminine writing that brings the historically unspoken to the textual surface.

Roig's early works will be studied in this chapter as testimonies of the historically unspoken and the metaphorically exiled. I take issue with the narrow definitions of feminism posited by Falcón as well as with Buckley's dismissal of a distinctly formulated voice in Roig's early works. That Roig's works have been misunderstood is an understatement, yet the erroneous reading of her texts is a predictable reaction from institutions and viewpoints created by dominant discourse. Roig's struggle to assert a nontraditional speaking subject in her narrative stems from historical patriarchal silencing of a unique feminine voice. Roig battles back by rereading, and thus reinterpreting History, the modern urban family, and canonical texts. The cross-generational feminist dialogue that Roig establishes blossoms directly from female appropriation of public urban spaces and provokes a questioning of socially imposed familial roles. Roig's first group of short stories, *Molta roba i poc sabó i tan neta que la volen,* [*So Many Clothes and Too Little Soap and They Want Them All So Clean*] (1970), introduces a cast of characters that she will develop in her next three novels that comprise the trilogy: *Ramona, adéu* (1972), *El temps de les cireres* (1976), and *L'hora violeta* (1980). Roig's female characters struggle to balance personal desires with socially scripted roles and responsibilities.

Through the development of feminine characterization and the reevaluation of traditional concepts of history, origin, and regionalism, Roig delves into epistemological questions concerning not only notions of ideologies but also socialization based on gender stereotypes. Roig questions the very political, social, and historical movements that women feel compelled to appropriate as their own such as feminism, socialism, and maternity. Her narrative does not promote random patronage to any social class, political organization, or gender, but she consistently brings to the surface of her narrative the seemingly lost feminine consciousness. She challenges the norm of women and men adopting ideologies blindly, without considering the underlying subconscious hierarchy of institution and dominant discourse. Roig suggests that any position worthwhile, be it political, emotional, or historical, deserves intense questioning and restructuring if it is to serve our needs as human beings. Kathleen McNerney comes closest to my own opinion concerning Roig's writing when she states that Roig's feminist revolution is much more difficult than merely subscribing to the latest set of radical notions. McNerney writes: "What is truly revolutionary, she [Roig] believes, and therefore threatening to people, is for people to live as women, with women's values, rejecting the structures and institutions that have been imposed upon us by the patriarchy."[13] McNerney does not elaborate in the brief introduction what she considers "women's values," however, Roig's texts clarify that these values include an interrogative intellectual capacity nurtured by relationships between women that lead to self-knowledge.

Biruté Ciplijauskaité defines this process as "el proceso de concienciación" [the process of gaining consciouness]. Ciplijauskaité discusses the novel of self-discovery written by women as a version of the traditional bildungsroman. In her analysis, women's versions use more innovative techniques than do men's.[14] Many of the narrative modes discussed in Ciplijauskaité's study define postmodern literature in general and not specifically the search for a feminine voice and include: criticism of social and historical hegemony, psychological reinterpretations of a mythical monolithic reality, and confronting the very nature of ideology or socially upheld truths.[15] However, Ciplijauskaité carefully delineates the ways in which feminine consciousness emerges through specific mechanisms employed by women writers. The development of a feminine consciousness resides in women's relationship to memory, her childhood, her movement into the sociopolitical sphere and her self-affirmation as a writer.[16] While all of these modes of consciousness appear in Roig's work, the cyclical nature of the narrative that disrupts chronological order locates women's relationship to the text not with time but rather with space. This idea is fundamental in Roig's rereading of mythical texts such as *The Odyssey* in *L'hora violeta*. Also on quite a literal plane, she rereads the space designated as female and domestic walls become permeable as the feminine subject moves into the social sphere and the act of writing, or being a writer, provides possibilities not only for emotional and intellectual release and stimulation but eventual means of economic independence.

Roig's works explore feminine revelation on various levels. Her characters come to realize the overwhelming influence of social and cultural inheritance manifested in generational shifts that can create opportunities for women while simultaneously promoting certain gender-specific myths woven tightly into the social fabric passed from one generation to the next. By addressing both the advantages and drawbacks of intergenerational relationships between women, Roig establishes the importance of the individual woman's genealogy. Even her most independent characters such as Ramona, who leaves her family to free herself of her past, or Natàlia, who abandons the suffocating familiarity of Barcelona, recognize the influence of the past as fundamental to their present situations and identities.

Ciplijauskaité compares the generational relationship cycle as an "'espejo de las generaciones' para mostrar cambio y continuidad en la existencia femenina"[17] [a generational mirror in order to show the change and continuity in feminine existence]. She goes on to cite Roig's *Ramona, adéu* as "un ejemplo muy logrado de la técnica de 'espejo de las generaciones'"[18] [a masterful example of the generational mirror technique] as it draws certain parallels between personal and political circumstances that defy chronological timelines. The circumstances that link the lives of the three generations of women in *Ramona, adéu*, all named Ramona (and nicknamed Mundeta), stem from personal disillusion, primarily with amorous relationships, set against a backdrop of political and social upheaval at different times in Barcelona's history. As Ciplijauskaité explains: "la evolución en las tres Mundetas se da no sólo en el nivel de la femineidad, sino también en cuanto a su conciencia social y política, transmitida con un estilo correspondiente a cada época"[19] [the three Mundetas' evolution isn't just on a feminine level but also deals with their social and political consciousness transmitted with a style that corresponds to each time period]. The political undercurrent supports Roig's insistence that women create a public space for themselves, yet her vision is far from utopian. Her characters struggle with already formed opinions of women activists and a patriarchal system rigid and resistant to ideas of change.

Roig plots femininity in her novels utilizing the changing backdrop of Barcelona over the course of the twentieth century. Her novels deal with the creation of a new woman demanded by a changing society. Juliet Mitchell claims: "As any society changes its social structure, changes its economic base, artifacts are re-created within it. Literary forms arise as one of the ways in which changing subjects create themselves as subjects within a new social context."[20] The cityscape and narrative voices in Roig's works change as Spain survives three major political incidents of the century presented in *Ramona, adéu* and alluded to in the following novels that comprise the trilogy. They are: the loss of Cuba, Guam, Puerto Rico, and the Philippines in 1898, the Spanish civil war in 1936, and the student uprisings in 1968. The narrative fuses political and social upheaval with personal development and yet the results are never consistent. Roig counterbalances political dedication with personal disillusion, group solidarity with emotional sacrifice, and social progress with personal failure. This contradiction of the personal and political becomes a central theme in the last novel in the trilogy, *L'hora violeta*, seen in Norma and Natàlia's continuous struggle to "estimar la humanitat i les persones al mateix temps"[21] [to love mankind and individuals at the same time]. Her point is to uncover the fleeting and transparent effects of patriarchal hegemony on personal growth, especially on women's development of an autonomous identity. Her disillusion with political and social systems, however, is remedied through the task of reinscribing women's experience into history through proactive writing. Not only do women appropriate urban spaces, they also assimilate history into the present, rewriting one-sided accounts of victory and defeat. Roig's political position that she imparts to her characters is malleable, varied, and changing with the passage of time. In this manner, Roig transforms traditional notions of chronological history with a fluctuating, objective point of reference. This is not to say that all history is relative but rather that reformulations of historical events distorted by collective memory comprise our past. The ordered, chronological rendition of history crumbles under Roig's intertwined narrative that combines female voices and generations to create one multifaceted feminist identity.

Within the framework of creating a specifically feminine genealogy, Roig focuses on ways in which women arrive at the consciousness of their own identity. One way involves movement from the passive recipient of patriarchal structured culture to active member and participant in daily urban life. During her successful career as a journalist, Roig published several historical accounts of women's history in relation to the city of Barcelona. In "La ciutat de Barcelona: Una mirada femenina" [Barcelona: A Feminine Perspective] Roig traces the process of women moving from behind windows, out onto balconies, and eventually into the workplace.[22] This social development for women mirrors the movement of her novelistic characters. Roig presents this process in the first two novels of the trilogy as arduous, painstakingly slow, and systematically beaten down by tradition and a solipsistic patriarchal society. Throughout the narrative process of the trilogy, urban locations become recontextualized into a feminine textual space. The appropriation of the traditionally male public space, the city, provides Roig's characters with a physical and intellectual liberation.

Women at home in the city who consume the urban setting, enjoy the bustling atmosphere, or identify themselves with the city are a major break from earlier female characters in Catalan literature of the twentieth century. Although Rodoreda's *La plaça del Diamant* unfolds in the urban setting of Barcelona, the protagonist doesn't seem to enjoy the city but is overwhelmed by it and until the final scene of the novel she is dominated by her fears of lost youth represented by the plaza, or the public meeting space. Maryellen Bieder describes the idyllic settings of the gardens and parks in Rodoreda's novels as a sharp "contrast to the frightening city with its noise, congestion and impersonality."[23] Cecília Ce from Rodoreda's *El carrer de les camèlies* wanders the streets confused, always an outsider and falling into the clutches of abusive men. The city dominates Cecília as she flounders in its vastness. Roig's women, on the other hand, actively soak in the urban environment of Barcelona, possessing its avenues, parks, buildings, and plazas. The city becomes a crucial space in the awakening of a feminine artistic identity for as women begin to inhabit the streets and public spaces they gain new perspective on the gendered division of private and public life.

The second way in which women gain access to a truer identity, seen most vividly in the last novel of the trilogy, *L'hora violeta*, is through writing themselves into history. The recuperation of a silenced past links together generations of women while documentation assures literary inheritance of a distinctly female history. Roig's use of the oldest Ramona's diary entries from the early twentieth century in *Ramona, adéu* acts as a written precursor to the interior monologues used to characterize the youngest Ramona of the sixties. The diary as a traditionally female genre loses its rigidness of propriety when juxtaposed with the typically postmodern less structured interior monologue. Roig combines these methods not to divide the generations along strict ideological lines but to show the similarities, the internal becoming external through different forms of writing. Roig writes self-consciously, that is to say she is aware of the text as artifact, as a form of permanent testimony. In *L'hora violeta* the point of departure for the narrative lies in the task of writing a book. Natàlia has asked Norma to write Judit's story, a life full of mystery and shrouded desires, from the diary and letters that Judit left behind. Ironically, Norma never finishes her book but Roig's inclusion of the diary entries and letters in the textual body of *L'hora violeta* leaves the pieces of Judit's life unedited and unorganized, exactly how she lived them and wrote them.

Patrícia Gabancho compares Catalan women writers to explorer Edmund Hillary "quan va arribar per primer cop a l'Everest, que li calia deixar testimoni de la seva presència"[24] [when he arrived for the first time at the top of Everest . . . he rightly left a testimony of his presence]. Roig has had to continually announce herself to the literary world. Faced with an often hostile environment in her own country, Roig consistently wrote in Catalan not only to vindicate her language but to establish a different subject position from which to counter the dominant language: Castilian. However, the recuperation of a Catalan female speaking subject suggests various other obstacles, for example, the unreliable tool of language that a woman must employ in order to share her findings from the exploration with a literary world dominated by stories of strictly male experience.

Gabancho suggests that all women share a common bond of a distinctly feminine reality and that "la dona reflecteix una experiència de dona quan escriu"[25] [women reflect female experience when they write]. She affirms that these are unquestionable factors but points out their flip side seen in literature written by men but never investigated in such a way: "La gràcia és que, si invertíem l'esforç, trobaríem un fil conductor semblant pel que fa a la no-dita literatura masculina"[26] [the funny thing is that, if we invert the formula, we find a similar line of thought in what is the never mentioned masculine literature]. Male literature inevitably reveals male experience yet this mode of narration has never been limited by a gendered analysis according to Gabancho, for male experience is simply understood as experience. Gabancho reveals the difficulty and ambiguity involved in defining experience. In fact, she herself falls into limiting feminine experience by granting the writer, an educated person of a certain class, with the power to construct contemporary Catalan feminine reality.[27] However, Gabancho proclaims: "un cop convençuts que no existeix la literatura femenina, es pot avançar cap a la reivindicació de la diferència"[28] [once we become convinced that feminine literature doesn't exist, then we will advance toward the vindication of difference]. In other words, women have to struggle to legitimize all types of female experience to salvage it from automatic marginalization or hierarchization within the prescribed world of feminine experience. The label *feminine* only serves to further marginalize women writers, according to Gabancho.

Roig seems to agree with Gabancho that difference only proves problematic for the progress of women writers. In her essay "¿Por qué no ha habido mujeres genio?" [Why Have There Been No

Women Geniuses], Roig discusses the tradition of philosophical inquiry that seeks to annihilate the "other," which she considers feminine. "El Yo masculino necesita mirarse al espejo y encontrar la imagen que él ha creado de la mujer, encontrar a su costilla, para así sentirse más seguro en un mundo que quizá le es hostil."[29] [The masculine "I" needs to look in the mirror and find the image of the woman he has created, find his rib, in order to feel sure of himself in a world that is perhaps hostile toward him]. Roig alludes to the fact that "the feminine" is a cultural construct that places "the masculine" on "el lado positivo del espejo, allí donde él cree que está la realidad, para convertirse en el único portador del pensamiento humano, en el único creador"[30] [the positive side of the mirror, where he believes reality lies, in order to convert himself into the only bearer of human thought, into the sole creator]. Therefore, Roig seeks to reinvent a literary woman from a privileged space of exile whose creativity extends beyond the assigned, legitimized role of maternity and beyond the comfortable assumption that "la mujer es creadora al parir poetas"[31] [women are creative when they give birth to poets].

The culmination of her historical concerns regarding the omission of women's voices lies in a pivotal moment of realization in *L'hora violeta*. The final novel of the trilogy acts as a synthesis of her literary project, for there she recontextualizes the historically canonical work *The Odyssey* through a female narrative voice. Natàlia, the protagonist, openly questions the silence imposed on women in Homer's epic that categorizes them into types: Calypso, Circe, or Penelope. What Roig intends with this rereading of a classical text is to tangentially expose the cultural ramifications of the literature that has formulated a false sense of female identity. Therefore, her attack of historical texts and the patriarchal culture they promote seems to threaten the established and accepted literary contract.

The institutionalized focus on biological differences, stemming from centuries of literary influence, that would seem to divide male and female creativity invariably leads to accepting behavioral differences between men and women as natural when the majority of gender differences are socially constructed.[32] Instead of biological determinism, Roig believes in the existence of a feminine literary space as a recognizable arena for women to become autonomous human beings. In order to achieve this, women must start from nothing, from the dark point zero where notions of normality and experience need to be reevaluated before women can occupy a genuine literary space not demarcated by patriarchal notions of abnormal, marginalized, or alternative. After all, she is not different or other to herself, but only in the dominant patriarchal literary language.[33]

Roig explores the emerging subjectivity of women and this dark creative space seen as a new subject position by weaving into her narrative the double vision of characters that are both female and writers. This technique will become paramount in the work of Carme Riera, who shares many feminist positions on language and writing with Roig.[34] In her three novels, *Ramona, adéu, El temps de les cireres,* and *L'hora violeta*, Roig develops the concept of female experience as part of a collective consciousness drawing on traditionally male experience of a public/political/social reality, internalizing its effects and regenerating externally a genealogy of a common feminine experience through writing. Roig's version of common experience is deeply rooted in her Catalan heritage and works on various levels. She is able to tap into a universal feminine condition through exploration of local conflict and growth in Barcelona during the twentieth century. Various stories from *Molta roba i poc sabó . . .* prefigure several characters and events later described in the trilogy. This self-referential style illustrates the conscientious restructuring of historically pertinent literary artifacts, such as letters and diaries that connect Roig's various works creating a family genealogy that exists outside of textual space. The recurring names, places, and events become familiar to the reader as they appear repeated in different texts. The reader in turn gains access to intimate family secrets, disputes, and desires as Roig's intertextual narrative unfolds.

RAMONA, ADÉU: THE GENERATIONAL MIRROR

In Roig's first novel of the trilogy, she sets up a trivocal narrative spanning three generations of Catalan women. Each woman shares with the reader through the text her most intimate secrets, desires, and sufferings, yet ironically through the various voices we become aware that the women don't really know each other at all. Elizabeth Rogers points out that "language has the dual capacity and function to reveal as well as to suppress the truth."[35] Language functions in the novel not to unite the plight of women but to show the need for empowerment found in written expression. Thus, the grandmother's life is told through a series of diary entries beginning on the eve of her marriage and ending with the death of her husband. The mother and granddaughter express themselves through first-person narration of selected memories. Yet as the text unveils the similarities and differences of these women's lives, it becomes a testimony to otherwise silent or silenced aspects of unthinkable female existence including sexual desire, loveless marriage, and disillusion with motherhood. The characters in the novel express their disdain of convention and socially correct feminine behavior through various acts of rebellion. The familial quarrels and unavoidable differences between the Ramonas only accentuate their sameness: the common struggle of all women within a patriarchal system. However, the text provides key information about each woman that the other characters do not know. This privileging of textual space over the fictional reality affirms Roig's intent of bringing a feminine genealogy to the forefront and recording the forbidden and the unspoken.

The mother Ramona functions as a pivotal character in the novel as she moves from youthful independence to a repressive marriage and family life. Her memories of past actions seem to conflict with her present outer persona that is timid and weak. Both older Ramonas express the same fear and disillusion in the face of motherhood, although they cannot share these feelings as a woman reluctant to bear children falls outside of "normal" and acceptable female behavior. Roig develops this theme from previous literary models, namely Mercè Rodoreda. The protagonist of Rodoreda's *La plaça del Diamant*, for example, finds pregnancy a strange and distancing experience and she feels as if she's been filled with "una cosa molt estranya"[36] [something very strange]. However, the unspeakable reality of a woman who fears and even loathes motherhood produces a dual reality for the characters. The grandmother Ramona actively maintains a public façade while revealing and recording her true reality privately in her diary. Women's repressed feelings that have been relegated to secretive texts become the focal point of Roig's narrative. She describes a separate, distinctly feminine history as "the perfume of history" that lives in and is revealed through women's connections with each other.

Critics of *Ramona, adéu* have underestimated the importance of the central Ramona, the mother. Elizabeth Rogers defines the grandmother and mother as two women who "live apart from official History" and that the mother "is totally ignorant" of the significance of political activities around her.[37] Ana María Brenes García concludes that the female body, as represented by the characters of different generations in the novel, mirrors the Catalan nation's oppression, suffering, and eventual liberation. Therefore, the oldest generation symbolizes the oppression of Primo de Rivera's dictatorship and the middle generation embodies the promise of human rights associated with the liberal Second Republic and the fall to the post–Spanish civil war conservatism of Franco's dictatorship. The youngest generation comes of age in the post-Franco, sociodemocratic era. However, Brenes García considers the middle generation, that experiences brief liberation and then sudden oppression under the Franco regime, best represented in a minor character, Kati, who appears much more developed in *L'hora violeta*. Although Brenes García's argument is convincing, she omits the middle Ramona when she decides that the nation's identity during the Second Republic and immediately after the civil war is best molded to Kati, a sexually and politically liberal woman who commits suicide. She writes that the Catalan nation can be considered "un cuerpo . . . que pasa a reconocerse y descubrirse y que, tras un breve período de goce—Kati—, se reprime durante casi 40 años"[38] [a body . . . that comes to recognize and discover itself and that, after a brief period of pleasure—Kati—is repressed for almost forty years]. While Brenes García correctly identifies liberal Catalunya with liberal Kati, she doesn't note that the mother Ramona passes through the very same experience and even more markedly than Kati in this particular novel.

Ramona, the mother, breaks most firmly with tradition by having a premarital affair in the 1920s. Her active pursuit of Ignasi leads her to dominate the urban spaces of Barcelona, an act she repeats later in her life when searching for her husband Joan after a bombing. She remembers her affair as euphoric, sweet, and idyllic: "tot en una mescla exultant de follia i de resignació, la Mundeta pensava que Barcelona era una flor oberta i quasi cosmopolita que es desfullava . . . més que una ciutat, semblava una promesa de ciutat"[39] [everything in an exciting mixture of insanity and resignation, Mundeta thought that Barcelona was an open flower, almost cosmopolitan, that lost its petals . . . more than a city, it seemed the promise of a city]. Her love affair with Ignasi, a young anarchist, awakens her desire, yet she realizes that Ignasi will soon leave to join the military and that any chance for an enduring love relationship is out of the question. Nevertheless, they love secretly and she remembers to herself that "Ningú no sabrà el nombre d'abraçades que ens donarem, les besades que ens regalarem. Ningú no les podrà comptar" (113) [No one will ever know how many times we hugged, or the kisses that we gave each other. No one will ever be able to count them all]. Ramona never reveals her secret love to any other character throughout the narrative; therefore it remains trapped in her memory as the secret it was always meant to be. Ramona's personal memory of Ignasi expressed as an inner monologue is the only textual evidence of the affair and therefore the reader accesses this crucial information that the other characters cannot.

Ramona the mother's insistence on maintaining her clandestine love affair leads her to discover her independence and decision-making capabilities. On the afternoon that she is secretly to meet Ignasi at the Café Tostadero, she plots to invite her Aunt Patrícia to *La reina Cristina de Suecia*, one of Greta Garbo's most controversial films establishing her as an icon of female independence. Ramona reinvents herself as Mundeta-Greta inspired by "la Greta, la divina, el mite" (128) [Greta, the divine one, the myth]. By appropriating a female persona of mythic proportions, the mother Ramona finds herself able to break away from the restrictive eyes of her Aunt Patrícia as they are on their way to the cinema and to meet Ignasi at the Café Tostadero. She sees this meeting with Ignasi as a test of her will and wit; in order to make an appearance she will have to literally escape from her aunt. The narrative here shifts to third person, creating distance that elevates the heroic Ramona: "l'empenyia una fúria nova, el desig de veure l'Ignasi, de comprovar, amb la presència física de l'home que l'estimava, com es difuminaven les boires que l'havien atrapada tota la vida" (143) [a new force pushed her, the desire to see Ignasi, to finally prove with the physical presence of the man she loved, how the fog that had trapped her during her whole life had lifted]. Her escape results in a consequent navigation of the city: "la Mundeta-Greta remuntava les Corts, cada vegada més a prop de la plaça de la Universitat, atabalada, absent de l'espectacle públic, atreta per una sola idea (143) [Mundeta-Greta went up las Corts, every step took her closer to the University Square, she was nervous, detatched from public spectacle, obsessed with only one idea]. Her Aunt Patrícia quickly disappears behind her and Ramona arrives at the café for what will be her last meeting with Ignasi, for he later commits suicide.

Roig's description of Ramona's small rebellion allows the reader to enter into the mind and machinations of the young mother Ramona's daring act of defiance. Perhaps she is inspired by love but her desire to act leads her to break with accepted norms of female composure. Ironically this act will be lost to her memory and to the page as her marriage catapults her back to the oppressive patriarchal structure similar to the one under which her own mother lived. But this feeling of independence, echoed again in the monologue when she searches alone for her husband, counterbalances her unhappy marriage. The mother's premeditated movement from active lover to passive wife parallels Brenes García's notion of the passage of the Catalan nation from the Second Republic, a period of recognition, to the dictatorship and forty years of repression.[40]

The same city that was once full of promise for Ramona appears drastically different in the monologue that opens and closes the novel. The novel begins and ends with the mother's voice, set off from the rest of the text by italics, describing the events of 17 March 1938 when she searches Barcelona for her husband after a particularly destructive bombing. While this monologue frames the novel, it also serves as a connecting thread emerging again at the midpoint of narration and bringing together the three main characters. Roig relies on the daughter's viewpoint in the body of the novel to raise questions about her mother's valor and her obsession with the past. Her daughter wonders:

Per què una dona eclipsada i temorenca es reviscolava quan es parlava de la guerra? No solament quan recordava el dia en què hagué de buscar el seu marit entre els morts d'un bombardeig, sinó quan amania la pasejada per la ciutat destruïda amb una infinitat d'anècdotes que augmentaven de to i de color cada vegda que es disposava a explicar-les. (81)

[Why did a woman so overshadowed and fearful show such vitality when she talked about the war? Not only when she remembered that day when she had to look for her husband among the dead, but also each time she recounted the story about her wandering through the destroyed city with innumerous details that increased in tone and color each time she told it.]

While the daughter criticizes her mother's embellishments of worn war stories, she acknowledges to the reader her lack of complete comprehension regarding her mother's struggle. Only the readers know of the recurring image of Ignasi, the mother's secret love, during the search for her husband. The version of the story that the mother tells her daughter and the truth remain inconsistent. Thus language has been employed to manipulate and censor the ideas that construct the truth of the situation. The text and the textual reality become separate here to demonstrate the lasting effects of silence passed from one generation to the next. The daughter's disgust and disdain for her mother as a "dona eclipsada y temorenca" adds a new, warped dimension to the generational mirror. The daughter cannot see herself in her mother; she only sees a weak woman that she despises, thus the mirror becomes curved showing a distorted image just as Valle-Inclán's *esperpento* reflects a deformed, demented side of society.[41] The daughter sees in her mother what she herself does not want to become and although she does not understand nor know her mother entirely, she constructs her own truth regarding the past. She constructs her mother as weak and timid in order to rebel against her.

The only scene in the novel where all three women appear simultaneously exposes the esperpentic notion of the generational mirror. The frustrations of each woman emerge as she relates her identity to her specific socialized upbringing. Nevertheless, the effect is to unite the women's experience and although they argue, the similarities of what they say become evident. Each feels misunderstood by the others as well as cheated by history. The daughter wants to leave home and her mother and grandmother try to dissuade her. This scene is yet another way in which Roig brings together the painful break with tradition. The scene is not just one of youthful rebellion but of recognizing the necessity of change. The grandmother explains: "tu no has viscut la meva època, allò sí que era terrible. Tot el dia amb la mamà, fent comèdia. Nosaltres, les dones, a callar. Però ara! Si feu el que voleu!" (137) [you haven't lived through my time, that, yes, that was terrible. All day long with mother, playing the fool. We women had to shut up! But now, you do exactly what you want!] The juxtaposition of the exclamation *ia callar*! with the textual evidence of the grandmother shouting seen in the exclamation points that follow, works to undermine her own upbringing and suggest that she too has emerged out of silence by decrying the rules of silence imposed on her youth. In her diatribe she exercises the opposite of what she was taught. She speaks out and does not remain quiet, thus allowing the granddaughter access to her repressive past.

The mother then chimes in: "Si haguessis viscut una guerra, sabries què significa passar fam, com la teva mare. Tot un dia escorcollant els morts, molts d'ells cadàvers completament cremats, per trobar el teu pare . . . , i amb una gana que tenia!" (137) [If you had lived through the war, you would know what it means to be hungry, like your mother. One entire day spent rummaging through the dead, many of them completely burned corpses, to find your father . . . and I was so hungry!] This moment links the heart of the novel, this confrontation between the three women, to the monologue that frames the narrative. The mother expresses her impressions about that day in 1938 when she was independent, directly involved in the results of a very real war and her sensorial memory serves to maintain the past moment of epiphany in the present. However, at this moment the daughter erupts: "Se me'n fot de la guerra i dels vostres embolics! Això d'ara és diferent, comprens?" (137) [I don't care about the war or all of your problems! Things are different now, don't you understand?] While the daughter has expressed her disgust with the obsessions of her mother and grandmother, she affirms that her time or era is different, "això d'ara és diferent." Roig masterfully collapses the entire narrative into this one-page climax of the novel. From this point the narrative telescopes out into personal internal renderings of the specific eras brought to life in this small scene. The mirror of generations reflects the struggle between women when change is inevitable. The scene acts as a superficial account of generational bickering while it underlines the aggressive interaction between three women who have no profound knowledge of each other. The overwhelming silence regarding key events of their lives that envelops the characters becomes hyperapparent in this scene as they argue senselessly. Their misunderstanding of each other stems from the fact that they have never shared with each other their individual pasts, specifically those details of their pasts that break with socially acceptable feminine behavior.

In the monologue that opens and closes the narration, Ramona the mother describes her first meeting with Joan, her husband, while she is searching Barcelona for him after the bombing. She remembers her monotonous relationship with her husband: "Les dones de la colònia anaven a esperar els marits a l'estació i s'asseien, totes, als jardinets del costat de l'estació" (20) [The women in the colony would go to wait for their husbands at the station and they all would sit in the little gardens just beside the station]. The women waiting for the men to return from work are defined by the promise of male presence that ensures a passive female role in the relationship. This public image of Ramona the mother is exactly that which her daughter so loathes. Ramona's marriage to Joan, which she describes in the opening monologue, becomes even more oppressive and mundane when she reveals one hundred pages into the novel what Ignasi, her lover, had written to her before he left to take up arms with the Republican cause: "et desitjo que no et converteixis en cap d'aquestes dones que van a esperar els marits a l'estació . . . " (115–16) [I hope that you don't become one of those women who goes to wait for her husband at the station]. Roig's technique of withholding information and disobeying chronological order provides the reader with small moments of epiphany throughout the unraveling of the story. With the insertion of Ignasi's comment toward the middle of the novel, the events from the beginning, such as Ramona's search for her husband and prior to that, her marriage to him, become tainted with remorse and nostalgia of the secret adolescent affair. What holds the narrative together is the consciousness of the characters, the mental recollections that together create an entire, multidimensional text.

In her monologue, the mother moves from her assigned domestic space out into the streets and public buildings of Barcelona. She remembers what her husband told her upon leaving the house: "Em va dir, avui, tu, ben quietona a casa. En Joan em diu sempre que jo sóc una bleda i una beneita i que sort en tinc d'ell, que m'acomboia per la vida" (9) [He told me "today, you stay at home." Joan always tells me that I'm silly and naïve and that I'm lucky to have him, that he leads me through life]. Joan's words seem cruel and oppressive but, given the radical contrast between the words and the circumstance in which they are uttered, the tone becomes ironic, for Ramona wanders the streets alone yet determined to find Joan. She has actively defied his order to stay at home and has proven to be intelligent in deducing his possible whereabouts. Also, he is absent during this crucial time and isn't there to "guide her through life" nor does she require his help. The roles are reversed; she is the one looking to save him. The irony is heightened at the end of the novel, which is the conclusion of the mother's monologue. She abandons her search to rest in the hospital, waits for the dead to be identified, and ends up listening to an old man tell war stories, which spark her interest in politics and lead her further away emotionally as well as literally from finding her husband. She muses: "Podia ser que mai més no tornés a veure en Joan" (165) [Perhaps I'll never see Joan again] as she begins to make her way home in the light of the breaking day. She sees a woman fighting with a dog for a piece of bread and as a final symbolic act of independence and rebellion against defeat she says: "Vaig arrencar a córrer i vaig ajudar la vella a guanyar la batalla del tros de pa" (166) [I began to run and I helped the old woman win the battle of the piece of bread]. With these words the novel ends, signifying not only Catalunya's entrance into lean years of economic and social repression but also the beginning of the metaphorical battle with injustice and repression that the youngest Ramona inherits.

Another aspect of the repression expressed by the grandmother Ramona is the disillusion with motherhood. Roig creates a similar mood in her novel as did Rodoreda in *La plaça del Diamant* when Natàlia describes her pregnancy as a strange and oddly distancing experience as if her body were not her own. Remedios Varo's previously discussed depiction of motherhood in *The Celestial Pablum* also draws a somber picture of motherhood as the exhausted woman trapped in a tiny isolated tower feeds stardust to a waning moon. The grandmother Ramona struggles with the same sense of detachment when she thinks she is too old to have a child and that "És com si ella m'hagués robat un bon doll de la meva sang, m'hagués deixat buida per dintre. No sé si me l'estimo, la nena." (145) [It's as if she (the baby) has robbed me of a good portion of my blood, as if she's left me empty inside. I don't know if I love her]. The continuation of an antimotherhood discourse formulated by Rodoreda and Varo links Roig to the work of her predecessors in two ways. First Roig creates a character that speaks for a generation gaining consciousness of the overwhelmingly oppressive nature of biological determinism. Rodoreda's Natàlia, Varo's figure and Ramona the grandmother discover that motherhood sometimes isn't the answer to a woman's lack of identity. Second, Roig propels the dialogue forward, which pays homage to her predecessors and at the same time expands the theme and thus acknowledges its importance. The implications of a multigenerational configuration of characters allows for the development of particular themes within the novel just as extratextually Roig is aware of her literary ancestors and the genealogy of women writers in Catalunya. Roig expresses the burden and promise of literary inheritance through the voice of the grandmother: "Els fills són com un mirall. En ells veus la teva fi. La seva presència te n'adverteix contínuament. I la meva infància, feliç i tranquil.la, s'allunya dins el record i es converteix en la cara desgraciada de la nova Mundeta" (146) [Children are like a mirror. In them you see your demise. Their presence reminds you of it constantly. And my childhood, happy and peaceful, fades into memory and becomes converted into the unfortunate face of the new Mundeta]. The negative generational inheritance becomes symptomatic of women's repressed position in marriage and family structures.

The grandmother Ramona succeeds in hiding her true experience behind social decorum required of her by dominant male society. Roig creates her diaries in order to reveal the grandmother's feelings that contradict her outward persona, which is consequently the image that her daughter and granddaughter consider true. As Christina Dupláa notes:

Allí, en ese mundo íntimo están los diarios, las cartas, las conversaciones que para Roig tienen el valor de *documento* y que le permiten reconstruir esa historia de mujeres, con códigos que funcionan totalmente al margen del mundo masculino-público-político.[42]

[There, in that intimate world are the diaries, the letters, the conversations that for Roig are documentation and they allow her to reconstruct women's history, with codes that function totally on the margin of the masculine-public-political world.]

Roig's women insert themselves into the public and political in ways other than with codified masculine behavior. They do not act like men but that negation of patriarchal surrender doesn't marginalize women from History in Roig's narrative; conversely it allows women to repossess history and make it theirs. Dupláa does, however, pinpoint the importance of Roig's intertextuality, the creation of a documentation of women's genealogy, not a recounting of events, marriages, children, and deaths, but a body of texts that attests to the very existence of the fissure between voice and silence.

The mother has no knowledge of the grandmother's loveless marriage, for after the death of her husband, the grandmother created a myth around his public image yet as her diary reveals: "ell m'irrita amb la seva dèria del *Vals de Coppelia*!. . .papalloneta, em diu. I jo m'aixeco d'una revolada i me'n vaig a sopar sense fer-li cas." (96) [He really bothers me with his obsession of *The Waltz of Coppelia! . . .* my little butterfly, he says, and I get up quickly and go to eat supper without paying any attention]. The grandmother's affair with a young student that produces such fear and guilt is restricted to the pages of her diary. She expresses her fear and desire: "Necessito morir d'amor" [I must die of love] and "Tinc por de desaparèixer, d'anar a l'infern" (112) [I'm afraid of disappearing, of going to hell] and "No vull tornar a pecar" (134) [I don't want to sin again]. Her emotion, desire, and fear, all blatantly honest in her diary, do not formulate in any way her social reality.

While her diary admits that "En Víctor (her young lover) també representa el meu Amor Ideal" (118) [Victor represents my Ideal Love], the confabulated reality that the grandmother has provided for her family is that which the granddaughter remembers: "L'avi Francisco era el mite de la branca Ventura: un home prudent, honest, i amb un profund sentit de l'honor" (119) [Grandfather Francisco was the myth of the Ventura clan: a prudent, honest man with a profound sense of honor]. The granddaughter even becomes jealous of her grandmother's love: "Evocava l'avi com una dona enamorada i la Mundeta l'envejava. Envejava l'amor pacífic que es desprenia de les paraules de la vella" (120) [She talked about grandfather like a woman truly in love and Mundeta was jealous. She envied the peaceful love released by the old woman's words]. Therefore, the discrepancy between what is written and what is believed to be true by members of the family once again underlines the false reality fabricated through spoken language and the underside of that reality found in the truth of the written testimony.

The youngest Ramona contemplates the mysterious side of her own mother: "Era un enigma, la seva mare . . . Semblava que

hagués comès un pecat molt greu, algun fet imperdonable de joventut"(125) [Her mother was an enigma. It seemed as if she had committed some grave sin, something unforgivable in her youth]. She
doesn't know anything about her mother's affair with Ignasi, but
her awareness of her mother's silenced past, "algun fet imperdonable," suggests the possibility of comprehension. Likewise, neither
the grandmother nor the mother is privy to the granddaughter's
involvement with the student protests, her love affair with an indifferent student leader, Jordi, or her growing unrest. When the
youngest Ramona finds Jordi in bed with her friend Anna, she seeks
revenge by picking up a stranger and having sex with him for
money. As she rips up the money she thinks: "Bon vent i barca
nova" (107) [Good wind and a new boat], a saying implying satisfaction at a deed well done. This action inscribing a "newer self-
awareness"[43] fills the void created by the disconnection between
and misconception of her mother and grandmother. The reader
understands her desperation, her newfound identity and independence free from Jordi and from a false sense of love and consequently from her family and past. Yet the silence surrounding the
relationships between the women creates a tension engendered by
the ignorance of pivotal moments in each of their lives.

Silence appears as a major theme in Roig's first collection of
short stories entitled *Molta roba i poc sabó i tan neta que la volen*
(1971) [*So Many Clothes and Too Little Soap and They Want Them
All So Clean*]. In this collection of stories Roig introduces the cast
of characters that will appear in the trilogy about the families Claret
and Miralpeix.

The first, story entitled "Breu història sentimental d'una mad-
ama Bovary barcelonina nascuda a Gràcia i educada segons els nostres millors principis i tradicions" [A Brief Sentimental Story of a
Barcelona Madame Bovary Born in Gràcia and Educated According
to Our Best Principles and Traditions], begins with the death of
Mundeta Jover i Almirall, the grandmother Ramona. Intertwined
with descriptions of the wake and funeral are pieces of a letter that
Ramona wrote to her friend Teresa recounting her wedding to
Francisco, their honeymoon in Paris, and the birth of their daughter. The text compares Ramona's life with her death as representations of the proper and silenced female existence. The narrative
voice of the story describes minute details and the "tocs definitius
per a enllestir-la eternament"[44] [little touches that will keep her

memory alive eternally]. The symbols of her conservative marriage and lifestyle include rosary beads "llargs, negres, i amb una creu de fusta al capdavall, que hom li entrelligà a les mans" (15) [large, black and with a cross on top, that she held laced around her hands]. In order to link Ramona's death to her marriage and life, the narrative voice points out: "Tots aquests detalls, banals i fútils, serveixen per a il.lustrar el lector, que no és agosarat de mena si es tracta de matèria d'imaginació, de l'extraordinària vulgaritat de la mort de na Mundeta Jover i Almirall." (15) [All these details, banal and futile, are intended to show the reader, who isn't blessed with skill when it comes to the imagination, the extraordinary vulgarity of Mundeta Jover Almirall's death]. The narrative voice criticizes not only Mundeta but also the reader for lacking imagination. The superiority and candor with which the narrative voice addresses the reader achieves two ends: the text becomes removed from the reader's dominion, that is to say, the reader shares the same level or plane of existence as Mundeta and the other characters, which is inferior to that of the narrative voice. Also the unsettled reader rises to the challenge if only to prove herself adequately skilled when dealing with material of imagination. Ironically, Roig uses the banality of Ramona's death to pay homage to the imagination as an integral part of history. In order to do this she needs the reader's cooperation and participation and therefore proposes a challenge by equating the reader to Mundeta in order to universalize her mundane existence. In this sense the narrator exorcises the alienated position of the reader who falls into a metatextual exile from the work itself. The reader must realize her part in the production of the narrative as an outsider, who is accused of lacking imagination, but is necessary for the development of the work.

In order to construct a literary genealogy Roig depends on an active intertextuality that draws the exiled reader in while breaking textual codes and narrative strategies of sequence and closure. "Breu història sentimental" relies on letter fragments to document the events of Mundeta's life while in *Ramona, adéu* her diary relates many of the same occurrences and circumstances. In order to maintain her social status and decorum the grandmother writes letters that sometimes gloss over the detailed descriptions and her emotional response to the same events found in her diary including her illicit love affair and her true feelings toward Francisco, her husband. For example, in one letter to Teresa that forms part of

"Breu història sentimental," Mundeta claims: "Quan ell dorm i el sento roncar al meu costat, perquè ronca, saps, penso en les nostres vides i no em sé avenir de tot plegat. El veig com un desconegut . . . ai, no sé pas perquè t'ho dic això" (31) [when he sleeps and I hear him snore at my side, because he snores, you know, I think about our lives and I can't believe it. I see him like a stranger . . . oh, I don't know why I said that]. Nevertheless, in *Ramona, adéu,* Mundeta's profound disgust for Francisco emerges in the pages of her diary:

> Les seves mans tremolen i suen molt. Se m'arrapa com una llagasta i sento, a cau d'orella, el seu esbufec. El seu alè desprèn les olors de l'estómac. Jo me n'aparto i en Francisco s'atura. Ja no en sento el bleix. En Francisco, aleshores, fa mitja volta i s'adorm . . . i ronca. En Francisco ronca tota la nit. (*Ramona,* 96)

> [His hands tremble and sweat. He grabs me like a tick and I hear his panting in my ear. His breath gives off smells from his stomach. I pull away and Francisco stops. I can no longer hear his panting. Then Francisco rolls over and falls asleep . . . and snores. Francisco snores all night long.]

The link between these two texts depends on the silence enforced on Mundeta by her family and by society. She is not at liberty to discuss her unhappy marital situation with her friend in a letter, the only place she can voice her opinion is in a private textual space. The diary text then becomes a subaltern testimony, the unspoken, silenced reality that exists beneath the public testimony of letter writing.

Another example of the socially mediated wording and tone found in the letter to Teresa of "Breu història" occurs when Francisco discusses the significance of the millennium with Senyor Domingo. "El senyor Domingo va arribar a la conclusió que, si el segle començava amb el 1901, aleshores el 1900 no existeix. Ves quines coses! ("Breu història," 32) [Mr. Domingo arrived at the conclusion that if the century begins with the year 1901 then 1900 didn't exist. Can you believe it?] On the other hand, when Mundeta writes about the same conversation in her diary she expresses her feelings with more conviction and disapproval: "De vegades trobo que els homes fan unes reflexions molt poca-soltes" (*Ramona,* 101) [Sometimes I find that men just say the stupidest things].

A moment that appears equally disturbing in both her letters and diary revolves around the birth of her daughter. Mundeta tells her friend Teresa: "Confesso que hauria preferit un noi. Almenys un home és lliure. Pot fer el que vol" ("Breu història," 36) [I confess that I would have preferred a boy. At least men are free. They can do what they want]. In her diary, Mundeta also laments the fact that her baby is a girl: "Si haguéssim tingut un nen . . . Un home és lliure, pot triar el seu camí. Una dona no hi té res a fer, al món." (*Ramona,* 145) [If only we had had a son . . . a man is free, he can choose his path. A woman doesn't have anything to do in this world]. Mundeta's detachment from motherhood, her daughter, and her own status as a woman in a patriarchal society defines a fundamental part of her personality. Her willingness to show her disapproval of the gender of her child reveals her own unsatisfactory life and her surrender to the female condition proclaimed by the men in her life and by society at large.

In "Breu història," after the family has left the cemetery and returned to "el món dels vius" [the world of the living], a different voice, defined by italics, speaks directly to the dead grandmother beginning with "*tu te n'has anat per sempre d'aquest món de vius*" (37) [you have left this world of the living forever]. The new voice serves to vindicate the mundane, sad life of Mundeta Jover by bringing her story back from the dead. This voice belongs not to Roig, but to the conceptual reality of women writers, that is to say, the challenge that women face to bring silenced lives into a newly formulated sense of history.[45] The voice continues: "Tots plegats et dictaren les normes que haurien de menar la teva vida pels viaranys de la inconsciència" (38) [Everyone together dictated the norms with which you should have conducted your life through the paths of unconsciousness]. The narrative voice seeks to salvage and preserve within the pages of the text a consciousness that allows all of the Mundetas to claim a place in history. The final sentences of this story attest to Roig's clear vision of her own project as a writer and with these words she prepares the reader for the numerous texts about these women that follow:

Perquè tu no ho saberes, tot això, perquè passares pel món en silenci, imperceptiblement, amb la lleugeresa pròpia dels qui parlen per dintre . . . I ara, des d'una Barcelona que comença a perdre fins i tot la nostàlgia d'aquell to de reina destronada, intentaré d'edificar per a tu el perfum de la història. (38)

[Because you didn't know all of this, because you went through the world in silence, imperceptible, with your own ease of those who talk to themselves . . . And now, from a Barcelona that begins to lose even the nostalgia of that dethroned queen, I will try to construct for you the perfume of history.]

Encapsulated in this portion of text lies the importance of the city and of the power of language that the writer utilizes to mold and reform a sense of history. Roig directly addresses the need to incorporate into history the woman exiled from language. That silent figure, resigned to nothingness and excluded from the world, resides in all of Roig's characters, and by writing them into being she breaks with the code of female resignation.

Christina Dupláa also detects a declaration of intent in Roig's words and explains: "ya anunció cuál iba a ser su propósito en relación a la literatura y su ciudad"[46] [she already proclaimed what would be her purpose in relation to literature and the city]. Yet Dupláa goes on to define "ese perfume de la historia es esa Barcelona entrañable y nostálgica de toda su obra"[47] [this perfume of history is that beloved and nostalgic Barcelona in all of her work]. Dupláa's definition captures the importance of the city in Roig's work as well as in her worldvision of literature, nevertheless the questions of history and the vindication of women within its rigid framework surpass the confines of any one city.

Susan Merrill Squier defines the relationship between women and urban spaces when she cites Carl Schorske, who points out:

No man thinks of the city in hermetic isolation. . . . He forms his image of it through a perceptual screen derived from inherited culture and transformed by personal experience. Hence the investigation of the intellectual's idea of the city inevitably carries us outside its own frame into a myriad of concepts and values about the nature of man, society, and culture.[48]

Squier equates this observation, despite its assumption of a male viewpoint, to the analysis of a city's treatment by women. The city then becomes a "symbol of culture, or as the nexus of concepts and values determining woman's place in history and society."[49] Therefore, Roig's Barcelona becomes metaphorical of every urban setting, a universal location of passing history where the women scramble to insert themselves into the equation. The perfume of history then may not be Barcelona, but the unnamable underside of urban life and the history that belongs to women.

This is also evident in the connection between Roig's use of the phrase "perfume of history" and its origin. The opening epigraph to "Breu història" discloses how Josep M. de Sagarra defines the phrase in his novel *Vida privada* [*A Private Life*] as "allò que no es veu i només es respira: el perfum de la història" (11) [that which cannot be seen but only breathed: the perfume of history]. In a sophisticated intertextual play, Roig has associated the dead Mundeta with the widow Xuclà from Sagarra's novel, described in the epigraph as "una dona vella que ha viscut molt manté, més que un home, l'empremta del passat" (11) [an old woman who has lived a long time and maintained, more than any man, the fingerprints of the past]. By borrowing the elusive and enigmatic "perfume of history," Roig links her text to that of Sagarra. This connection works on a textual level as well as on an ideological level that links all women to the feminine historical void represented by the "fingerprints of the past." As evident in Roig's reconstruction of female genealogy through diaries and letters, and in accordance with Sagarra, she affirms that women maintain the past through memory more effectively than men and this effort to document it translates into literature.

The carefully woven threads of women, silence, and problematic history emerge throughout the collection of short stories as well as throughout the trilogy of novels that follows. The textual sharing of characters, and terms, and a continual rupture with phallogocentric history create coherence and persistence, giving form and voice to the silenced female "perfume of history." In this way Barcelona functions in the narrative to locate women in a particular circumstance at a particular point in time, bringing familiarity through a recognizable city to the circumstance of Roig's women. This familiarity in turn allows the reader passage into the daily lives and routines of the women in the Claret and Miralpeix families. The specifics of Barcelona provide details that connect to the reader's own circumstance. While Barcelona remains an important focal point for Roig, its urban spaces become universal as they begin to incorporate feminine experience.

EL TEMPS DE LES CIRERES AND *L'HORA VIOLETA*: RECONSTRUCTION
AND DEMYTHIFICATION OF CULTURE

Through Roig's meticulous observation of detail, *El temps de les cireres* [*Time of Cherries*] and *L'hora violeta* [*The Violet Hour*] form a complex interweaving of characters, places and events held together by the central figure Natàlia Miralpeix. As a photographer, Natàlia spends her life observing and trying to preserve moments of history with her camera. In *El temps de les cireres* several voices emerge throughout the narrative, including Natàlia's father Joan, her brother Lluís and his wife Sílvia, her Aunt Patrícia, and Natàlia herself. The one character whose absence acts as an overwhelming presence and who permeates the thoughts and emotions of the other characters is Judit, Natàlia's mother. A shroud of mystery surrounds Judit, who swiftly declined physically and emotionally after a brain aneurysm left her incapacitated. Judit also mourns the death of her young son who had Down's syndrome for whom she felt immense pity at the expense of her other children, Natàlia and Lluís.

However, the central theme of Judit's friendship with Kati spans both texts, establishing the focal point of the narrative discourse on female relationships. Judit's friendship with Kati, an eccentric Marxist who sought social and political freedom through sexual promiscuity, is built up in *El temps de les cireres* as an axis around which revolves the relationship between women that society deems enigmatic. In fact, the female relationship exemplified in Judit and Kati's secretive bond places female friendship on the outside of cultural acceptance. Women who share a deep connection exist in a realm exiled from society's prescribed place for women. Roig challenges heterosociality as the dictated social norm and through Judit and Kati provides a poignant example of how women are separated by forces beyond their control.

What Roig constructs in *El temps de les cireres* as formal historical accounts of the family's development is reinvestigated in *L'hora violeta*. Barcelona as a physical reality becomes less important as it gives way to the narrative space of the writerly construction of the past. The mystery surrounding Judit and Kati's relationship as well as Joan's obsession with his dead wife are told through the male character's perspective in *El temps de les cireres*. Conversely, in

L'hora violeta entries from Judit's diary and letters from Kati reveal the true nature of their relationship and their attitudes and fears toward imposed familial and societal duties. In the latter novel the act of writing supersedes all political, personal, or familial bonds that are strained, broken, or in some way twisted. Roig implies that while the past cannot be corrected or relived, the tragedy lies not in the violent acts of abandonment, such as Natàlia leaving her family and refusing to return for her mother's funeral, or Judit ignoring her healthy children while doting on Pere, her son with Down's syndrome, or even Kati's sudden suicide but rather in the threat of forgetfulness if the lives of these women remain unrecorded, unwritten, and therefore unlived.

In order to arrive at a distinctly feminine narrative voice, Roig disrupts chronology with nontraditional narrative devices such as the insertions of memories, flashbacks, letters, and diaries that are fundamental to the structure of the first novel of the trilogy *Ramona, adéu*. However, in the consequent novels the time frame encompasses two texts, defying spatial and temporal limitations of the written page. Familial love contrasted with nationalistic pride and political commitment clash in both novels and personal love and a love of humanity emerge as troublesome opposites most vividly in *L'hora violeta*. Even though Roig concentrates on love as the main source of conflict in the lives of her female characters, the questions she poses use relationships between women as a springboard to arrive at a more profound sense of feminine creative identity. The urban spaces of Barcelona in *El temps de les cireres* that possess moments of Natàlia's youth and define her familial relationships remind her of the limitations of her past. In *L'hora violeta* these spaces seem to evaporate, the street names lose importance, Natàlia spends time on an unnamed island, and several characters escape the mundane urban code through death. In this novel the critical space of the text and language replace the urban landscape as testimony to the past.

In these two ways, through the demythification of spatial relationships between the individual and the city combined with the liberation found through female friendship, Roig begins a dialogue between women and writing concluding that through writing women can conquer love, fear, and even death.

In an interview with Geraldine Cleary Nichols, Roig discusses her reason for writing both novels:

El temps de les cieres fue una novela de premonición; cuando la escribí estábamos en un momento de gran euforia porque había muerto Franco y nos creíamos realmente que íbamos a construir la sociedad perfecta . . . Al mismo tiempo tenía la idea de reconciliarme con la generación anterior; de entender por qué ellos habían sido vencidos y se habían declarado a sí mismos vencidos, y era porque tenían que sobrevivir.[50]

[*Time of Cherries* was a premonition; when I wrote it we were in a euphoric moment because Franco had died and we believed that we were going to construct the perfect society. At the same time, I had the idea to reconcile with the previous generation; to understand why they had been beaten and had declared themselves beaten, and it was because they had to survive.]

The notion of the novel as reflective of a specific historical moment in Catalunya's history emerges in the detailed descriptions of Barcelona that impress Natàlia upon her return from England. The disillusion with Marxist socialism and its hollow promise of a perfect society leaves the characters in the novel adrift in directionless political liberty and personal crisis. Roig also addresses in the interview the antecedents to and her personal investment in *L'hora violeta*:

La hora violeta es la única de todas mis novelas que me ha salvado a mí; parece todo muy exagerado pero fue así. . . . En broma decía que mi marido me había dejado por su amante y mi amante por su mujer. Total, pensé en suicidarme. Pero no me suicidé; primero, por mis hijos; segundo, por lo que ya podía escribir. Pensaba; hay que dejar constancia de todo esto.[51]

[*The Violet Hour* is the only novel of mine that has saved me; it seems a bit dramatic but that's how it was. . . . As a joke I said my husband had left me for his lover and my lover for his wife. In any case, I thought of suicide. But I didn't commit suicide; first, for my children, second, for all that I could write. I thought: I have to record all of this.]

In Roig's own words the healing effects of writing and of giving experience form and presence release the lost sense of identity produced by either the civil war or by failure in love. Notably what stands out in Roig's testament to her work as well as in the novels themselves is not the love triangle, not that women love more intensely than men, not that women give themselves over more completely to love but rather the absolute necessity for women to write themselves into the social fabric and create documents that attest to the validity of feminine experience.⁵² It is this act that reclaims a literary space for the emotionally exiled writer.

At the beginning of *El temps de les cireres*, Natàlia returns to Barcelona after living in England for twelve years. Leaving the airport on her way to her Aunt Patrícia's house, Natàlia observes several landmarks that situate her physically and emotionally in her native city: " 'hi ha un mural d'en Miró' reconegué els trets màgics i suposadament infantils del pintor català i va somriure, 'ja sóc a casa' "⁵³ ["there is a mural by Miró" she recognized the magic and supposedly infantile trademarks of the Catalan painter and smiled, "I'm home"]. Her relation to the city lies in the concrete space of her Aunt Patrícia's house: "Quan la Natàlia va tornar a Barcelona, va preferir anar al pis de la tia Patrícia, que era a la Gran Via tocant a Bruc" (9) [When Natàlia returned to Barcelona, she preferred to go to her Aunt Patrícia's house on the corner of Gran Via and Bruc]. Her Aunt Patrícia's garden that serves as a symbolic Eden of Natàlia's youth has been sold and the lemon tree that appears at specific key moments throughout the retelling of the women's history is gone. As Natàlia tries to readjust to a new city she feels dislocated and isolated. Her observation that "Barcelona era un immens cadàver esventrat" (97) [Barcelona was an immense, disembowled cadaver] reflects not only Natàlia's relation to the city but also to what the city represents, her childhood and her family. Natàlia's mother, Judit, has died and her father lives institutionalized due to his strange erratic behavior.

However, Natàlia's struggle to readjust to a city that has changed and bears the scars of her own personal familial disasters becomes the source of an epiphany. Natàlia wanders the same streets of the Barrio Gótico that she loved as a teenager with her nephew, Márius. The narration is exact in locating the two characters within the actual streets of the old Barcelona neighborhood: "Deixaren endarrera el carrer de Flassaders i tornaren a voltar Santa Maria del Mar, la Natàlia pensà que la gent jove també estimen els carrers de Barcelona" (215) [they left behind Flassaders Street and rounded Santa Maria del Mar again, Natàlia thought: young people love Barcelona's streets too]. When Natàlia reaches out to Márius, who threatens to run away from his family, she offers a bit of advice: "jo també creia que aquesta ciutat s'enfonsava però a fora he comprès que la ciutat, la portem a dintre" (216) [I also thought that this city was collapsing around me, but while away I understood that you carry the city inside of you]. The Barcelona of concrete and stone has been transformed into an internal spatial realm of memory that comprises one's past.

Another reference to the city and its specificity as a marker of the past lies in the repetition of the Café Núria mentioned in both *Ramona, adéu* and *El temps de les cireres*. Squier cites the importance of the public gathering spaces: "cities at least hold out the possibility of sisterhood, as women who have escaped from the private home gather in public spaces to work, to play, and to discover that . . . they like each other."[54] In the novel *El temps de les cireres* when Joan and Judit first meet they go to the Café Núria where Judit explains that the women gathered there are "unes amigues de la meva germana Patrícia . . . la que riu tant es diu Kati" (*El temps,* 149) [some friends of my sister Patrícia . . . the one who laughs so much is Kati]. One of Patrícia's friends is Mundeta from *Ramona, adéu*. The public space of the café appears as a central meeting place for the women in *Ramona, adéu*: "La Mundeta Ventura, amb un vestidet de crespó de dues peces, la faldilla combinada en plecs, esperava la seva mare per anar al Núria" (*Ramona,* 36) [Mundeta Ventura, in her crepe suit complete with pleated skirt, waited for her mother to go to the Núria]. Thus the reemergence of the locale crossing textual spaces establishes the discourse of public gathering, which empowers women with a sense of community.

Roig also defines urban spaces through linguistic domination. Bourdieu's term "linguistic market" refers to established language and its implied hierarchies: "the structures of the linguistic market . . . impose themselves as a system of specific sanctions and censorships."[55] The contrast in Roig's use of Catalan and Castilian serves to separate the ideologies supported by each linguistic market. Bourdieu's concept of a linguistic market delineates specific social, cultural, and economic groups of people who communicate in ways particular to their community and in ways that express and support a certain ideology. For example, when Natàlia recalls her experience during the student riots in 1968 when she and her boyfriend Emilio are taken into the police commissary for questioning, the noted presence of Castilian remains vivid in her memory. The story of her incarceration occupies about thirty pages of the novel and also reveals her initial confrontation with the conflict of personal and political interests. The police speak only Castilian, which appears in the original Catalan version of *El temps de les cireres* in italics. This separation of languages enforces the reality of the military, brutal tone that Castilian carried for Catalans. In addition, the police speak crudely about Natàlia: "*las mujeres estáis más bonitas con faldas, con pantalones parecéis marimachos*" [you women are prettier in skirts, in pants you look like tomboys] and another policeman who overhears this shouts "*dejadla que es muy fea*" (114) [leave her alone, she's really ugly].

Roig expresses her opinion concerning the fissure between the Castilian and Catalan in her interview with Nichols: "Para mí, el castellano es siempre una lengua impuesta, comenzando con el colegio. Era la lengua del poder, del dominio, mientras que la lengua del amor o del afecto era la catalana."[56] [For me, Castilian is always an imposed language, beginning with school. It was the language of power, of domination, while the language of love or affection was Catalan]. Therefore the separation of languages into a domestic hidden language and an official language used for law enforcement, government, and schooling sets up a radical dichotomy between the writer's private and public identity and her relationship to and position in the "linguistic market" depending on which language she chooses to employ. In Roig's case she clearly states that her linguistic preoccupation lies in the vindication of Catalan as an official and literary language. By inserting moments of Castilian in the Catalan narrative, the Castilian becomes an aberration, the presence of the enemy in relation to the main characters of the narrative.

Another example is when Natàlia is in a cell waiting to be released and she hears: "Natalia Miralpeix, accentuat damunt de la i car el que cridava deuria ésser castellà" (118) [Natàlia Miralpeix, accented on the i, whoever was yelling had to be Castilian]. The night before when Natàlia and her boyfriend were arrested for throwing rocks at the police who were breaking up a student demonstration, they witnessed several policemen beating a young girl. The policeman who releases Natàlia threatens her in Castilian: "*y la otra también está fuera. Comprenderás que el compañero estuviera muy nervioso,¡los habíais recibido con piedras! La chica está bien, el médico la ha visto, conque, aquí no ha pasado nada, ¿eh?*"

(119) [and the other one has been released, too. You understand that my partner was nervous. You were throwing rocks at him! The girl is fine. The doctor saw her, so nothing happened here, okay?] The language of social authority and oppression that the policeman uses forces Natàlia into silence concerning the incident of police brutality. Yet within the context of the narrative, the Castilian loses prominence and narrative authority and is reduced to a symbolic representation of the injustice of the police system.

While Roig manipulates accepted notions of Castilian as the official language in Spain, she empowers Catalan as the language of narrative and the reconstructive idiom of the past and history. Other forms of oppression in the novel grow out of the rigid familial system and related repressed sexuality experienced by both men and women. Roig clearly does not draw gender distinctions in the severity of sexual oppression fomented by Catholic doctrine but instead uncovers the painful reality of relationships forged under strict sociocultural restrictions. Her solution to the misunderstandings between people exposed in *El temps de les cireres* appears in her following novel as a need for female solidarity. Nevertheless, in *El temps de les cireres* the social oppression of a sexual nature remains embedded in the familial lining as deep dark secrets kept by certain family members.

Aunt Patrícia and Uncle Esteve, Natàlia's sister-in-law Sílvia (daughter of Ramona-mother), and Joan Miralpeix harbor sexual feelings that they fear are abnormal by society's standards. Natàlia's abortion becomes common knowledge to her family but serves as a breaking point in her relationship with her father and a manifestation of the fear and medical danger that engulfs the characters during Franco's oppressive dictatorship.

The second part of the novel *El temps de les cireres* is entitled "Aroma de tardor" ["Aroma of Autumn"] and tells the story of the troubled matrimony of Patrícia and Esteve Mirangels. Patrícia narrates the section with delicate decorum, that is to say her language is not offensive or accusatory because she herself accepts her social position as wife. Because of her love for her husband's friend Gonçal Rodés, she considers herself to be the cause of her marital unhappiness. Patrícia represents the older generation of Roig characters. She finds herself in oppressive, socially constructed situations yet fails to act or react because of her acceptance of tradition and primarily of marriage as a sacred, religiously sanctioned pact between man and woman. She sees herself as exiled emotionally from the myth of a harmonious marriage but cannot act to reaffirm her own identity.

Patrícia takes for granted the hierarchical nature of her marriage including the fact that her husband verbally abuses her, ignores her, and makes unwanted displays of sexual aggression. Esteve comments on her physical appearance: "Els Miralpeix . . . sembleu gent de mala vida . . . Us marciu abans d'hora" (65) [You Miralpeix . . . you all seem like vagrants . . . you all wither before your time]. He only comments on how pretty her hands are "quan passava una temporada que no la volia fer gruar" (65–66) [when he was in one of his moods when he didn't want to offend her]. Esteve's indifference to his wife stems from his privileged position as the male in the matrimony and from the fact that he married her for economical reasons, considering her a bargain.

In her later years, after Esteve's death, Patrícia begins to drink "per empassar-se les penes . . . Ella vol espantar els mals, els mals són com corbs que la fiblen" (67) [to drown her sorrows . . . she wants to scare away evil, evil like crows that peck at her]. Roig inserts this information early in the chapter, planting the idea that there is an overwhelmingly painful experience that Patrícia has not shared with anyone else in her family. Eventually the reader learns of Esteve's aggressive sexual behavior on their wedding night:

"li premia les espatlles i la llençava damunt del llit. Ella serrava les cames i s'arrapava amb les seves mans, tan blanques i tan belles, als llençols brodats a mà. Però ell ja era al damunt, amb el colze li estrenyia la gola i amb el genoll, clavat al pubis, feia per obrir-li les cames." (72)

[he pressed down on her shoulders and threw her on the bed. She closed her legs and her hands, so white and lovely, clutched the hand-embroidered sheets. But he was already on top of her, with his elbow he pressed down on her throat and with his knee, dug into her pelvis, he tried to open her legs.]

Patrícia accepts this behavior as normal interaction between men and women and never reveals the unpleasantness to her family or friends. However, the more important and romantic secret that she never revealed to anyone is her love for Gonçal Rodés.

Clearly Patrícia internally feels violated, humiliated, and subordinated by her husband's behavior even if she never confides in a friend or family member. Her attraction toward Gonçal reveals her longing for respect for she claims that Gonçal "no cridava mai, com cridava l'Esteve, i deia 'dispensi', 'em permet', en Gonçal era un home diferent, suau i delicat com un núvol" (84) [never yelled like Esteve yelled, and he said "excuse me," "allow me." Gonçal was a different kind of man, soft and delicate like a cloud]. Patrícia's fantasy excludes any sexual contact, which she considers associated and restricted to marriage under Catholic law, but rather resides in the possibility of courtesy and respect shown by Gonçal. They do exchange a kiss out in the garden that turns into a memory of eternal pure love for Patrícia. However, Patrícia's secret love for Gonçal becomes overshadowed by the final events in the chapter. The narration prepares the reader to accept the woman's depression as result of her failed marriage and unfulfilled love, yet this is soon proven to be only part of the hidden story.

One day Patrícia and her sister-in-law Sixta are out for an afternoon stroll. Patrícia knows that Gonçal will be at her house visiting Esteve discussing politics, literature, or poetry, as they commonly do, so she lies to Sixta, telling her she feels ill as an excuse to go home. When Patrícia arrives home, anxious to see her beloved Gonçal, she finds the house silent: "travessà el passadís, fosc i silenciós, el rebedor, i obrí, plena d'inquietud, el dormitori. Respiraven, en Gonçal i l'Esteve, com 'el bressoleig de les fulles del llimoner', sota el cobrellit de setí estampat amb unes enormes flors blaves" (90) [I crossed the hall, dark and silent, the sitting room, and I opened, very troubled, the bedroom door. Gonçal and Esteve were breathing like "the rocking of the lemon tree leaves" on the satin mattress patterned with enormous blue flowers]. Although Patrícia is unable to describe what she sees and resorts to an awkward metaphor of rocking leaves on the lemon tree, she at once understands her husband's lack of affection toward her. The underlying truth of Patrícia's personal story represents the hidden unspeakable past that Roig intends to record. The reader gains access to Patrícia's past through her nostalgic interior monologue. The information that Patrícia has shelved in her own mind is so disturbing because it disrupts her formulation of marriage and sex, as well as places her outside of the homosexual intimate bond. Her husband's actions not only alienate her from the marriage formula but also subvert the very nature of male sexuality as dictated by the social collective. Roig includes this very short scene in order to suggest various repressive tendencies of Catalan society. Patrícia's unwillingness to discuss or even acknowledge her husband's homosexual experience enshrouds the concept in mystery, inflating its importance beyond a mere act to a manifestation of the unspeakable. The familial structure that relies so heavily on socially constructed roles cannot allow for such sexual aberration and therefore ignores it. The superficiality of their marriage is now cemented and they continue to play out the roles assigned by the institution. Roig uncovers the problematic limitations of homophobia on men who are unable to express their sexual nature and the consequences suffered by the women who are forced into complying with the silence and taboo because of their inferior position in the familial structure.

Sílvia, who is married to Natàlia's brother Lluís, also experiences sexual suffocation under the socially imposed rules of marriage. Sílvia lives an economically privileged life although she resents the fact that her husband made her give up her career as a dancer. However, her resentment seems placated by visits to an expensive gym where she can commiserate with her friends. Her acceptance of her inferior status as a wife becomes apparent as she chats with her friends about Lluís's interests in the "Automòbil Club" and his comments about her weight gain. She adds: "Com que en Lluís no em deixa que treballi . . . no em faria res de tenir un altre fill però no hi ha manera" (175) [As long as Lluís won't let me work . . . I wouldn't mind having another child but there's no way].

The idle banter between friends turns to the recently released movie *Last Tango in Paris* (1973), which presents for the women a type of voyeuristic release from their sexually oppressed relationships. All of the women comment on the crudeness of the character played by Marlon Brando in his sexual encounters with the young female protagonist. However, the superficiality of the conversation becomes inverted when Sílvia and Natàlia later in the chapter have a conversation at the Café Samoa. The conversation turns to the movie *Last Tango in Paris*, suggesting that Sílvia is perhaps a bit obsessed with its content. She confesses to Natàlia:

saps que em vaig quedar d'una peça quan vaig veure que en Marlon Brando feia a la noia—i que tothom diu, quina marranada—el mateix que en Lluís m'ha fet a mi des que ens vam casar? A en Lluís, només li agrada fer-ho pel darrera i jo em pensava que això passava en molts matrimonis. Però quan ho vaig veure a la pel.lícula, fora de mi, vaig sentir tant de fàstic . . . La Sílvia tenia espurnes als ulls, per això no em quedo embarassada. Oi que hauria de tenir un amant? (182)

[you know how astonished I was when I saw that Marlon Brando was doing to that girl—and everyone says, "How disgusting"—the same thing that Lluís has done to me since we've been married? Lluís only likes to do it from behind and I thought that this went on in a lot of marriages. But when I saw it in the movie, outside of myself, I felt so disgusted. Sílvia had tears in her eyes, that's why I never get pregnant. I should have a lover, shouldn't I?]

Sílvia's sense of betrayal surfaces when she becomes convinced by a movie that her husband's sexual preferences are abnormal. The hierarchy expressed outwardly in their marriage through her restriction to the domestic work and childrearing also takes form in a sexually oppressive relationship. Sílvia feels debased not because of the sexual act, for she only learned to reject the idea because of her friends' reaction to the movie, but because of her absence in the act itself. Her complete inability to communicate verbally or sexually with her husband leads her to consider the situation unchangeable. Her lack of true feeling for her husband convinces her that any woman in her right mind would seek a lover.

Roig not only weaves into the narrative the socially constructed terms of marriage but also the socially rendered patriarchal construct of heterosexual physical relationships. She implies that the normal and abnormal are encoded in popular culture and ingested unconsciously by the consumers of the upper middle class. The complacency with which Sílvia approaches her own sexuality promotes the oppressive nature of matrimony as well as blind acceptance of the socially rendered images of a misogynistic male sexuality.

Joan Miralpeix, Natàlia's father, also suffers from dark sexual secrets. Joan serves as an example in Roig's narrative of a complex male character whose emotions substantiate significant character development. In the father figure, Roig crosses gender boundaries to include the same sense of isolation and detachment from reality that many women in the novel express. The novel ends with Joan alone in his room in a hospital, caressing some silk stockings that he believes belong to Judit, his dead wife. The tenderness with which he remembers his wife, even in the days after her stroke, becomes vivid and touching in the scenes that Roig writes in his voice. His family, nevertheless, cannot put up with his sexually explicit behavior toward the end of his life, namely masturbation and fetishism. Judit, Joan's wife, collected and cared for dolls perhaps as a substitute for her dead son, Pere, and her friend Kati who committed suicide in 1939. After her seizure, Judit mutilated the dolls' faces and then cared for them as if they were children, "I, com més les feia patir, més les estimava" (161) [and the more she made them suffer, the more she loved them].[57] After her death, Joan continues his wife's doll fetish, dresses one up in silk underwear, and places it on Judit's side of the bed. The doll "de porcellana que no tenia ulls ni mans" (229) [porcelain doll that didn't have eyes or hands] serves as a sexual memory for Joan yet seems so abnormal to the rest of the family that his son places him in a mental hospital.

Natàlia considers her brother's actions impulsive and even cruel. But the information that neither Lluís nor Natàlia nor any other member of the family knows is the troubled sexual education of their father. Roig reveals Joan's impotence and fear of sex that Judit was able to cure with her aggressive sexuality. As a young child Joan saw his father and Remei, a young woman who worked in the house, involved in "una escena tan rara que, de primer, no la va acabar d'entendre. Per què el seu pare havia lligat la Remei al capçal del llit i semblava com si li gratés l'esquena mentre anava a cavall? (164–65) [a scene so strange that at first he didn't understand. Why had his father tied up Remei to the headboard and looked like he was scratching her while riding horseback?] The beating that the young boy receives upon questioning his father is what confuses him and implants the dark, forbidden, dirty thought of sex in his mind. As he matures, "En Joan Miralpeix no creia en l'amor, creia que les dones eren com bestioles. Per això va lligar aquella mueca, l'Elvira de ca la Rita" (166) [Joan Miralpeix didn't believe in love, he believed that women were like little animals. That is why he tied up that whore, Elvira, from Rita's place]. His sense of love and sex is completely separate: "el sexe eren escenes brutes i tristes, plenes de grinyols i de somiqueigs" (167) [sex was brutal and sad, full of squeals and whimpers]. Fortunately for Joan, Judit changes his attitude and convinces him that sex can and should be an intimate, positive experience. Roig again reveals the devastating effects of socialized concepts of sexuality. She implies that the patrilineal inheritance of misogyny also forces men to suffer from patriarchal silence surrounding sexual identity. Marriage is presented as a type of binding contract for Patrícia and Sílvia but for all of the characters suffering from sexually oppressive, unhealthy relationships marriage only acts as an institution condoning silence. Men and women in Roig's narrative live secret lives, never fully understanding the roots of their own insecurities that lie in silent, socially unacceptable moments of their pasts.

The narrative sequence containing Natàlia's abortion is another way in which Roig seeks to uncover and recover the forgotten past of the social consciousness. Even though Natàlia feels isolated and removed from her family after her abortion, Roig intends to bring her experiences to the forefront of the struggle against the silencing of women's issues. Abortion in Spain in the early 1970s was illegal and women with money went to England for the operation. The only other option was to visit one of the houses of prostitution where inexperienced *comadronas* or midwives operated small, clandestine, unprofessional clinics. Natàlia's experience at the *comadrona* proves to be one of the worst-case scenarios. After the procedure she suffers from high fever and continual bleeding. A recurring nightmare about a hairy spider engulfs her in her room: "l'aranya que bategava les potes tot davallant del sostre de la cambra il.luminada pel focus, cada vegada més grossa, la cenyia, l'estrenyia ben fort, les potes de l'aranya eren peludes, llefiscoses, cada pota deixava anar milers i milers de potes peludes. . . . (136) [the spider that trembled and descended the wall of the room lit by a spotlight, growing bigger and bigger, squeezed her, it held her very tightly, the spider's legs were hairy, sticky, and from each one sprouted thousands and thousands of hairy little legs]. The hairy spider is the horrible dark secret, not only of her abortion, but also of her cultural heritage. It is that which is abhorrent, undesirable, yet a driving force of culture itself: the abject. Roig's incorporation of the abject to reveal a cultural silence parallels the abject employed by Rodoreda in her short stories "La meva Cristina" and "La salamandra."[58] Natàlia struggles with this demon externalized in the spider that in turn grows to symbolize the suffocating secrets of her entire generation. When Natàlia's condition worsens, she calls her sister-in-law Sílvia for help, but before she divulges any information she swears Sílvia to secrecy: "M'ho promets, que no diràs res a en Lluís (137) [Promise me that you won't say anything to

Lluís]. Sílvia promises to keep her secret but immediately tells Lluís out of fear for Natàlia and worry about hiding a family secret from her husband (138).

Years later, after Natàlia's return from England, she and Sílvia discuss the episode. Natàlia asks her why she told Lluís about the abortion and Sílvia replies that she was afraid. Natàlia thinks to herself: "La maleïda por . . . la por d'aquell temps tan gelat i ombrívol, la por semblava un vent immòbil . . ."(182) [Damn fear . . . the fear of that frigid and somber time, the fear that seemed like a still wind]. Roig consolidates and defines a specific fear of a certain time. By dividing the book into encapsulated moments of specific events and then revealing Natàlia's reactions to those events, Roig establishes the connections between these moments of change. A recognition of the unspeakable past, the text becomes a testimony to the progress of documenting the dark secrets that define a person outside of his or her social positioning.

Natàlia's character acts as a bridge not only between the two novels in question but also between the two generations represented by the older Joan Miralpeix, his wife Judit, Aunt Patrícia, and Esteve and the younger generation full of hope seen in Sílvia and Lluís's child, Márius. Natàlia reconciles with her past that includes several fleeting love affairs, a botched abortion, the indifference toward her mother, and resentment toward her father by embracing the relationship between her mother, Judit, and the enigmatic Kati in *L'hora violeta*.

The novel's title is taken from lines 215–20 of *The Waste Land* by T. S. Eliot that serve as an epigraph for the novel. "At the violet hour, when the eyes and back / Turn upward from the desk, when the human engine waits / Like a taxi throbbing waiting, / I Tiresias, though blind, throbbing between two lives, / Old man with wrinkled female breast can see / At the violet hour . . ."[59] Eliot's own notes prove especially revealing considering Natàlia's connecting role as the observer of the family saga. Eliot states:

> Tiresias, although a mere spectator and not indeed a "character," is yet the most important personage in the poem, uniting all the rest. Just as the one-eyed merchant, seller of currants, melts into the Phoenician Sailor, and the latter is not wholly distinct from Ferdinand Prince of Naples, so all the women are one woman, and the two sexes meet in Tiresias. What Tiresias *sees*, in fact, is the substance of the poem.[60]

The violet hour is that moment freed from chronological historical time constructs when the coming together of the masculine and feminine in form of the old man with wrinkled female breast illuminates the story in order to relate it to others. Natàlia combines masculine and feminine attributes by fusing the traditionally gendered roles of woman in her devotion to love with those traditionally male traits of pursuing a professional career, independence, and sexual liberty. Although unlike Eliot's Tiresias in the poem, Natàlia is clearly a character in the novel, her return to Barcelona in *El temps de les cireres* and more important her quest to write an unwritten history in *L'hora violeta* place her at the axis of the action as the mediator between other relationships. In *L'hora violeta,* Natàlia defines herself as the seer: "Em sembla que m'he passat la vida observant el que succeïa al meu davant com si algun déu m'hagués col.locat en una butaca de llotja"[61] [It seems as if I've spent my life observing what goes on around me, like some god has set me down in a balcony seat]. Her moment of understanding opens the novel *L'hora violeta* as she realizes the importance of telling Judit and Kati's story. By soliciting the help of her writer friend Norma, the binary equation that draws a parallel between the older generation, Judit and Kati, and the younger generation, Natàlia and Norma, establishes the fundamental observations of the novel: namely that female solidarity and documentation of the misunderstood relationship between females conquer the fear of oblivion.

Carme Riera, however, warns of oversimplifying Natàlia's character. She pinpoints the commonality between Roig and her character, Natàlia. Both the writer and fictionalized character carry the essence of Barcelona within their being, Roig so much so that "li va servir com a marc de tots els seus textos de ficció"[62] [it served as the framework of all of her fictional works]. Despite this parallel between writer and creation, Riera affirms that she will not fall "en la temptació de suposar que la Natàlia era Montserrat Roig ni tan sols un *alter ego*, o una prolongació o potser una màscara . . ."[63] [in the temptation to assume that Natàlia was Montserrat Roig, or that she was an *alter ego* or an extension or even a mask]. The separation of writer and character that Riera emphasizes in her article redirects the reader's attention away from a possible autobiographical analysis and toward a closer textual reading. Despite the tenuous autobiographical nature of Roig's writing, which she openly acknowledges as secondary to the text, the intricate textual structures and narrative technique attest and give precedence to the artistic consciousness of the writer rather than to the personal experiences and feelings of the author.[64]

If Roig uses her personal experiences as blueprints for more developed narrations, the same can be said about her essays. She seems to play off her own question posed in her book of essays *¿Tiempo de mujer?* (1980). She ponders in an essay from this collection: "Yo, que ya no sé quien soy. A quién pertenezco. Cuál es mi mundo. Yo que quisiera llamarme todos los nombres de las mujeres. Y no llamarme nuinguna. Y quisiera saber si ahora ha llegado, de verdad, el tiempo de la mujer"[65] [I still don't know who I am. To whom I belong. Which world is mine. I wanted to be everything for all women. And I am no one. And I would like to know if now, finally and for real, the time for women has arrived]. While Natàlia and Norma in *L'hora violeta* struggle individually with extramarital affairs and a resulting identity crisis, there is no doubt that the time has come for them to reinscribe their ancestors into what C. B. Cadenas calls the "counter-saga" or the unknown underside of history.[66] If we understand Roig's "woman's time" to mean a movement to reinscribe a communal feminine genealogy into the social network by disturbing the established order of things then the answer to her own question lies in *L'hora violeta*: the time of woman has indeed arrived.

The urban spaces of Barcelona and the social/sexual oppression discussed in *El temps de les cireres* become transformed in *L'hora violeta* into a more fluid textual space where the reconstruction of traditional texts occurs and a personal liberation found through the loyalty of nonsexual relationships emerges. Roig involves in her reconstruction the prototype of the male hero and female survivor found in *The Odyssey*. Through a deliberate inversion of the Penelope myth, Roig uncovers and eventually subverts the gendered roles that her characters play inspired by Homer's universally embraced epic. Roig alludes to the epic in an interview with Pep Blay from 1991: "Pero todas las grandes preguntas ya las plantea Homer: en *La odisea* hay absolutamente todo"[67] [All of the great questions are already posed in Homer: absolutely everything is in *The Odyssey*]. The importance of *The Odyssey* to Roig's novel is not necessarily debunking Homer's heroine, Penelope, but rather rereading the philosophical implications of the gendered roles that have endured to our own times. Roig's narrative recognition of the

Homerian prototypes of women offers not only a rereading of the traditional Circe, Calypso, and Penelope, but also provokes a reconsideration of the unconditional acceptance of any "master" narrative.

The second chapter of the novel, entitled "L'hora perduda" [The Lost Hour] introduces the theme of *The Odyssey*.[68] The chapter's subtitle reads, "La Natàlia llegeix *L'Odissea* en una illa del Mediterrani" (23) [Natàlia Reads *The Odyssey* on a Mediterranean Island]. The naming of a specific text but not of a specific island minimizes the importance of the literal spatial and geographical location while heightening the importance of the textual space. Obviously it is more important for the reader to be aware of the book *The Odyssey* than where Natàlia is while reading. Natàlia addresses her married lover Jordi as she reads the epic, equating her situation to that of Circe or perhaps Calypso. Jordi has confessed to Natàlia that he does indeed love his wife, Agnès, and will return to her permanently, signifying the end of their adulterous relationship. Therefore the equation that Roig establishes and develops throughout the novel until the final, revolutionary scene is: Jordi as Ulysses, Natàlia as Circe/Calypso, and Agnès as Penelope.

However, Catherine Bellver has noted the fluidity between the identities of the three Homeric women in Roig's text and that in fact "Natàlia conjectures she is part Calypso and part Penelope."[69] The crossing and melding of identities tie in with Eliot's fusion of characters in *The Waste Land* especially when the poetic voice claims "all the women are one woman."[70] Bellver, however, confirms the presence of the Penelope syndrome in the novel and as part of Roig's project. "For Roig the social and psychological destiny of women still centers on awaiting the return of an adventure-seeking or wayward mate."[71] Nevertheless, Roig's project in this novel rises to much more radical heights of textual and cultural reinterpretation notwithstanding Agnès's final rejection of Jordi and of her Penelope status that occurs at the close of the novel symbolically leaving the questions unanswered and the future unwritten.

Natàlia's thoughts about the female characters in Homer's epic seem to align her more strictly with Circe and Calypso and she posits Agnès definitely in the Penelope role. Roig challenges Homer's text by interspersing quotes from Homer's epic in Natàlia's musings about the victimized women.

Jordi, saps una cosa? M'agradaria sentir-hi els plors de Circe, la bruixa, a qui els historiadors han titllat de dolenta perquè convertia els homes en animals. Potser el seu únic pecat ha estat d'estimar Ulisses. Jordi, t'adones com utilitzo la paraula pecat? Circe encantava els homes perquè era una deessa i no sabia usar les armes del sofriment. Circe no volia ser una dona-víctima. Jordi, a mi no m'agrada ser una dona-víctima. Tampoc Calipso no volia sofrir. El poeta conta, Jordi, que deixà anar entre llàgrimes el guerrer que l havia enamorada. Mira què diu aquí:

> Sou implacables, déus, i més que altra cosa gelosos!
> No perdoneu a les dees que el llit dels herois comparteixin
> a la clara, si una se'n fa espòs i l'estima. (24)

[Jordi, you want to know something? I would like to hear Circe's laments, the enchantress, who has been branded evil by historians because she converted men into animals. Perhaps her only sin was that she loved Ulysses. Do you realize, Jordi, how I use the word "sin"? Circe loves men because she was a goddess and didn't know how to use the weapons of suffering. Circe didn't want to be a victim. Jordi, *I* don't want to be a victim either. Calypso didn't want to suffer either. The poet tells, Jordi, of when she tearfully let the warrior, with whom she had fallen in love, leave. Look at what it says here:

> You all are relentless gods, and moreso jealous!
> You don't forgive the goddesses who sleep freely
> with the hero they have chosen and who they love.]

Not only is this passage of fundamental importance to the novel in that Natàlia comments on the historical "otherness" of the women, but it also lays bare Roig's own disillusionment with classical interpretations of canonical works. Her reworking of the epic in her own text through the mind of a female character who is a writer seeks to vindicate and empower the traditionally powerless.

The text speaks to the reader who becomes hyperaware of the textual limitations and inability to correctly express female suffering. Natàlia concludes in keeping with Homer's moral that "I a la fi va vèncer Penèlope. I és que era una dona sàvia. Aquesta dona constuïa la gàbia més subtil amb el seu teixir i desteixir al voltant del record de l'home que tornava" (24) [And in the end Penelope won. The fact is that Penelope was a smart woman. A woman who constructed a subtle cage, with her weaving and unweaving, around the memory of a man who was coming home]. However, Natàlia's conclusion doesn't ring true. Only her sarcasm and anger directed toward Jordi seem sincere. "Ei!, no hi vegis comparances amb la teva dona, que no és el cas." (24) [Hey, can't you see here the similarities with your wife? It's the same thing!] Roig reveals through her character Agnès/Penelope the false wisdom of stoic waiting and the true courage of action when at the end of the novel Agnès rejects Jordi with a smile after his long absence.

Agnès either systematically describes herself in terms identifiable with Penelope or is referred to as such by an omniscient third-person narrator. Agnès recalls her mother's words when she told her that Jordi had abandoned her and her two children: "és un bon noi, tornarà per què en tu ha trobat el que no trobarà en cap altra dona. Has de tenir paciència"(34) [he's a nice boy, he'll come back because he's found in you what he won't find in any other woman. You just have to be patient]. Patience eventually engulfs Agnès, swallows her whole, and leaves her in "un silenci total, un silenci dens, com de mort" (51) [a total silence, a dense silence, like death]. The patience and waiting become physically unbearable for Agnès as she imagines herself covered in a thick dust that "li entra per tots els forats del cos" (78) [enters through every opening of her body] and she claims her ovaries hurt "com si hi tingués una bèstia que es cargola i recargola sense parar, una serp que s'embolica com un tortell" (78) [as if she had in there an animal that wound itself up and then unwound itself incessantly, a snake that rolled itself up in a tight ball]. The serpent and suffocating dust emerge as constant physical sensations throughout the passages dedicated to Agnès. These physical renderings of her incapacity to act parallel the hairy spider that plagued Natàlia in *El temps de les cireres*. Her emotional inability to take action leads her to imagine her oppression in physical, tangible forms that she can visualize and therefore understand.

When Agnès meets a charming young neighbor, Francesc, her nightmarish visions disappear (81). Even though Francesc appears fleetingly in the novel and in her life, his presence allows Agnès to move beyond waiting for her Ulysses to return. Her realization that she can live without a man comes at the violet hour of the morning after she has slept with Francesc. "Va ser la primera nit que no va tenir cap malson. Es despertà a trenc d'alba, quan la llum és de color violeta, i va veure que en Francesc se n'havia anat. Ja no el va veure més . . . I l'Agnès per primer cop des de feia molt de temps, va somriure" (87–88) [It was the first night that she didn't have a nightmare. She woke up at the break of dawn, when the light has a violet color, and she noticed that Francesc had gone. She never saw him again . . . And Agnès, for the first time in a long while, smiled]. Following Eliot's epigraph, Agnès "sees" and understands at the violet hour, the hour of literal and spiritual awakening.

Agnès's actions in the final paragraphs of the novel inspire hope and courage as they completely subvert the conventional passivity of the waiting Penelope, grateful for her husband's return. Throughout the course of the novel, Natàlia has lashed out at Jordi for leaving her and going back to Agnès while Norma divulges her disappointment and inexplicable sense of loss after her divorce from Ferràn. Both women act freely, taking lovers, divorcing or never marrying, yet they both still search for the tranquility that Agnès seems to possess at the end of the novel. Jordi says to Agnès: "crec que podríem refer-ho tot una altra vegada. I l'Agnès tardà a contestar. Al cap d'una estona, només va dir, no. No, què?, va fer en Jordi. Però ella només deia, no, no." (231) [I think we could work it out again. And Agnès hesitated to reply. After a pause she said, no. No what? asked Jordi. But she just said, no, no]. Jordi assumes that there is another man involved and asks her whether this is the case and whether she is in love with him. This time Agnès doesn't even reply and the novel closes with the triumphant inversion of Penelope simply smiling ironically: "I l'Agnès només va somriure" (232) [And Agnès just smiled]. Agnès's action of freeing herself from a false sense of obligation and liberating herself from a loveless marriage brings a different perspective to the novel. The one woman who has upheld tradition in the sense of matrimony, children, and submission to her husband is the one who completely subverts the hierarchy in the end.

Roig suggests that the Penelopes of the world have the most power to undermine the system completely and totally. While Norma and Natàlia have tried socialism and feminism and been disillusioned with both, (Norma complains while trying to understand her destructive love affair that "feminism hadn't dealt with the facts") Agnès has not been seduced by the patriarchal "isms" that promise liberation for women. Instead she is freed from her own personal demons, the serpent and the dust that represent the cruelty of her marriage, her fear of abandonment and oppression. Roig affirms here that institutionalized forms of freedom are primarily *institutions*, which hinder any intended sense of freedom.

Norma claims: "No puc dissimular més, la lluita entre eurocomun-
istes i leninistes no és la meva lluita. És una lluita entre
homes"(150) [I can't pretend anymore, the fight between the euro-
communists and the Leninists isn't my fight. It's a fight between
men]. The division of the political party, its pejorative attitude
toward women as well as the sometimes strict confines of a rigid
feminism do not provide answers according to Roig. Only once
freed from social obligations, including marriage, socialism, and
feminism, can women hear their own voice and emerge truly liberated.[72]

One textual space that allows women this kind of freedom from
dominant culture is in the exploration of friendship between
women. In her collection of essays entitled *Digues que m'estimes
encara que sigui mentida: Sobre el plaer solitari d'escriure i el vici
compartit de llegir* [*Tell Me That You Love Me Even If It's a Lie:
About the Solitary Pleasure of Writing and the Shared Vice of Reading*], Roig explains her fascination with the unspeakable, unex-
plainable female friendship.

> Les dones, avui, hem descobert l'amistat entre nosaltres, la complicitat,
> el secret per fi compartit. Enraonem en veu alta, hem deixat de xiuxi-
> uejar. I hem confós l'amistat amb l'amor. L'amor és massa cruel perquè
> tingui la tendresa de l'amistat. . . . estimo massa les dones, algunes
> dones, per a enamorar-me'n.[73]

> [Women today have discovered friendship amongst ourselves, complic-
> ity, the secret finally shared. We speak out loud, we've stopped whisper-
> ing. And we have confused friendship with love. Love is too cruel for
> the tenderness of friendship. . . . I love women too much, some women,
> to fall in love with them.]

But, what is the secret finally shared between women? What happens when we finally realize that women's time has arrived? The
friendship at the center of *L'hora violeta*, that of Judit and Kati, is
a narrative attempt by Roig to capture the fleeting moment of this
enigmatic relationship that seems to surpass love by removing the
term from the symbolic order, beyond the definable and into the
semiotic.

The section of the novel dedicated to Judit and Kati's story bears
the title "La novel.la de l'hora violeta" [The Novel of the Violet
Hour], implying that this microcosm inside of the actual novel is

a novel that Norma will someday write. Also the title plays on the revelatory powers of the violet hour as described by Eliot in the epigraph suggesting that the novel of the women's relationship includes the epiphany, or the moment of understanding that Natàlia intends to uncover through Norma's written version of the story. The epiphany of Roig's metanovel lies in this chapter as well.

Pieces of Judit's diary from the years 1942 to 1950 are interspersed with third-person narrative from 1958, after Judit had stopped writing. A first-person testimony about Judit and Kati appears in Aunt Patrícia's voice as well as in a letter dated 27 October 1938 written by Kati to the love of her life, Irish brigade soldier Patrick, who dies at the front and disappears in the Ebro River. The letters and diary in this section serve as found documents, worthy of study and compilation. This metatextual link to the other official document, *The Odyssey*, places the texts written by Kati and Judit into the realm of "official" literature. When Natàlia presents the documents to her friend Norma at the beginning of Roig's novel, she writes a letter of explanation saying: "La literatura no és història. La literatura s'inventa el passat a partir d'uns quants detalls que han estat reals" (13) [Literature isn't history. Literature invents the past based on a few details that were true]. Natàlia also documents in her letter to Norma her own motives for requesting the novel about her mother and Kati. She imbues Judit and Kati's documents with the power of revelation, with the key to the secrets of the past. She admits that "Per a mi, escriure podria ser el primer pas cap a la serenitat" [for me, writing could be the first step toward serenity], but she is afraid that she would lie too much if she herself tried to write the story (15). Therefore, before we are presented with the pieces that make up the past and reveal the hidden lives of these two enigmatic women, Natàlia has convinced Norma, the reader of the letter, and us, the readers of the novel, that these testimonies are truthful. The written word becomes a tool that the writer uses to reconstruct the past, or at least a version of it.

Judit's diary recounts the birth and death of her son Pere, whom she loved deeply. She considered him "un fill de la guerra" (101) [a child of war] who suffered through life silent and ignored. Judit identifies with her son, for she too feels stifled and useless. Judit also equates Pere with Kati, who has been dead for five years when Pere is born. Pere is a son of war because Judit's husband lived in a concentration camp for five years and when he was released and

came home Pere was conceived. Yet Judit relates Pere's condition
to her own empty existence since Kati's suicide, spurred by the
death of Patrick in the war. Judit affirms that "Ningú no me'l pren-
drà" (101) [no one will take him away from me] and her absolute
possession of her son gives her reason to continue living.

She describes how he follows her all around the house "com un
gosset . . . seu a la cadireta de boga al costat del piano. Per a ell
interpreto les sonates de Chopin . . . Avui he pensat en la Kati més
que mai" (102) [like a puppy . . . he sits in his little rocking chair
beside the piano. I play Chopin's sonatas for him . . . today I've
thought about Kati more than ever]. Kati permeates her thoughts
and the pages of her diary connecting her days with Pere to those
she spent during the war with Kati. She remembers how Kati used
to ask her to play the piano and that "tocava per a ella com ara ho
faig per a en Pere. Només per a en Pere" (104) [I played for her
just like I play now for Pere. Only for Pere]. It is in the private space
of her diary that she can remember her relationship in detail and
mourn the death of her friend. She writes about Kati: "El seu op-
timisme la va matar. No vam guanyar la guerra, i d'aquell temps
m'ha quedat el meu Pere, que em segueix per tot arreu com un
gosset" (102) [Her optimism killed her. We didn't win the war and
from that time all I have is my Pere, who follows me everywhere
like a puppy]. Since the war has left Judit alone, without Kati, she
replaces her friend with her son, who loves her unconditionally.
His sheer dependence on Judit fills her otherwise empty existence
with meaning.

The only other source of fulfillment that Judit has is her writing
and music. She confesses in a diary entry on 15 February 1947 that
"en Pere m'ajuda a viure. I aquestes notes. Quan escric em sento
tan lliure com davant del piano" (103) [Pere helps me to live. And
this diary. When I write I feel as free as I do in front of the piano].
The act of writing for Judit revolves around the act of remembering
her past, thus allowing her to relive the memories and then safely
hide them away. She writes: "El silenci m'ajuda a recordar. M'enyoro dels dies passats a la guerra, amb la Kati. No sé per què penso
que vaig ser tan feliç, durant la guerra." (104) [The silence helps
me to remember. I miss those days of wartime, with Kati. I don't
know why I think I was so happy during the war]. The inversion of
the negative collective memory of war suggests a rereading of the
historical events. While most members of Judit's family and com-

munity certainly wish to forget or avoid memories of what she her-self defines as "l'època en què vaig veure més mort i més tristesa" (104) [the era in which I saw more death and more sadness], Judit associates the war with the liberating politics of feminism that Kati espoused. The freedom from her husband and the intimacy found with a friend proved satisfying for Judit, who suffers under the rigid confines of the normality that has returned with the end of the war. Through Judit's view of the war Roig presents an interesting shift in how women view history.

Mary Nash comments that the social upheaval benefited radical social movements such as feminism by supporting women's proac-tive role during the war.[74] Judit even entertained the thought of running away with Kati, who refused to live in a Barcelona taken by fascist troops. Judit remembers when Kati proposed the plan and she asks: "Què hauria estat de mi si hagués fugit amb la Kati quan ella m'ho va proposar? Tenia tanta por. . . . " (105) [What would have become of me if I had fled with Kati when she made that pro-posal? I was so afraid. . . .]. Once again Roig focuses on the paralyz-ing fear that women face in asserting any form of life-changing initiative. Natàlia's words come to mind when Sílvia admits her fear about Natàlia's call for help with her pain from the botched abor-tion: "La maleïda por . . . la por d'aquell temps tan gelat i ombrívol, la por semblava un vent immòbil . . . "(El temps, 182) [Damn fear . . . the fear of that frigid and somber time, the fear that seemed like a still wind].

Judit didn't flee with Kati and ends up alone. Pere dies when he is five years old, exactly ten years after Kati commits suicide, and Judit is again left alone. She declares that she will never play the piano again (107) and in this moment she understands the futility in writing because she will never capture the essence of her son nor of her relationship with Kati. Judit ponders the inexpressible nature of her relationship with Kati: "Ella comprenia què volia dir, jo, quan parlava del que volia descriure sense haver d'interpretar. Una música silenciosa, que em venia de dins i que en paraules no ho sabia explicar" (107) [She understood what it was I wanted to say, when I spoke trying to describe something, she understood without interpretation. A silent music that emerged from within and couldn't be explained with words]. The music of the piano acts as a mode of communication between Judit and Kati and later be-tween Judit and Pere. Where words fail to describe the relationship, where dominant discourse cannot express the inexpressible, music becomes the means of communication. Judit decides to give up writing and stops playing the piano, and stops communicating with those who understood her. "En Pere és mort, la Kati també. Ho enterro ben endins, mai més no tornaré a tocar" (108) [Pere is dead, so is Kati. I'll bury it deep down inside and never play again]. This is a concrete example of how Roig shifts her narrative from the symbolic power of words to the semiotic expression through music.[75] She suggests that women communicate by other means, through a certain intuition or knowledge pertaining to another kind of discourse. In this sense women, exiled from dominant language, find their own means to come together, share their lives, and exchange ideas.

At the end of the chapter Roig reconstructs the scene when Kati tells Judit that Patrick has been killed and suggests that they run away together. Judit's memory has prepared the reader for the actual dialogue of the scene, which becomes much more intense because the reader understands the repercussions the scene will have later on in Judit's life. As a possible turning point that becomes a missed opportunity, the exchange between Kati and Judit reveals the reason behind Judit's depression and loneliness in later life. For the reader, Judit's desperate feelings become compounded with the knowledge of her love for Kati. Judit refuses to go because of her family. Kati cries out before she leaves: "S'ha acabat! . . . no ho suportaré, el que vindrà. Ara que tot començava a ser diferent . . . però no va poder continuar" (143) [It's all over! . . . I won't be able to stand what is in store. Now that everything was starting to change . . . but couldn't continue]. As a sad echo of her friend's desperation, Judit writes in her diary eighteen years later: "Prou, s'ha acabat. Ja no escriuré més. Continuaré" (144) [Enough, it's over. I'll never write again. I'll go on].

Judit and Kati not only have a close friendship but also unconsciously share the same discourse of resignation. In the face of fascism Kati commits suicide, in the face of a loveless, lonely life, Judit commits a kind of literary suicide, depriving herself of the only outlets that she has, her writing and music. Natàlia realizes the loss that these two people have suffered and therefore her efforts to understand them even though she admits her love/hate relationship with her mother (16) reside in recording their history. She claims: "Totes les dones del món que s'havien perdut o estavellat. Em sem-

blava que calia salvar per les paraules tot allò que la hisòria, la Història gran, o sigui la dels homes, havia fet imprecís, havia
condemnat o idealitzat" (17) [All the women in the world have either gotten lost or been smashed. It seemed to me that it was necessary to save, with words, all that history, big History, I mean men's
history, had made imprecise, had condemned or idealized]. Natàlia's words at the beginning of the novel set the stage for the rest
of the narrative. That which men, or perhaps more accurately the
patriarchy, have overlooked is what Norma defines: "els homes heu
perdut el valor de l'amistat" (156) [you men have lost the value of
friendship].

Earlier, Norma voices the importance of friendship when she describes to Natàlia her experience with some kids who were doing a
survey about what people value most highly in life. Norma reports
that the majority of people responded that health, happiness, or
love were the most important things and when Natàlia asks her, "I
què els vas dir, tu?" Norma replies, "Doncs, l'amistat" (50) [And
what did you say? (Norma replies) Friendship]. Norma deviates
from the three accepted answers when she replies "friendship"
and this central moment of the novel encapsulates Roig's literary
project.[76] The unspoken experience of women cannot be represented by dominant culture for there is no comprehensible way to
define it through patriarchal language.

Catherine Bellver concludes that Norma and Natàlia's response
to the found diary and letters "transcends mere readjustment to
include re-creation, if not actual realization of a female reality, for
they establish, within patriarchal, andocentric culture, the existence of a rich female social and cultural context."[77] While Bellver's observations are fundamental to the study of Roig's work, I
would add that the relationship between women that Roig explores
lies outside of, not within, patriarchal culture. Roig has shown us
how it cannot possibly exist within the patriarchal confines of marriage, socialism, or even within a complacent brand of feminism.
Instead, Roig advocates an active search, through writing, of wom-
en's past. Roig seeks not to separate men from women but to reevaluate the very nature of relationships between the individual and
society. She does this by renegotiating the presence of the author
and reader not only within the confines of a text but with the larger
idea of texts and testimony in general.

Roig's texts themselves can be considered a generational mirror into which readers peer searching for cultural and historical identity. The refraction of cultural institutions such as marriage, motherhood, and women's public and private realities inspires various rereadings of patriarchal history. Therefore, Roig's criticism of literary history resides in an ironic subversion of historical "texts." Her appropriation of male authored and authorized texts such as Eliot's poem, Homer's *The Odyssey*, Bertolucci's film *Last Tango in Paris*, and Sagarra's novel as well as institutional texts such as marriage and family contracts destabilizes certain cultural values. While her literary project achieves an intense level of cultural questioning, she has also been misunderstood by the dominant culture.

Critics who fail to hear Roig's literary voice do so because of institutionalized expectations. They long for one subject to declare one position and rally for a cause. Primarily because Roig refuses to blindly accept but rather criticizes movements and institutions such as socialism, marriage, or even heterosexual love, she becomes alienated from the writers who represent contemporary peninsular literature mired in tradition and who constantly look for approval in a male-dominated international literary market. Her search for a feminine writing, in line with the insertion into history of a feminine viewpoint outlined in the idea of *écriture féminine* posited by some French theorists, lies in the uncovering of a female past hidden by patriarchal discourse. In Spain, she represents one of the very few writers experimenting with sophisticated French theory and successfully challenging the rigid power structures that have consumed even supposedly liberal movements. Keeping in mind the presence of an overtly oppressive dictatorship in Spain until the mid-1970s, Roig's work emerges at a crucial time in Spanish history when the reassertion of lost voices may have threatened the socially desirable act of forgetting that would perhaps rapidly heal the wound of a fascist government. The importance of her trilogy is that she exemplifies the silent voids in history contrary to a social conscious that yearns to forget. Through her use of a minority language, Catalan, and women's traditionally male-dependent identity, Roig creates a dual discourse empowering the regionally marginalized as well as the oppressed gender. Her ability to see commonalities in both situations places her work in a category of its own.

Therefore, Roig's exile is a self-imposed one. Her works suggest that she cannot write as a woman within the perimeters of Catalan identity and literary history and thus must force herself outside of the dominant discursive labels in order to better see, evaluate, and understand the conditions in her homeland. As Ilie suggests, both the exiled and the abandoned territory, in this case patriarchy, experience the loss and void: "Cada segmento (el exiliado y la nación) está incompleto y ausente del otro"[78] [Each segment (the exiled person and the nation) is incomplete and lacking the other]. As Roig intends to point out, her issue is not with men, but with the institutions that promote a fissure between the sexes. Systems that keep women in a dark and voiceless place also hurt family and by extension society in general. Roig's metaphorical exile places her on the edge of dominant discourse, bringing to light the voices of another, feminine past.

The common thread holding the trilogy *Ramona, adéu, El temps de les cireres, L' hora violeta,* and the collection of short stories *Molta roba i poc sabó . . .* together is the recovery of the generational link between women that has been silenced and forgotten. Certainly Roig's interest in documentation and testimony stems from her career as a journalist, for her novels fuse the power of testimony with the seduction of the imagination. Roig proclaims through her character Natàlia that retrieving the past through recognizing diaries and letters as testimonial documents and writing the "counter-saga" or unofficial history brings Catalan women's multiple voices into a distinctly feminine and legitimate textual space.

3

Authorial Exile: Reformulations of the Author/Reader Contract in the Narrative of Carme Riera

¿Cómo comenzamos a narrar? ¿Cuándo sentimos la necesidad de vernos narrados? [How do we begin to narrate? When we feel the need to see ourselves narrated?]

—Montserrat Roig

Los seres humanos no somos más que impura memoria y vacilante voz. [Human beings are nothing more than impure memory and fluctuating voice.]

—Luisa Cotoner

As a contemporary of Montserrat Roig, Carme Riera also delves into textual questions regarding female subjectivity. However, Riera steps outside of the privileged authorial role, in an act like that of Roig of self-imposed exile, in order to manipulate and bend the historically fixed author-reader relationship. This act of voluntary separation comes from an ideological stance that not only forces Riera outside of dominant discourse but also allows her to express a depoliticized view of literary history. Riera takes on readerly expectations by reformulating the traditional epistolary genre in her texts; therefore her project lies in the reevaluation of the act of reading itself. She proclaims herself a feminist yet her writing extends beyond the social boundaries of the political and enters into the unstable, provocative arena of language, meaning, and text.

In her short novel *Qüestió d'amor propi* [*A Matter of Self-Respect*], Carme Riera creates a character, Àngela, who locates her own epistolary within a larger historical framework when she says: "El text no és més que un pretext amorós"[1] [Text is nothing other than amorous foreplay]. Àngela's self-conscious double billing of literature as text and pretext breaks the sanctity of text as document or testimony, a position firmly held by Montserrat Roig, by pointing out the fluctuating nature of meaning. Nor do we see in Riera's work the generational mirror, a fundamental element in Roig's work, reflecting the binding matrilineal inheritance that defines women's history and locks us into certain destructive emotional patterns. For Riera, the text loses its authoritative dimension as a recorder of certain hidden or lost realities and instead becomes an idea, a process full of contradiction and friction. The multilayered textual realities that bifurcate into writerly desire and readerly (mis)conception directly confront the very notion of a "writer." Creative posturing and intertextual game-play give way to a demythification of the writer who breaks down the façade of an innocent storyteller and gatherer of forgotten images and experience. Riera seeks to redefine the idea of the woman writer through her innovations within the epistolary genre. Her aim parallels Linda Kauffman's approach to the epistolary mode. Kauffman describes the epistolary exchange as that which is "mourning the inadequacies of language, transgressing generic boundaries, subverting gender roles, staging revolt through the act of writing."[2] The traditionally feminine, highly codified world of letter-writing becomes exposed as an effective and dangerous tool that provokes and seduces the reader into renegotiating ideas of gender and genre while reconsidering the tenuous relationship between writer and reader that both gender and genre imply.[3]

Riera acknowledges her fascination with literary seduction in an interview with Luis Racionero: "escribo naturalmente para seducir al lector, para atraerle desde la primera página, si es posible, para conquistarle y hacerle mío."[4] [I write naturally in order to seduce the reader, to draw him in from the very first page, and if it is possible to conquer him and make him mine]. As Akiko Tsuchiya points out, the seductive powers of the text that elicit desire in the reader have often led to self-reflexive discourses. The construction of the reader/writer relationship based on erotic models produces a text that exposes "the narrative mechanisms upon which the narrator's seductive power depends in the first place."[5] Kathleen Glenn proposes that the epistolary novel is a way to present an intimate portrayal of the inner workings or psyche of the narrator. Glenn's analysis reveals the double seduction of Riera's narrative; the fictional seduction instigated by a letter-writer of another fictional character and the "real" seduction of the actual reader.[6]

Mirella Servodidio describes Riera's narrative as driven by "the seductive power of ambiguity."[7] This ambiguity resides not only in the movable subject positions the author embraces but also in the leveling of hierarchical paradigms traditionally inscribed in the author/reader discourse. Servodidio concludes: "literature is an act of erotic seduction, first arousing and then sustaining the desire of the Other."[8] In citing the necessary role of the Other, Servodidio suggests the networks of power implicit in the critical discussion of seduction at hand. However, by reinterpreting the epistolary genre Riera reimagines traditional notions of authorial power.

As Foucault explains, the author-function is itself a construct "tied to legal and institutional systems that determine, circumscribe and articulate the realm of discourses."[9] Therefore, the author becomes a vessel through which a collective discourse emerges. Riera's use of literary seduction serves not to exercise a personal writerly power over her readers, but to expose the commonality of the erotic discourse, the extreme importance of the reader's or Other's presence in the creative process. In this case it is her status as a writer, beyond a question of gender, that forces her into a textual exile, a position outside of and separate from genre.

What Montserrat Roig considered a private love affair between the writer and reader Riera reformulates as a public spectacle, the artifice of literature as common knowledge and therefore an area to be explored and exploited. Roig maintains a careful distance from her reader when she claims that the author's function is to remember and evoke the past.[10] Roig also sustains the bipolar power structure placing the author in a superior position: "Sentim un gran plaer quan mentim. Quan fem la mentida creïble, quan seduïm l'altre, que potser sap que mentim i que ens està demanant que continuem mentint."[11] [We get great pleasure from lying. When we make the lie believable, when we seduce the other person, who may very well know that we are lying but pleads with us to continue]. Riera's narrative departs from the discourse of author and Other by uncovering the dishonest mechanisms that create a literary lie. The art of seduction is not as much an art or artifice as it is a textual unveiling of layered voices and social power play.[12]

In this chapter I will analyze several short stories and a short novel written in the epistolary form in order to reveal Riera's conscious dismantling of the power hierarchy implied by erotic seduction. By stepping outside of traditional literary constructs, Riera enables herself to analyze, destabilize, and criticize the notion of authorial intent. Even though she herself employs a type of seduction within the narrative discourse and extratextually through linguistic and subject position manipulations, her narrative works toward a commonality of experience uniting reader and writer within a larger sense of programmed culture. Instead of resisting institutionalized society, Riera breaks it down into comprehensible parcels thus exposing not only our individual prejudices but also the social machine that produces an accepted discourse. Riera's seduction therefore is actually a progressive unveiling that entices the reader to comprehend a previously occulted or unexpected subreality instead of remaining ensconced in a socially acceptable discourse.

However, in some cases seduction can be considered as another theoretical framework that follows the debilitating path of hermeneutics in its insistence on implying a subject/object relationship. The necessity to radically rethink the subject as a series of positions in constant motion thus unable to bring a standardized set of "pre-understandings" to a text becomes fundamental in the study of Riera's works.[13] The elitist precept of a type of reader immediately relegates historically oppressed and marginalized sectors of society to an inferior level of misreading and consequently misunderstanding. Therefore the reader is systematically exiled from theoretical discourse and what might be labeled as "true" understanding. Instead of a seduction in terms of an erotic deception, Riera produces texts that reinscribe the social reality of language and cultural artifact with a literary presence that is in and of itself theoretical. Her narrative destroys boundaries of reader, writer, text, and social reality. Riera takes up the challenge of dismantling the monolithic, historically rendered subject.

Fredric Jameson's brand of social-Marxist theory heads most convincingly in this direction. His ideas about the text as a manifestation of repressed historical revolutionary moments aid in a feminist reevaluation of a one-sided patriarchal history. Jameson also takes to task the "basic underlying problem of the *subject*, which it assumes as nonproblematical and as a given from the outset."[14] By problematizing the subject, Riera explores these theoretical boundaries that necessarily create divisions and ultimately exclusions. William Dowling pinpoints Jameson's criticism of Freud as the "'problematics of individuality' that arose from Freud's untroubled acceptance of individual identity as an ultimate category."[15]

Julia Kristeva seems to solve Jameson's quandary regarding Freud's individual identity with her idea of the never fully realized subject, the nonsubject, or subject-in-process/on trial. Kristeva explores negativity as a "conflictual state" that attests to the heterogeneity of the semiotic function. Therefore, as she explains, the "use of the term 'negativity' is to designate the process that exceeds the signifying subject."[16] While negativity seems to help locate and define the subject of enunciation or the speaking subject, rejection she describes as "characteristic of the subject in process/on trial."[17] This subject is not a fixed point and cannot be located through negativity but rather vacillates, emerges and disappears through the text's organization. The subject on trial decenters the very notion of an individual consciousness by proposing a continually evolving subject position that moves within the realm of the text where the "*chora* of the process is represented."[18] Kristeva provides a piece of music or a work of architecture as the best metaphor for the chora. The unnameable organization of sounds or geometric patterns that construct a piece of music or a building alludes to the absence of language for communicative purposes. Yet these constructive elements are fundamental in the totality and eventual comprehension of meaning. The *chora* can be understood as a transparent rubber cement that holds together the text but remains "unseen." Riera plays with language in this sense. She deprives the words of literal meaning, and by forcing the reader to consider their relation to each other, to the textual space and to the movement of the narrative, she engages the reader in a discovery of the semiotic *chora*.

An embracing of the subject on trial and a devaluation of the speaking subject distinguish Riera's narrative from that of her contemporaries. Riera's innovation lies within her totalizing vision of marginalized humanity and the Kristevian notion of rejection that proposes a different relation between the subject and culture. Therefore, various levels of marginalization, such as race, gender, sexual orientation, and class attest to a cultural development of their own and not as oppositional forces to a dominant history.[19] In this way her narrative is not reactionary or political, but revelatory in how it assumes the reader's pre-"misunderstandings," to modify

Roman Ingarden's term. Riera's narrative posits as cultural universals the unthinkable and the illogical. Her epistolary narrative proposes a new feminist thinking, or as Kristeva describes it, a new "signifying space, a both corporeal and desiring mental space."[20]

TE DEIX, AMOR, LA MAR COM A PENYORA

Mirella Servodidio discusses the various publications of Riera's first collection of short stories. *Te deix, amor, la mar com a penyora* [*I Leave You, My Love, the Sea as a Token*] is a collection of stories published in 1975 followed by *Jo pos per testimoni les gavines* [*I Give as Testimony the Gulls*] in 1977. In 1980, Riera translated into Castilian and reissued both collections of stories under the title *Palabra de mujer* [*Woman's Words*]. However, according to Servodidio, Riera "significantly altered" the two title stories and the "original story sequences are not universally upheld."[21] Moreover, the two title stories translated as "Te entrego, amor, la mar como ofrenda" and "Y pongo por testigo a las gaviotas" appear sequentially, thus creating a more obvious continuity.

The first story is a letter written in retrospect by a young woman to her former teacher and lover. The second story, "Jo pos," opens with a letter to the actual flesh-and-blood editor of the first story, Alfons Carles Comín, requesting that the enclosed letter be forwarded to "la senyora Carme Riera autora de 'Te deix, amor, la mar com a penyora'[22] [Mrs. Carme Riera, author of "I Leave You, My Love, the Sea as a Token"]. The letter to Riera discloses the writer's surprise at the similarities between the story and her life, but the signature is illegible. Following the letter is another version of the "Te deix" story told from the teacher's point of view. However, in Riera's Castilian version of her own Catalan stories, she omits the framing device of the letter to the editor and to the author Riera. Servodidio sees the omission of the letters as a maneuver that protects the "principle of oneness and continuity" between the two stories.[23]

However, in order to restore the original format, another Castilian compilation of the two original collections of Catalan stories appeared in 1991 under the title *Te dejo el mar*, translated and with an introduction by Luisa Cotoner.[24] While Cotoner rearranges the sequence of some of the minor stories, she maintains the integrity of the original Catalan version of the two separate books. By opening her collection with "Te dejo" and its subsequent stories and then introducing as a second part of the book the stories of the "Y pongo" collection, Cotoner emphasizes the textual space as it relates to the marked temporal references of the stories. The introductory letters to "Y pongo" are also restored, enhancing the metafictional and multiple-voiced qualities of that story. An investigation into Riera's reasons for the rigorous self-editing and rewriting apparent in her Castilian version, *Palabra de mujer,* would prove insightful and are well worth consideration, however, due to the limited scope of the present study as well as the focus on multi-level textual readings and the question of the unstable subject, in my analysis I will refer to Riera's original Catalan versions of the stories.

Luisa Cotoner defines in her introduction the main theme of "Te deix" as "el virgiliano *fugit irreparabile tempus*" [Virgil's theme of the inevitable passage of time] that spawns a plethora of subtopics related to aging, such as solitude and resigned memory.[25] She also mentions the fundamental theme of love that permeates the collection. The two stories that formulate one experience function in tandem linked primarily by the theme of silence. This theme of imposed silence reaches a new height in the works of Riera yet it is clearly a development of earlier instances of silenced females seen in the works of Rodoreda and Roig. The passage of time becomes unbearable for both protagonists of Riera's stories primarily because of the overwhelming silence surrounding their love affair. Consequently, their unfulfilled love becomes an obsession only because it is prohibited, silenced, and resigned to unreal exaggeration by memory. Therefore the subthemes of longing, love, memory, and the uncontrollable passage of time really fit under the cultural silence that dictates female behavior.

The first story, "Te deix, amor, la mar com a penyora" is a letter written by Marina, who is on the verge of giving birth to her first child. Marina writes to a former lover and teacher with whom she had a fleeting but emotionally intense affair when she was fifteen years old. An important aspect about the letter is that the gender of the recipient, her former lover, is not revealed until the last lines of the story. Only then does Marina address her lover as Maria, thus undermining the reader's culturally formulated expectation that the teacher is male. Riera plays with readerly expectation from a position outside of tradition and narrative norms.

The letter has a lyrical, poetic quality that recounts minute details of their meetings and breakup, bringing the past events into vivid focus and suggesting that these moments have been replayed in Marina's mind constantly throughout the years. The longing for a past, idyllic time when youth allowed indiscretion becomes the focus of the letter. She writes: "Erem més joves, menys conscients, plens d'una innocència perversa, quasi maligna, d'àngel rebel"[26] [We were younger then, less aware, full of a perverse, almost deadly innocence of a rebellious angel]. The eloquent oxymoron, perverse innocence of a rebel angel, invites the reader to decode Riera's brand of seduction. Riera mentions in an interview that: "I believe that it is not with strength, but with weakness that one seduces. Strength leads to rejection. I believe that the seducer's weakness at times manifests itself in not displaying power but dissimulating it and making the other person think he or she is the central figure, when in reality the seducer is."[27] Jean Baudrillard seems to agree with Riera's view when he differentiates challenge and seduction. He writes: "the strategy (?) of seduction consists in drawing the other within your area of weakness, which will also be his or hers."[28] The perverse and deadly innocence that Marina refers to suggests that this weakness lies in the inevitable passage of time that taints or disproves innocence. Therefore, seduction does not operate as a unilateral power tool to coerce someone into something, but rather in Riera's text it sublimates desire to weakness, drawing the reader into a world of emotion and uncertainty, which explains the overwhelming silence surrounding the affair.

Silence also formulates part of the seduction as it suggests and refers to the absent. The textual reader of Marina's letter as well as the actual reader embrace the moments of silence because those moments are the only allusion to the truth about the amorous relationship and its unspeakable and inexpressible nature: a cross-generational lesbian affair. Also, the negativity of the opening paragraph establishes the counterpoint to the present time as well as the inversion of the present identity of Marina. "Des d'aquí, des de la meva finestra, no puc veure la mar. Només uns níguls de mal color . . . Res de bo." (19) [From here, from my window I can't see the sea. Only dark clouds . . . Nothing worth seeing]. The emphasis on the negative and inability to see repeats the narrator's sense of nonbeing in the present. She cannot see the sea but envisions it as "Endolada, greixosa, quasi pudent . . . Aquesta mar no s'assembla gens a la nostra" (19) [mourning, greasy, almost disgusting . . . that sea doesn't look at all like ours]. The sea becomes symbolic not only of their love but of another time and space, for with the passing of years even the sea has changed. The sea that she cannot observe embodies all that her present reality lacks.

Marina also invents a specific time frame for herself within the textual reality of her letter when she writes: "vaig fabricar-me un calendari d'ús personal on els anys, els mesos, els dies, començaven al mateix instant, al punt exacte en què la blavor era perfecta, el teu cos de seda, tèbia, dolça, suau la llum que s'escolava . . ." (20) [I made up a calendar for my own use in which the years, the months, the days all began in the exact moment of that perfect blue, your silky body, warm, sweet, and the soft light that filtered through]. Her invention of a personal time frame that incorporates the textual space and remains unfinished, indicated by the points of suspension, suggests a calendar that marks a different kind of time that exists beyond closure, outside of social demarcations and only within memory. This same self-conscious creation of an altered or appropriated sense of time emerges in Marina's approach to language.

Marina's linguistic innovations revolve around trying to give voice to the unspeakable. She remembers the moment when "vaig tancar els ulls i vaig dir-te que t'estimava. Tu em feres callar; com un autòmat et sortien les paraules de la boca" (24) [I closed my eyes and said that I loved you. You told me to be quiet. Like some automaton the words came out of your mouth]. The preprogrammed words of the older woman reject the sincerity of Marina's unabashed declaration of love. Maria, the teacher, tells her that their relationship cannot continue because it will amount to nothing. The prohibited love between two women cannot be expressed in patriarchal language; it must be hushed and avoided. To counter this silencing, Marina reinvents her method of communication exhibited when she returns to school after a summer vacation imposed by her father to separate the two women (a physical way of silencing the relationship). In a large auditorium, Marina spies her lover on the stage with all the other teachers and from her position in the last row of the theater she tries to communicate nonverbally with Maria: "et mirava; crec que no te n'adonares, de la meva pre-

sència, malgrat els esforços que feia per comunicar-me amb tu"
(28) [I looked right at you; I don't think you even noticed my presence despite the effort I was making to communicate with you].
Even though language has failed her, the young Marina does not
abandon her unspeakable desire for her teacher; instead she dili-
gently displaces communication into a nonverbal realm.

Other moments in Marina's letter recall the silent nature of their
love. She recalls: "l'amor de què mai, per aquella època, no parlà-
vem" (23) [the love that we never spoke of] and she writes love letters to her teacher but hides them in a box locked with a key that
Servodidio points out as "the figurative equivalent of their closeted
affair."[29] However, these textual silences serve to accentuate Maria's own overbearing extratextual silence. Riera defined letter-
writing in an interview with Neus Aguado as "la carta no es más
que un diálogo aplazado."[30] [a letter is nothing more than a postponed conversation]. Therefore, in order to complete the textual
totality implied by the epistolary that in itself instigates a dialogue,
the reader bears a double identity: as the stand-in for the fictional
recipient of the letter and the voyeur/reader with access to a private
text. The rupture that the identification of the teacher as female
brings to the last few lines of the story jolts the reader into a completely unexpected subject position. Not only are we, the readers,
transgressing the boundaries of public and private but we realize
that throughout the course of the letter we have been participating
in a doubly marginalized affair defined as a cross-generational
teacher/student taboo lesbian love.

Another linguistic play that decenters the individual subject
combines and blurs the identity of the two lovers. Marina recalls
the day when the two women were on a ferryboat together and un-
dressed for each other. In the moment of disrobing the subject also
becomes stripped of her specific, individual identity. Marina recalls: "ens esperava la bellesa, que es confonia amb la teva-meva
imatge quan em mirava a l'espill de la teva carn" (25) [beauty
awaited us, becoming confused with your/my image when I saw
myself in the mirror of your body]. The image of Maria's body as a
mirror for Marina doubles her identity. It reflects her body, thus
confusing her sense of self. She embraces the confusion of my/your
image absorbing the union and totality of love manifested in the
mirroring of the bodies. Catherine Bellver locates the notion of
doubling in the symbol of the sea as a replica for the lost lover. She

links Marina's longing for her lover to her yearning to see the sea and claims: "The invisibility of the sea announced in the first sentence of the story duplicates the absence of the lover."[31] However, Riera herself explains her purpose of doubling when she writes:

> Tal vez ha sonado para la mujer una nueva hora en que dejando de ser habladas comencemos a hablar con la boca de nuestra cara, sin olvidar que tenemos otra, a través de la cual fuimos también silenciadas y sometidas. Recobremos nuestras dos voces, la que nos conecta a la razón y muestra nuestra capacidad intelectual, y la que nos une al atavismo, al mito, a la profecía.[32]

> [Perhaps a new time has come for women in which we are no longer talked about but we begin to speak with the mouths on our own faces, without forgetting that we have another to which we have been subjected and silenced. We will recover both voices, the one that connects us to reason and shows our intellectual capacity and the other one that ties us to atavism, to myth, and to prophecy.]

Therefore, Marina's instinct to see herself in her lover and to celebrate a sense of totality reflects Riera's understanding of the dual nature of woman. The proliferation of mirror images and doubling in her writing revealed by Bellver is one narrative technique Riera uses to uncover the complex nature of the woman writer appropriating and inventing her own literary language.

Riera also reinvents the notion of textual space. At the end of the collection of stories that began with "Te deix . . ." Marina's narrative voice reappears in a short paragraph (121). The same lyrical voice of the first story suggests that perhaps each previous story has formulated part of the long letter intended for her lover. Or perhaps it is the author's way of reintroducing the individual experience of each story in a culmination that rejects finality. Marina ends this final paragraph by declaring her love associated with an eerie suggestion of death: "Tancar els ulls amb la son suficient per a somiar-te un altre cop tan sols i lliurar-te després com una ofrena, no penyora, no mar, a l'oblit necessari on tants de cops t'he esperat." (121) [To close my eyes just tired enough to dream you alone one more time and then to deliver you as an offering, not a token, not the sea, to the necessary oblivion where so many times I have waited for you]. The desperate tone of these final words seems to suggest a type of closure to the cycle of memory. Yet instead of signing her name to the letter, she writes: "Començo a inventar-te . . . (continuarà) (121) [I begin to invent you . . . to be continued]. The narrative defies traditional closure at the end of the collection of stories and instead proposes rebirth and continuity with an imagined text. Thus "end" becomes void of meaning as the short text subverts the notion of closure. Meaning in language has become unreliable and ironic, just as the words Marina used to voice her love were ineffectual. The end of the narrative symbolically refers to death in the image of closing eyes, the dream and oblivion while the textual reality propels the story forward, negating any real sense of finality and instead convincing (seducing) the reader into actively inventing the continuation of the text.[33]

Jo pos per testimoni les gavines was published in 1977, two years after the publication of *Te deix* . . . The two letters that introduce the second version of the love story provide a metatextual commentary on the authenticity of the past events. The body of the narrative in the story "Jo pos" retells the fated love between Marina and Maria from the teacher's point of view. However, we assume that the teacher is Maria, despite the illegibility of her signature, because the events described are similar to Marina's version. But the absence of the author's name, or in this case the unrecognizable signature, allows for unlimited possibilities regarding the narrative point of view. By refusing to name the writer of the letters as well as the author of the second version of the story, Riera universalizes the conflict. The individual struggle against time and loss becomes nameless, coercing us, the readers, to place ourselves in the text.

The textual distancing provided by the introductory letters serves to create a fictional writer as well as an illusion of correspondence between editor, writer, and reader. However, this writer is also a reader, just as we are, of the first story. The fictional reader, in this case the teacher, becomes a writer of letters and an authoritative voice that confirms the events of the affair. The boundary between author (authority) and reader (submissive receiver) becomes crossed as the previous reader of Riera's story writes a new, corrected version of the story. The roles are in fact inverted: the reader writes to the writer who becomes a reader. Therefore, the flesh-and-blood Riera surrenders narrative authority as well as seductive power over her reader and we, the real readers, become meta-authors as we piece together events from "Jo pos" and "Te deix" in order to create a unifying version of the textual truth.

The metatextual commentary in the letter written to Riera that opens the story "Jo pos" establishes the framework for the recounting of events that follows. The nameless reader writes: "no es pot imaginar la sorpresa enorme que em causà veure'm gairebé retratada" (10) [you can't imagine my surprise when I saw myself almost perfectly depicted]. Riera's imprecise narration, according to the writer of the letter, fails to render a true portrait of the affair, thus warranting a second version of the past events. The second version of the love affair between Marina and the woman we assume to be Maria focuses on how the frenetic passage of time fails to erase past feelings. The textual links also encapsulate time into words taking us back to the first story and then compounding the leap of time back to the days of the affair.

"Jo pos" begins with a contemplation of the last page of the previous collection of stories, *Te deix, amor, la mar com a penyora*. The writer directly addresses the writer of the first story: "Li sabria greu que començàs aquesta història amb paraules manllevades? Amb paraules de la nostra història—seva perquè vostè l'escriví i meva perquè jo l'he viscuda—amb paraules emprades per vostè a les darreres ratlles, abans d'escriure 'continuarà'?" (11) [Would it seem rude if I started this story with some borrowed words? With the words of our story—yours because you wrote it and mine because I lived it—with the words that you used in the last lines, before writing "to be continued"?]. She goes on to quote the passage alluding to death, the closing of the eyes "per a somniar-te un altre cop" (11) [in order to dream you one more time]. By repeating the words from the previous story, the text establishes a linguistic bridge between the two narratives. Words become mobile, not locked onto a page or into one setting. They move fluidly from one text to the next, defying any sense of authorship and belonging to no one. Likewise, references to past experiences already set forth in "Te deix" examine the dual nature of the text in its efforts to correct, that is contradict, and simultaneously confirm the persistent emotional impact of the past.

In "Jo pos" the writer imagines a more idyllic time and place "enllà de la mar gran, on és possible encara el miracle de les sirenes, i els paradisos marítims . . . on els homes-peixos són lliures, feliços i s'estimen." (12) [beyond the high sea, where the miracle of mermaids and a maritime paradise are still possible . . . where the fish-people are free, happy, and love each other]. This fantastical rendition of a lost paradise echoes the epigraph of "Te deix" that reads "Jo era a la vegada arbre i ocell, / al.lot i al.lota, peix mut / dins la mar—Empèdocles" (5) [I was at once tree and bird, / boy and girl, mute fish / in the sea—Empedocles]. The fusion of animal and human and male and female challenges and subverts cultural norms of bipolar divisions. Only in a world of fantasy and idealization (the underwater paradise) can these worlds not collide but gently fuse into one harmonious being. Thus the impossibility of Maria and Marina's love, rendered hopeless by society because of their gender, the difference in their ages and respective roles, accentuates the underlying forces that pull apart and separate terms that don't fit into the socially acceptable equation.

Several other moments of textual sharing between the two versions of the love story heighten the reader's sense of textual fluidity and create a shared experience that seems to exist beyond the written page. The authority of both narrators, Marina and Maria, removes their experiences from a literary context in order to make it seem more "real." Because we, the readers, have already accessed the information that Maria refers to in her version of the affair, the events become part of the readers' collective memory. In "Jo pos" Maria refers to "un passeig vuitcentista cobert de fulles grogues, isolat entre un vells murs de color ocre, murs de convents" (14) [an antiquated path covered with yellow leaves isolated between old cream-colored convent walls]. This observation strikes the chord of memory as Marina describes the same walk in "Te deix" as "Les fulles dels plàtans eren quasi grogues al passeig vuitcentista" (28) [The plantain leaves were turning yellow on the antiquated path]. In both descriptions the yellowing leaves signal the arrival of autumn and the symbolic death of the affair.

However, the two women react differently to a chance meeting in public. Maria acts cautiously while the young student abandons all sense of public decorum upon sighting her love. In "Jo pos" Maria describes the meeting upon remembering

L'estrident xiscle d'uns frens aferrant les rodes sobre l'asfalt a un pam del seu cos. Vaig sortir espantada i m'abraçà amb tanta força, amb tanta desesperació, que gairebé em tirà a terra. La gent ens mirava. Em sentia incòmoda, ens podien conèixer. (14)

[The screech of brakes and tires on the pavement, inches from your body. I got out of the car shocked and you hugged me so suddenly, with such desperation that we almost fell to the ground. People were watching us. I was uncomfortable, somebody could have recognized us.]

While the older woman worries about her social status in the town and what people will think if they see her hugging her young student, Marina reacts on pure emotion. She describes the scene in "Te deix" with innocent enthusiasm: "Un cotxe frenà a un pam del meu cos: era el teu. Sortires amb cara d'espant . . . Amb tanta força, amb tanta ràbia et vaig abraçar que et tomballares. No em convidares a pujar" (29) [A car stopped inches from my body: it was yours. You got out looking horrified . . . I hugged you with such force, such fury that you trembled. You didn't invite me to get in]. The common events of the story are purely narrative, the car stopping only a few inches away from the girl and her spontaneous embrace. Both narrators reveal their personal reaction to the situation, thus formulating a whole scene with both reactions present. We can now imagine the total effect of Marina's unabashed signs of affection and Maria's worried expression and lack of response.

However, both fictional writers, Maria and Marina, also use similar images throughout their respective narrations, which confirm the intensity of their love. For example, Maria confesses her regret about breaking off relations with Marina but she claims that her complaints are useless: "el vent se les enduu lluny, ben lluny fins a donar-les eco" (15) [the wind takes them far away, very far away, and they become only echoes]. Marina confesses her endless love for Maria in a long letter that she wrote one night but never sent. Instead she ripped it up into tiny pieces: "A mil bocins, bocins petitíssims, se l'endugué el vent des de la meva finestra" (32) [in a thousand pieces, tiny little pieces, the wind carried them away from my window]. The wind as an intangible element represents the shadowy memory of their love. It is ever-present and felt, but its very essence defies capture and possession. Maria alludes to their experience on the ferryboat as another fleeting moment that produces guilt yet plagues her as a moment forever lost. Maria reveals that the two women never actually made love that day on the boat, primarily because of her own feelings of guilt. She struggles with the socially constructed moral straitjacket that robbed her of what she thinks would have been a truer experience. "I no el rebutjaria com aleshores amb frases de moral a l'ús, en què tampoc no creia, mentre per dintre em negava als fortíssims reclams del desig, mentre esquitxava l'ànsia immensa de fer-me seva, de fondre'm dins l'espill de la seva carn . . ." (16) [I wouldn't reject it, like I did back then, with moral conventions that I didn't even believe in, while I denied myself from within the burning call of desire, while I avoided the immense longing to abandon myself to her, to submerge myself in the mirror of her skin . . .]. Nevertheless, her words echo the doubling identity that Marina expressed in "your/ my image" as she sees herself in the mirror of her skin. The delicacy of the relationship as expressed in the textual tension between desire and moral duty brings a certain purity to the memories. Maria can only regret that which she has not done and this regret may be what has kept her memory alive for so many years.[34]

In both cases the women feel compelled to write the story and send it to a reader in search of the second part of the dialogue that would affirm the text's existence. Therefore we see in the sequence of events as told by both narrators that writing provides a certain level of catharsis. Yet by structuring the story in an epistolary mode each writer assumes a reader who will interpret the written word. This interpretation or mere recognition of the text legitimizes the story that is in a sense reborn with each reading. Each letter proposes a dialogue to a fictional reader. It is up to us, the real reader, to complete the dialogue through textual clues and bring each part into its place among the totality of the text.

However, Riera's narrative goal is not to create two perfectly interlocking pieces to a puzzle. Her aim is to disturb convention and disrupt our readerly expectations. At the end of "Jo pos" Maria directly addresses the author of "Te deix." In fact she challenges the authenticity of the first version and in doing so claims complete narrative authority and knowledge of the truth. In a sense Riera is deconstructing her own identity as a writer and tangentially the identity of all writers. Maria writes: "Marina desaparegué quan tenia disset anys—no va morir de part com vostè insinuava, no tengué cap nina, tampoc no es casà" (18) [Marina disappeared when she was seventeen years old—she didn't die in childbirth as you insinuated, she didn't have a daughter, she never even got married]. Thus, Riera's Marina from "Te deix" becomes a mere characterization of a "real" Marina who committed suicide quite young. This narrative trope of holding up one's own writing to a judgmental light puts all writing, specifically the art of storytelling, into question. We know the same author, Riera, wrote both texts but her textual world becomes so self-sufficient that the ability to question authorial omniscience occupies center stage. But if Maria the writer seems to know the truth of the situation, once again her reliability becomes overshadowed by doubt.

Maria admits early on in her letter that she voluntarily has committed herself into a psychiatric hospital. She claims she is happy there and that she likes her surroundings for they enable her to "posar en ordre la memòria, dedicar-li tot el temps . . . la memòria ho és tot per a mi" (13) [put my memory in order, dedicate all my time to it . . . memory is everything for me]. With this knowledge, the reader must view the inversion of the events at the end of Maria's story with a wary eye.[35] But this unreliable narrator does not in any way confirm as more legitimate the version of the story in "Te deix." On the other hand, the marginalized world of Maria only confirms the social marginalization of most of Riera's characters. But as Luisa Cotoner points out in her introduction, Riera's marginalized characters reflect upon a society that is foreign to them instead of rebelling against it. She states: "ese factor de marginalidad se dé únicamente en el ámbito de su intimidad, de sus propios estados de ánimo o de sus propios sentimientos, ello hace que, por otro lado, sean perfectamente reconocibles en las coordenadas histórico-sociales señaladas"[36] [this marginality factor is apparent only in the realm of their intimacy, in their own emotional states and feelings, this fact, on the other hand, makes the historical and social context of the stories perfectly recognizable]. Therefore, Maria's version of the affair cannot be trusted as entirely true because it only reflects her relationship to dominant culture. Thus all writers face an extremely difficult task in establishing the truth outside of social and cultural boundaries, yet Riera continually succeeds in challenging our preconceived notions of reality and truth. Riera's characters, who are mostly writers and readers, create an intimate textual world primarily due to the epistolary nature of the narrative, which establishes a displaced dialogue. In her other epistolary narratives, Riera constructs the same type of intimate world playing with the notions of dialogue and extratextual cultural values brought unconsciously to the text by the reader.

FALLEN LANGUAGE IN "PRINCESA MEVA, LLETRA D'ÀNGEL"

In Riera's 1991 collection of short stories *Contra l'amor en companyia i altres relats* [*Against Love with a Partner and Other*

Tales], most of the protagonists are professional writers and most
are women. In "Princesa meva, lletra d'àngel," [My Princess, Angel
Writer] Riera deviates from this norm and not only subverts the
writing profession but also reveals how unstable and malleable language itself can be. By exploring the possibility of a simultaneous
dual discourse within a single text, Riera arrives at what can be
considered the seduction of language itself. Words evolve into sites
of polysemantic chaos with no resolution and therefore any sense
of meaning relies on the complexity of the textual totality.

"Princesa meva, lletra d'àngel" departs from Riera's other epistolary narratives in a radical way. The implied postponed response
from the reader of the epistolary narrative actually appears in the
story in the form of an epistolary dialogue. The relationship established through a series of misunderstandings revealed in the epistolary dialogue uncovers the inconsistencies of language. Epistolary
literature in general represents one voice and consequently one
point of view about certain events, thus the response or possible
responses become fundamental to the reader's reconstruction of
the textual truth. Riera explains that the tone of the literary letter
has little to do with the events narrated and much more with "el
destinatario y de la relación que a través de la carta se establezca
entre emisor y receptor"[37] [the reader and the relation that the
writer establishes through the letter with the reader]. The relationship between the writer and the intended reader that is implied
through one letter and then developed in another appears in
"Princesa meva, lletra d'àngel" as the point of deception and mis-
communication.

The story revolves around everyday propaganda that arrives by
mail. The company Catalanitat sends out various mass-generated
letters advertising cheap trinkets and books symbolic of Catalan
pride to a targeted market. An older gentleman, Sr. Antoni Barba i
Callicó, receives such a letter, thinking that it is a personal letter
from a distanced family member because the last name that appears at the closing of the letter is the same as his own: Cèlia Callicó i Alavedra.[38] The letter from the company adopts a friendly,
intimate tone and defends Catalan nationalistic pride and linguistic
normalization. The letter begins: "Benvolgut amic: M'adreço a
vostè perquè sé que és una persona interessada per la cultura catalana i que àdhuc ha demostrat més d'una vegada la seva catalanitat"[39] [Dear Friend: I write to you because of your interest in
Catalan culture and because on more than one occasion you have

demonstrated your Catalan pride]. In order to maintain the fabricated sense of intimacy, the company decides to close the letter with a proper name, representing a person behind the sentiments. Mary Vásquez points out that there are two distinct discourses at work in the story. She observes that Antoni "receives this text but reads another, superimposing on the commercial discourse of the offer a discourse very much his own."[40] She sees the explicit generation gap exaggerated in the innocence of a man who has not entered into the capitalistic mass production of advertising and therefore cannot understand the "profit motive" ideology of the company.[41]

Antoni's confusion with language introduces the reader to the events of the story. The opening paragraph is actually not part of the epistolary exchange, but rather a furious diatribe Antoni directs at the fictional writer, Cèlia Callicó. He begins: "Princesa meva, lletra d'àngel, per què m'has fet això? Bruixa, meuca, mala puta, jo mai no t'havia enganyat. Sóc pobre i vell, tu ja ho sabies (23) [My princess, angel writer, why have you done this to me? You witch, you tramp, you slut. I never lied to you. I'm poor and old, and you knew it all along]. Already the semantic contradictions display Antoni's confusion. His fabrication of a person who doesn't exist drives him to a delusional state. Cèlia is just a fabricated name and a computerized program churns out the letters. Vásquez concludes that another sign of the generation gap is the bipolar categorization of woman as either saint or whore, seen in Antoni's vacillation between the two: he calls her "angel" and "slut."[42] However, after reading the correspondence that makes up the body of the story, we realize that Antoni's opening speech takes place at the offices where he thinks he will find Cèlia. He speaks to a secretary: "Miri, miri si és de debò: aquí té les cartes, Ja ho pot mirar. I les meves" (25) [Look, look and see if it's true: here you have the letters. Look at them for yourself. And here are mine]. Antoni has gone to visit Cèlia, taking their correspondence as proof of their relationship. Even though the relationship cannot materialize, for Cèlia doesn't exist, the relationship established between writer and receptor does exist. The letters from the company say one thing, but mean something completely different to Antoni. As readers of Riera's story, we know the outcome before the events unravel, yet this technique heightens the relevance of each small revelation in the letters written and exchanged between Antoni and "Cèlia."

The marketing technique employed by the company involves establishing a relaxed, friendly conversational tone in the letters. Riera describes tone as the mode of the narrative voice, which in turn relates to the point of view of the narrator.[43] The first letter of the story opens with "Benvolgut amic" [Dear Friend] and incorporates the intimate tone that becomes recognizably false and intrusive when paired with the overt advertising in the letter. The first offer is for a three-volume history entitled *La Gran Història de la Sardana* described as "una obra escrita precisament pensant en persones com vostè per importants especialistes" (25) [a work written with people like you in mind by important specialists]. None of the important specialist authors are named, suggesting that the target group of lower income retired men probably do not have an affiliation or familiarity with the academic world. The last section of the letter explains different payment and delivery methods. Yet the tone is flattering and with the closing of the letter, "Rebi la meva sincera amistat" (26) [With my sincere friendship], Antoni feels compelled to write back.

His first letter maintains the casual, congenial tone of his "new friend" Cèlia. He writes: "Benvolguda amiga: Em va fer molta il.-lusió la seva carta. Per què va pensar en mi? (26) [Dear Friend: I was so happy to receive your letter. Why did you think to write to me?] With these words, we understand the comprehension gap and the pieces start falling into place. Antoni continues in his own secluded textual fantasy world volunteering personal information about his life, his wife, and his commitment to the Republican cause during the Spanish civil war. The illusory receptor augments the pathetic nature of Antoni's letter. However, by creating an imaginary textual reader, we, the real readers, become the sole receptors of Antoni's letters. It is doubtful that anybody at the company would have time actually to read his letters and take interest in their content. Yet as readers of the narrative we have committed ourselves to entertain Antoni's fantasy. Although we remain outside the textual exchange of letters, we witness the irony of the relationship and at times chuckle at Antoni's innocent mistake. The reader occupies the textual space of the secretary from the beginning of the story who is handed the letters as written proof. The sincerity of Antoni's letters, his honest admiration for Catalunya, and his need for a friend become a source of a pathetic humor in the context of the story. Riera has constructed a narrative where all textual components, words, paragraphs, images, and metaphors cease to function independently of the larger, more radical context. Each part functions persuasively in her equation to subvert the intimate discourse of letters and the commercial discourse in terms of a textual totality. Antoni's letters are often touching in their honesty, yet knowing that he has been duped into writing them and that no one will read them undermines the apparent, superficial meaning of his letters. The correspondence between Cèlia and Antoni becomes layered with meanings as the voyeur/reader, in a position of omniscience, watches as Antoni comes to realize his error and in a startling twist of logic pursues his skewed, invented line of thinking.

Another reason for Antoni's insistence on maintaining the fictional relationship with Cèlia may be to calm his own fears of death. As Vásquez has discussed, the obvious allusions to the generation gap between the young, democratic, commercialized Spain and the battle-worn idealist Republican emerge at various points in the correspondence. However, Antoni's interest in Cèlia erupts into an obsession toward the end of the story, for she is that youthful part of him that he seeks to revive.

Antoni's willingness to open himself emotionally in his letters acts as a cry for companionship. He continues to speculate about the details of Cèlia's physical appearance even after she has refused to answer his letters personally. He thinks that perhaps she is blonde or maybe brunette (30) and at one point desperately confesses to her "Vull veure-la" (31) [I want to see you]. Antoni has created a mythic "other" who confirms his own existence. His epistolary responses divulge an anxious desire to establish an intimate relationship with a young woman; perhaps his reaction would have been different had the name read "Carles Callicó." In the case at hand, Antoni feels compelled to seek the affirmation that woman as "other" provides. In the letter announcing his wife's death he promises to go to Barcelona and find Cèlia. He admits that "a ella no li hauria agradat que tot d'una me n'anés a veure-la a vostè" (33) [she wouldn't have liked that I'm going to see you right away], suggesting that his wife discouraged him from pursuing this crazy idea of going to meet Cèlia. Yet Antoni immediately replaces his wife with the dream of Cèlia, for he says to her that she is the only woman, "una noia d'ànima de princesa i lletra d'àngel" (34) [a girl with the soul of a princess who writes like an angel] that deserves the $250 golden rose pin offered in Cèlia's previous letter.

The letter from the company describes the gold rose gift as "una rosa que vostè voldrà fer lluir sobre l'escot de la dona estimada" (32) [a rose that you will want to see shine at the neckline of your loved one]. The rose pin "que mai no es marceix" [that never withers] is compared with the short-lived and disappointing natural rose that "es marcia, poc després en uns instants" (32) [wilts after a while in just a few moments]. The juxtaposition of a natural rose with the gold rose pin furthers Riera's social commentary on the new, commercialized Spain. A drive to preserve youth and stop time with money produces commodified tokens of sentiment. This is another point that Antoni cannot understand, for he takes Cèlia a fresh rose, one of the best from his town, and claims angrily: "Meu no tindràs res, t'ho ben juro. Res. Cap rosa d'or, princesa meva" (36) [you'll never have mine (my rose) believe me, never. Nor any golden rose, my princess]. Antoni clearly privileges the fleeting beauty of a natural rose over the impressive economic symbol of the gold rose. His own generation can be compared to the natural rose, withering away and undesirable, soon to be replaced by a shiny fake fetishist symbol of prosperity.

In order to preserve his own fleeting youth, Antoni refuses to accept his error. At the end of the story, he repeats parts of his initial monologue, especially his cursing of Cèlia. When the secretary explains to him Cèlia's invented identity and that "No existeix, senyor Barba, no l'enganyem" (35) [she doesn't exist, Mr. Barba, we're not lying], her ironic words have a double meaning. She tells him the truth about Cèlia yet the discourse presented in the letters is indeed molded to coerce the reader into buying a product, to trick him into buying Catalan pride, love, and entrance into a new commercial era. Antoni continues his one-sided relationship with Cèlia. The story ends and he is still addressing her, condemning her, and accusing her. He claims: "perquè sóc vell i pobre no has volgut sortir, no m'has volgut conèixer" (35) [because I'm old and poor you didn't want to come out, you didn't want to meet me]. Antoni places the blame on Cèlia for rejecting him, for he cannot comprehend the greatness of his own misinterpretation. The invented receptor of his letters legitimized all of his written feelings, including his pride in past experiences he wrote about, his desire to meet Cèlia and to create a life for himself beyond the reality of a poor old man. Thus the image of Cèlia must remain a truth for him, for if she were to dissolve into nothingness, so would his own persona transcribed in his letters. Therefore, epistolary discourse, even though it may represent one voice or one point of view, can never really be one-sided. The mere desire to transmit information immediately creates an "other." In Antoni's case the effects are confusing, disorienting, and pathetic, however, in Riera's other epistolary narratives this doubling of discourse leads to camaraderie and liberation.

QÜESTIÓ D'AMOR PROPI AND "ESTIMAT THOMAS"

In Riera's epistolary narrative Qüestió d'amor propi, she pursues similar issues concerning discourse and the cultural power structure inscribed in language. Riera also subverts the traditional notion of the epistolary as a realist genre for women documenting their lives in nineteenth-century Europe. In an interview I held with her in October 1998 she explained her fascination with developing a nonlegitimate aspect of the epistolary. I had asked her about the relevance of the ending of Qüestió d'amor propi and if Àngela can be considered satisfied or compensated by the act of writing the letter and not necessarily getting even with Miquel. She replied:

> Yo creo que hay diferentes cosas, la primera es que no sabemos si la historia fue así porque solamente tenemos una voz. Por eso las cartas me gustan tanto a mí, me parece un género tan fácil porque no tenemos más que un único punto de vista y por eso no siempre tiene la razón la persona que escribe. Yo no sé si, pues no he llegado a saber si él realmente fue tan malo como dice Àngela que fue.[44]

> [I think there are differing things: the first is that we don't know exactly how the story went because we only have one voice. That's why I like letters so much, it's such an easy genre because there is only one point of view and therefore the person who is writing isn't always right. I don't know if, well, I haven't come to realize yet if he (Miquel) was really as bad as Àngela says he was.]

If the narrative voice of the epistolary may be considered unreliable as Riera indicates, then the truth of the story lies outside of the text. This places a more interactive responsibility on the reader. We become a form of audience, not only reading but also judging the sincerity of the narrative process. Therefore Àngela's letter becomes a performative act of catharsis as she reveals her personal disillusion with love, and more important, with the social conditioning she has fallen victim to as a woman. Her personal commentary may be tainted by her own egotism, yet her realization of a restricted social education provides the background for a collectively conscious act of reading. The act of writing, regardless of the impetus or response, proves a subversive form of liberation for the woman writer schooled by patriarchy to remain silent. Nancy Chodorow says:

> The sex-gender system is, just as any society's dominant mode of production, a fundamental determining and constituting element of that society, [it is] socially constructed, subject to historical change and development . . . Sex as we know it—[defined as] gender identity, sexual desire and fantasy, concepts of childhood—is itself a social product.[45]

The social product of gender identity that Chodorow defines draws upon and supports various cultural institutions challenged by Riera. These cultural structures that define our roles as men and women in society include marriage, sex, motherhood, and family. Riera focuses specifically on the role of the woman writer and academic who confronts these cultural structures searching for an authentic voice with which to accurately express herself. By probing the nature of the female role embedded in the framework of these cultural institutions, Riera uncovers the roots of social oppression. Her character Àngela tries to defy the apparently inevitable social role-play and instead take charge of her particular situation. This liberation leaves behind the traditional passive female stereotype and ushers in a new age of action.

Riera eloquently brings to light the struggle that women writers face in creating their own literary space through language. She asserts that there is a difference in how women and men write, but that ultimately literature is creation through language.[46] The problem for women writers therefore lies in language itself as a patriarchal construct that supposedly limits any true, original female expression. However, she attempts to redefine the presupposed limits of patriarchal language. Women writers must manipulate language to express the inequality that women experience in heterosexual relationships as well as to reveal the inherent conflicts with domestic life that women encounter while working in the public sphere. Through language, Riera liberates the women in her narratives, although not by simply inverting the language hierarchy and giving women the power of the "masculine" word, but rather by closely scrutinizing certain cultural expectations. Through the act of writing, her female characters assert themselves as artists and this creative action empowers them.

Qüestió d'amor propi is a short novel written in epistolary form. Àngela, a writer and critic from Barcelona, writes a revealing confessional to her friend Ingrid in Denmark. Àngela has suffered a torturous breakup after what seemed to her a passionate, profound love affair with Miquel, a young, successful writer. Miquel abandons Àngela and then adds fuel to the fire by publishing a novel obviously based on their short-lived relationship entitled El canto del cisne [Swan Song]. Miquel's novel features a washed-up, aged, and foolish female romantic lead. Àngela immediately sees herself in Miquel's characterization of the desperate older woman. In a state of despair Àngela writes to her friend Ingrid, breaking a year of silence between them, and asks for help to seek revenge on Miquel. She explains to her friend that Miquel will soon be traveling to Denmark and he is sure to seek out Ingrid, who is an expert on Scandinavian culture. Àngela proposes to her friend that she feed Miquel false information about the customs and culture of Denmark so that when he publishes a series of informative articles he has planned he will look ridiculous and incompetent, losing any chance he may have had to win the Nobel Prize.

Riera's novel ends with the closing of Àngela's letter to Ingrid. Therefore as readers, we don't know Ingrid's reply or the outcome of Àngela's vengeful plot. Will Ingrid help her heartbroken friend seek revenge or will she refuse to play the same kind of power publishing game that Miquel himself used to harm Àngela? Emilie Bergmann notes that the epistolary creates a more intimate narrative space, allowing the reader the unique perspective of a spy or voyeur who observes, in this case, a personal metamorphosis through the "subversive linguistic and political implications" of Riera's epistolary narrative.[47] Riera's subversion of the traditional epistolary involves reproducing bits of dialogue between Àngela and Miquel, parts of their phone conversation, and even excerpts from Ingrid's last letter written to Àngela. The inclusion of other narrative methods into the immediate present tense of the epistolary creates a narrative tension between the overtly structured sequence and the intimate framework of the epistolary.

Elizabeth MacArthur defines the epistolary as "present moments [that] are recounted without knowledge of the future, privileging metonymy over metaphor, sequence over closure."[48] Riera has broken the spontaneity by including references to the past and reconstructing a story yet, in accordance with MacArthur, closure remains superfluous to the goal of establishing dialogue. This proximity to Àngela, the writer of the letter, ultimately renders Ingrid's response unimportant to the story primarily because the end of the letter has resolved the conflict established. Àngela regains control of her situation by taking on a more active role and coming to terms with the various conflicting aspects of her own socially constructed identity. Whether Ingrid chooses to act on behalf of her friend or not doesn't change Àngela's newfound understanding of how society has coerced her into degrading role-play.[49]

This transformation is fundamental to the novel, as it suggests an awakening of consciousness in Àngela. Simply by voicing the pathetic nature of her dependency on Miquel and acknowledging the damage caused by her deprecating self-image, Àngela takes the first step toward change. There is a crucial moment toward the beginning of the letter when Àngela defines the socialization of women. First she divides women into two categories, those who view sex as simply another physical need, "com una necessitat" [a necessity], and those like herself "que són incapaces d'entrar en uns altres braços sense estar enamorades"[50] [who are incapable of lying in someone's arms without being in love]. This limiting polarization of women as types stems from the binary opposition of the whore/virgin archetype formulated by patriarchal culture and seen in "Princesa meva, lletra d'àngel." Women function sexually within the society completely dependent on a male opinion that strips women of sexual autonomy while prohibiting male recognition of female sexual desire. Àngela goes on to describe the contradictory nature of women's sexual desire as seen by men. Speaking for her generation, she claims:

> moltes dones de la meva generació i, de manera especial, les que passàrem per més intel.ligents, vam arribar a avergonyir-nos d'aquesta pro-

pensió vers la tendresa perquè ens pareixia una prova de debilitat, de feblesa femenina, i vam estimar-nos més mostrar-nos, especialment davant dels homes, fortes, fredes i autosuficients. (23–24)

[Many women from my generation and especially those of us who passed for the more intelligent ones, came to a point where this propensity towards tenderness was embarrassing because it seemed to us a mark of feminine weakness and we wanted to become and more important show ourselves, especially to men, strong, cool, and self-sufficient.]

However, this remolding of femininity as cold, strong, and independent is just another extreme that doesn't seem to fit with Àngela's vision of herself. There are two different cultural ideals at work here, the strong, independent woman and the submissive, nurturing partner. Most significant, however, is that for Àngela the two are in direct conflict, pushing her in opposite directions and completely obscuring any real sense of self. She completes this section of the letter by admitting that the one thing she has wished for all her life is to be diminished, objectified, and degraded. Her self-image covers the range of extremes and raises the question: Why would an intelligent woman desire to be "disminuïda, infantilitzada, quasi cosificada" (24) [belittled, childlike, almost objectified]? By raising this question within the narrative, Riera reveals the problematic social construct of femininity and how it restricts women, categorizing them as one patriarchal ideal or the other.

Psychologist Carol Gilligan observes: "Many women have a hard time distinguishing the created or socially constructed feminine voice from a voice which they hear as their own."[51] Riera explores in her narrative the social education that convinces women to conform to the institution of heterosexual marriage and family, which inherently forms a hierarchy with a male at the head. The woman either embraces the subservient position of wife or rejects the role, entering into a state of chaos and seen as undesirable or uncontrollable by men. The marriage formula or hierarchy is repeated in any heterosexual relationship into which the woman enters. Because the observations that Àngela makes about her own self-image and about the roles she feels forced to play appear at the beginning of the novel, the subsequent account of the truly degrading experience with Miquel takes on not only personal but social significance. Àngela's desire to be reduced and objectified is the direct result of the social structure in which she lives.

However, by writing the letter to Ingrid, Àngela breaks with the codified social norms of female silence. Yet at the same time her request to Ingrid to deceive Miquel leads her down the same path of trickery and deception that Miquel himself once walked. Akiko Tsuchiya has pointed out that Ingrid is in fact the object whom Àngela sets out to seduce, convince, and influence. In these terms the end of the novel can be read as a failed attempt on Àngela's part to gain true understanding because she merely falls into the same power game that was used to destroy her.[52] Sandra Schumm makes the case that the language in the novel actually "crosses gender distinctions" and fuses female and male voices in order for the protagonist to regain control of her situation. Thus Schumm establishes the relationship between language and control.[53] The problem that arises is that in the conclusion Àngela employs aggressiveness and patriarchal power over her friend through patriarchal language and therefore plays with the same emotional and professional manipulation as does Miquel. Kristeva points out that when women replace men in the hierarchy, that is to say, when women seek to exercise the same power that they are subject to, then women are settling for a false sense of liberation. Kristeva describes problematic feminism as an extremist movement that "does not analyze its own relationship to power and does not renounce belief in its own identity."[54] Kristeva's concerns lie in the relationship between the notion of the individual and power as a dominant ideology when she affirms: "We run the risk of creating within feminism an enclosed ideology parallel to the ideology of the dominant class."[55]

Nevertheless, if we look at Àngela's development within her social context, the success story lies not in her aggressive linguistic behavior but in her personal recovery from negative cultural baggage. Riera has carefully laid out in detail Àngela's situation, her problematic self-image, her insecurities as a writer and as an aging woman. Therefore, the moment when she decides to write to Ingrid and realizes that she has been treated unfairly, not only by Miquel but also by her social education and upbringing, is the moment of true revelation. This awareness of injustice on the basis of gender does not fit into the social prescription given to women, which Àngela has discussed so openly in her letter. The movement from passive to active, from suffering to scheming, from silence to writing elevates Àngela to a new level of consciousness which is not necessarily "masculine" but positive in the sense that it provides

Àngela with options other than the limiting roles social structures offer. The epistolary form as manipulated by Riera falls into what Margaret Jones defines as a feminist narrative strategy that uses "language to shape a female or 'other' experience and posit an alternative to the patriarchal language of control, with thought-provoking implications for friendship or relationships between women."[56] The reconnection between Àngela and Ingrid seems to overshadow Àngela's miserable past experiences and supports her newfound identity.

Àngela admits that she finds satisfaction not in revenge but rather in subverting the norm of what is expected of her. She writes to Ingrid: "En el fons no és el fet de deixar-lo en ridícul el que més em satisfà sinó estar segura que, cregut com és, l'única lliçó que treurà de tot això és que mai hom ha de confiar, perquè no en tenen, en el criteri de les dones" (87) [Deep down it's not really to make him look ridiculous that will satisfy me but rather to be sure that, as conceited as he is, the only lesson that he will gain from all this is that a man should never trust a woman's criteria, because she has none]. Àngela has reached a point at which she embraces the traditionally negative image of a resourceful, even spiteful, woman. Language and meaning become separated, for Miquel's misogyny as an anticipated reaction only categorizes him, confines him, and limits him to a certain rhetoric that he has created.

However, as Àngela continues to realize the socialization of her own behavior in her relationship with Miquel, she turns against language when she recognizes it as a false form of reality. She describes Miquel's inflated rhetoric of love as false and insincere. He whispers to her on one occasion: "El meu desig de tu és tan immens com la mar, més pregon que les simes abissals. T'estimaré mentre visqui perquè ningú mai no m'ha arribat tan endins" (39–40) [My desire for you is as vast as the sea, more profound than the deepest chasms. I will love you for the rest of my life because no one, ever, has touched me so deeply]. Àngela confesses to Ingrid: "Eren frases trivials, Íngrid, fins i tot cursis amb tuf de seminarista suat i retòrica de sagristia, però a mi em sonaren a música celestial, tal volta perquè les havia estat esperant, no des de feia cinc dies sinó des de mesos ençà, o potser anys, qui sap si des de tota la vida" (40) [They were silly words, Ingrid, really quite tacky and they stank like a sweaty seminary student and holy rhetoric, but to me they sounded like heaven, perhaps because I had been waiting for them, not for five days but for up to five months, or maybe for years, who knows, perhaps for my entire life]. Miquel's seductive words are turned on their head, the meaning inverted as Àngela dispels the myth of passion in a declaration of love. The metaphorical quality of Miquel's hyperbolic declarations seems insincere and rote when followed by Àngela's critical commentary. She criticizes not only his words, but also, more important, her own willingness to consider them truthful. She admits that she had been groomed for months or perhaps years to hear those very words from a man. Her social conditioning to believe in the rhetoric leaves her initially impressed and later doubly repulsed. Her disillusion with her lover actually becomes secondary to her realization of her own participation in the gender role-play.

As the epistolary narrative develops, Àngela's distrust of language and the verisimilitude of Miquel's novel call attention to her own letter as a superior form of literary composition. The contradiction inherent in Riera's epistolary narrative revolves around Àngela's mistrust of language yet total dependence on it to regain her dignity. Àngela and Miquel meet for the first time at a conference on the nineteenth-century realist novel from Spain. She explains her intervention and challenge to Miquel after his paper on *La Regenta*, a popular realist novel by Leopoldo Alas, otherwise known as Clarín, published in 1885. She describes her nerves before asking the question: "Fent un esforç inusitat per dissimular el meu empegueïnent vaig demanar la paraula per rebatre en Miquel" (32) [making a concerted effort to disguise my embarrassment I raised my hand to get the floor and challenge Miquel]. Her discomfort about speaking enforces her marginal position at the conference. Àngela's mixed feelings about herself are reflected in her comments about Ana Ozores, the protagonist from *La Regenta*. Her rebuttal to Miquel's remarks about Ana's sexual deprivation asserts that really the source of Ana's frustrations lies in "la falta d'afecte en què va créixer" (32) [the lack of affection in her childhood]. Both Àngela and the fictional character Ana Ozores are victims of a socialization that ignores the complexity of female sexuality and builds rigid social structures intended to dictate and control female behavior.

Àngela criticizes Miquel's novelistic world as made "de cartó pedra, sense cohesió moral" (56) [out of cardboard, without any moral cohesion], suggesting that his command of language is inferior to the truth that she herself is writing in the letter. Àngela continues her critique of Miquel's work and words: "Havia escrit la nostra relació, no l'havia viscuda. Tal vegada ni ell ni jo érem altra cosa que un munt de paraules que ara, de sobte, s'enfonsava amb dolor, renou i fúria per esclafar-nos" (57) [He had written our relationship instead of living it. Perhaps we were nothing more than a pile of words that now, suddenly, came tumbling down with pain, noise, and anger to flatten us]. The insincerity of Miquel's words, both spoken and written, contradict the open, confessional tone of Àngela's letter to Ingrid.

Riera's use of the epistolary as a tool to legitimize experience by presupposing a textual reader and a response seems to place Àngela's version of the love affair on a superior level. Her metatextual commentary on writing and words emphasizes her desire to express herself truthfully through language. Yet the language she employs undercuts patriarchal language by divesting it of power, stripping Miquel's words of influence and meaning. Therefore, Ingrid's approval or rejection of the idea of revenge makes no difference. Her anticipated reading of the letter fulfilled by us, the real readers, ensures that Àngela's version is heard and that she has found a voice. Àngela's literary project is, as she admits in the end, not so much to see Miquel squirm as to subvert the cultural ideal of female decorum.

Another epistolary narrative that subverts socially generated ideas regarding female decorum is a humorous short piece entitled "Estimat Thomas" [Dear Thomas] that tells the story of a young girl's passion. Nine letters written to Thomas while Montse is vacationing with her family contain countless references to her unbridled emotions. She writes in the first letter: "Quina ràbia, és el primer aniversari que passem separats"[57] [I'm so angry, this is the first anniversary we will spend separated] and recalls the first time they met and how Thomas walked next to her father so seriously. She swoons over his eyes, she delights in washing his back, she admits how his tongue drives her crazy "quan es posa en contacte amb la meva pell i puja per les cames, genolls, amunt . . . Thomas, Thomas, t'enyoro tant. .(84) [when it touches my skin and climbs up my legs, my knees, rising . . . Thomas, Thomas, I miss you so]. In one of her letters, Montse declares her love again despite what she considers Thomas's shortcomings: "No em sap greu que no em puguis escriure. No em fa falta, crec en tu. M'agrades com ets"

(89) [It doesn't matter to me that you can't write. I don't need that, I believe in you. I like you how you are]. She imagines what his writing would be like, large and filling the entire page with "t'estimo" (89) [I love you]. This moment provides the crucial connection between Thomas and Montse. Words cannot describe their love and Thomas's inability to express himself with language only increases Montse's desire to be with him physically, for what he cannot write he can express through touch.

The shock of this story resides in the final letter when we realize Thomas's true identity. Montse's sister has confiscated the letters and gives them to the hotel concierge, telling him to mail them to Thomas at the canine boarding facility in Barcelona. The receptionist asks Montse: "¿Vols dir que sap llegir es teu ca, nina?" (94) [You mean to say your dog knows how to read, little girl?]. Our readerly expectations, previously enticed by the subtle erotics of Thomas's pink tongue, come crashing down around us. Montse's love for her dog has been manipulated by the reader's assumptions and her affirmation at the end of her last letter, "T'estimo més que mai" (95) [I love you more than ever], proves her feelings to be more stable and constant than the trickery of her words.

Language becomes unreliable when the context of the fictional reality shifts with the reader's awareness as in "Princesa meva, lletra d'àngel" or without as in "Estimat Thomas." The vacillation of semantics can be located more concretely in the evolving and shifting subject positions created in the texts. Geraldine Cleary Nichols defines Riera's narrative upheavals or surprises as fantastic. She claims: "to start from the margins is a feminist or minority practice, and to deconstruct the integrity of the desiring subject is a typical practice of modern fantasy."[58] Nichols supports her argument by citing Rosemary Jackson when she says, "It is important to understand the radical consequences of an attack upon unified 'character', for it is precisely this subversion of unities of self which constitutes the most radical transgressive function of the fantastic."[59] Therefore, Riera's narrative innovations lie not only in the fluctuating stages of understanding and relation to an "other" that the characters or narrative voices experience but also, and perhaps more radically, the process that the reader experiences. The nature of the epistolary informs a textual reader, yet when that very reader becomes a fabrication or an animal, the extratextual reader's comfort as voyeur quickly becomes thwarted and we are not observing an initiation of a dialogue but rather the textual proof of the fictional writer's own semantic subversion.

Riera's reformulation of the epistolary incorporates notions of traditional letter-writing as an intimate confessionary tool as well as revolutionary approaches to bridging the gap between the emitter and receptor of the information. Her willingness to address such issues as the commoditization of the epistolary, as in "Princesa meva . . . ,'' and the absent and at times nonexistent reader (Cèlia and Thomas the dog) proposes a new kind of letter-writing where the possibility of dialogue sustains the writer's desire. Brad Epps discusses the writer's desire that takes a narcissistic turn in the excessive giving embodied in the text that "expects to get something, equally excessive, in return."[60] Epps refers specifically to Àngela in *Qüestió d'amor propi* but his analogy applies to all of Riera's letter writers; the letter becomes a metonymical tool representing not an implied dialogue but the infinite possibilities of dialogue. We can imagine each letter writer reacting quite differently depending upon who reads and comments on his or her letter, thus the speaking subject becomes unstable due to the imprecise nature of language. Riera celebrates the mystery and potential of language not as a monolithic exclusionary structure to combat but as a permeable arena of polyvocality that in its fluctuations can produce enlightening feminist texts.

By decentering the speaking subject and allowing various levels of possible interpretation or more important noninterpretation, Riera points to the failings of any homogeneous imagining of the writer or reader. The boundaries become blurred just as social boundaries that delineate gender, sexual preference, or marginalization disappear as the gradual unveiling of the narrative leaves the reader astonished and susceptible to the lie of language.

Riera's narrative is important in that it continues the feminist project of reinventing history by writing women into experience. Her narrative project can be understood as a departure from a fundamental concept in Jameson's thought: that of literary manifestations of historical repressions, for it goes beyond mere recuperation of history. However, Riera also plays into accepted and repressed cultural formulations of art, love, and history not unlike Jameson, who identifies the dominant institutions of the superstructure as partially dependent upon the ideology of a socially rendered consciousness.

As her story "Princesa meva" suggests, Catalunya, as a specific cultural space, must look forward to change instead of backward to the historically rendered errors of the past. In this way, Riera also intends to reformulate Catalan social consciousness regarding the tragedy of the Spanish civil war. The lasting effects of the war are perhaps most profoundly felt in the lack of an artistic and literary history stemming from the prohibition of the Catalan language. These repressions therefore coincide with the rise of the Falange under Franco. Riera treats the war in her narrative as just another socially constructed discourse that dictates certain behaviors to certain sectors of the population. Like any dominant discourse, its subversion lies in the dismantling of language and in the revelation of the unreliability of language. Riera's literary project seeks to bring Catalunya out from under the oppressive history of the Spanish civil war and into a more progressive theoretical arena of global consciousness.

Nevertheless, her narrations all take place in Barcelona or on the island of Mallorca. By writing specifically about Catalunya and Mallorca, she can not only inscribe the local into a global theory of culture and history but also can bring the international literary world's attention to her own region. Riera's ability to see beyond her own region and country's borders by relating Catalan historical shifts to a larger, less physical realm of cultural studies and theory distinguishes her literary voice. She is no longer a woman struggling to write and to express herself adequately with the clumsy tool of patriarchal language from a position outside of dominant culture. Her genre and gender innovations place her squarely within a developing international feminist literary movement. Yet only from this place of exile, of separation from genre and language, can Riera subvert traditionally historical norms of epistolary narrative. By distancing herself from authorial omnipotence, Riera is able to engage the reader in a new and meaningful way.

Conclusion

This World is not Conclusion.
A Species stands beyond—
Invisible, as Music—
But positive, as Sound—

Emily Dickinson

GENDER EXILE AS SEEN IN THE WORKS OF VARO, RODOREDA, ROIG, AND Riera refers to the alienation of an individual from her surroundings. I have demonstrated through close textual analyses the various ways in which these women approach their situation as an outsider looking into the patriarchal construct of language, which in turn maintains certain social institutions such as marriage, family, motherhood, and authorship. Despite the imposed disciplinary differences between art and literature, I have shown how Varo and Rodoreda both use ideas of confinement and escape to express their individual journeys of exile. The most subversive link between the two lies in their use of metamorphosis as a way to strip a character of gender and permit an exploration of alternative lands and experiences. Just as Natàlia from Rodoreda's *La plaça del Diamant* suffers from intense neurosis when enclosed in her own home and relates to the walls that surround her as a defining part of her experience, Varo's figure in *Double Agent* faces the wall unable to confront the mounting sexual tension in the room. These are the metaphorical walls that both women will break down in an attempt to define a feminine voice from a marginalized position. Both women seem to find a temporary answer to patriarchal demands through laughter. At the end of *El carrer de les camèlies*, Rodoreda's protagonist Cecília confronts her own fears of abandonment with shared laughter. Varo's humorous nods at the school of surrealists, who nurtured her artistic talent from a respectable distance because she was Benjamin Péret's mistress, take form in her paintings that mock the psychoanalytical fervor expressed by the founding members of the movement.

196

The works of the four women in this study considered as a whole prove revolutionary in terms of contemporary Spanish art and literature. By taking on paradigms such as religion in "La meva Cristina" by Rodoreda or canonical literature as in *L'hora violeta* by Roig the authors not only intend to insert female experience into the grand equation of social history but also to subvert traditionally embraced and accepted institutions. Riera provides an alternative to heterosexual love in both "Te deix, amor, la mar com a penyora" and in a more humorous way in "Estimat Thomas." However, the result is the same: nothing is sacred, not family, traditions, inheritance, gender, or genre. At a time when many critics are lamenting the "literary malaise" of post-Franco Spain[1] and even writers complain about the "poca atención que ha merecido la literatura española en los últimos ciento cincuenta años fuera de España"[2] [little attention that Spanish literature has received in the past 150 years outside of Spain] I hope to have shown here that there is no literary malaise in Catalunya and that the two women writing in post-Franco Spain draw from their postwar predecessors to form a coherent body of work that defies stagnant, one-sided art.

The scope of linguistic and iconographic subversion in the works of women writers and artists from Catalunya remains a vast, open field of possible inquiry. The proliferation of criticism and theoretical work currently aimed at unwinding the double bind of Catalan women artists stands as a testimony to the importance of understanding not only Catalan literary and art history but peninsular women's artistic identity and its role in the larger European community. I have traced the development and changes of women's artistic identity as exemplified through various literary and pictorial texts. The influence on Catalan women's identity exerted by the socially liberal Second Republic and the flourishing avant-garde movement in Barcelona allowed women a certain degree of liberty and equality not found in other parts of Spain.

Barcelona's geographical location acts as a bridge uniting Catalunya with France and metonymically with the rest of Europe and therefore the city functions at times as a mediator between cultures, fusing tendencies, languages, and customs. So the woman artist from Catalunya must resolve her marginalized status as female in a patriarchal society with her regionalism that separates her from the rest of Spain. Her texts and paintings bridge the gap between her double marginalization.

An important similarity in the lives and works of the four women in this study is the instinct to seek out female friendships as a way to express themselves artistically and emotionally. Through Rodoreda's correspondence with her friend Anna Murià we gain a sense of the moral support this friendship provided for both women during the difficult time of exile.[3] Only in these letters does Rodoreda divulge her true feelings for her married lover, Armand Obiols, a relationship that caused her much pain yet at the same time was a source of creative inspiration. A well-known fact about Remedios Varo's years in Mexico is her intimate friendship with the English painter Leonora Carrington. Varo's widower, Walter Gruen, has mentioned their deep affection for each other and Albert Blanco claims that perhaps only Leonora Carrington "had some insight into that world we call Remedios Varo."[4] The two women shared ideas about art and life while concocting special potions and experimenting with alchemy in the kitchen.

Montserrat Roig brings this aspect of female friendship to her writing as a possible solution to the oppressive social matrix of male/female relationships. While her novels do not investigate lesbian love as a subversive means of female expression, she does begin to hint at the benefits of a homosociality that privileges women's accounts of history, time, and narrative. Carme Riera also breaks socially constructed barriers of a heterosexuality that automatically places women in a disadvantaged position in the hierarchy. Her politics also find a way into her writing as she redefines the writer/reader relationship that parallels all human interaction. The connection between women expressed either through personal relationships or through various textual relationships suggests female empowerment.

The generational aspect of this study provides a framework for the progress and development of women's artistic identity in terms of male/female relationships evaluated from a position of exclusion or exile. The early generation represented by Mercè Rodoreda and Remedios Varo seems inevitably bound to the movements and men who formulated their first artistic endeavors. Surrealism and the Catalan avant-garde eventually became a stifling set of rules that disallowed true liberation for female artists and writers. While both Rodoreda and Varo seemed aware of the greater social issues that discouraged women to operate in the public sphere, they both spent their lives attached to men.

In the later generation represented by Montserrat Roig and Carme Riera, the dependence on a male counterpart becomes a point of contention in their narratives. Roig particularly expresses deep concern about the socialized nature of male/female relationships. She investigates the social and cultural phenomenons that breed such conflictive roles for men and women. Her narrative adheres to the city of Barcelona as a historical template that reacts and changes through the turbulent later years of Franco's dictatorship through the growing pains of socialism and into the new democracy. Clearly with Roig's work the political becomes personal and she looks away from her male counterparts and to a revision of history through the eyes of the marginalized in order to make sense of a feminine past.

Riera's work becomes less political but perhaps more subversive as she recreates the roles of men and women in her narrative. Most of Riera's social commentary is filtered through an unreliable narrator who exercises ulterior motives such as revenge or seduction instead of straightforward renegotiations of personal love relationships. Her interest extends beyond individuals to a cultural unconscious, an institutionalized relationship between people and society. Thus the generational development winds up in a postmodern vein, decentering the monolithic subject and breaking down the boundaries of cultural experience.

The rupture of the subjective "I" allows women not only to enter the creative scene as subjective beings but also to question the formulas imposed by the superstructure that define and oppress women, minorities, and subaltern voices. Through a diverse theoretical lens the relationship between the exiled subject and her reconciliation with language gains form and meaning. The theories of subjectivity posited by Foucault and Kristeva, among others, reveal a precarious space of individuality that helps define the feminist, subversive space from which these women produce art and literature.

The idea of gender exile then revolves around an axis of interrelated problems for a woman writer or artist and from her viewpoint as an outsider she is able to better define and attack these problems. The problems or obstacles include history, language, identity, socialization, and expectation. Paul Ilie claims: "el exilio interior es, en último extremo, una condición cualitativa con más partes recónditas y oscuras"[5] [internal exile is, ultimately, a qualitative

condition with hidden and dark parts]. These parts that Ilie describes bring us full circle to the words of Marguerite Duras, who
defines the "blackness" and "darkness" as the space from which
women write.[6] It is precisely this area that I have brought to the
forefront in this study: the unspoken, shadowy experience of
women that is in fact a gender exile.

Notes

INTRODUCTION

1. See Michael Ugarte, *Shifting Ground: Spanish Civil War Exile Literature* (Durham: Duke University Press, 1989). Ugarte provides detailed analyses of and connections between political and self-imposed exile, including a very informative chapter on Goytisolo.

2. Tabori gives an extensive overview of the history of exile from ancient times to the twentieth century in an effort to categorize and examine the experiences of mainly war-inspired exiles. Tabori, *The Anatomy of Exile* (London: Harrap, 1972).

3. Paul Ilie puts forth the fundamental reordering of the exile experience as he claims that those who are left behind, including those who inspired a state of terror for writers and artists after the civil war, experience an equal amount of trauma, loss, and identity crisis as those forced to leave their homeland. Ilie, *Literatura y exilio interior* (Madrid: Espiral, 1980).

4. María Lagos-Pope, ed. *Exile in Literature* (Lewisburg: Bucknell University Press, 1988), 7.

5. Ilie, *Literatura*, 11.

6. Marguerite Duras, interview by Susan Husserl-Kapit, *New French Feminisms*, ed. Elaine Marks and Isabelle de Courtivron (New York: Schocken, 1981), 174.

7. Foucault's ideas of genealogy are put forth in his *The History of Sexuality Parts I and II* (New York: Pantheon, 1985). Kristeva's notion of the *sujet en procès* or the subject in process/on trial is explained at length throughout her book *Revolution in Poetic Language* (New York: Columbia University Press, 1984). Kelly Oliver also defines the idea in *Reading Kristeva* (Bloomington: Indiana University Press, 1993).

8. For a detailed explanation of the semiotic see Kristeva's "The Semiotic and the Symbolic," in *Revolution in Poetic Language*, 21–106.

9. Kathleen McNerney's *Voices and Visions* (Selinsgrove: Susquehanna University Press, 1999) is a collection of critical essays on the narrative and poetic works of Rodoreda. In 1994, McNerney and Nancy Vosburg coedited a collection of essays entitled *The Garden across the Border* (Selinsgrove: Susquehanna University Press, 1994), which contains several crucial essays that have shaped the study of Rodoreda's work. Three important biographies of Rodoreda are: Carme Arnau, *Mercè Rodoreda* (Barcelona: Edicions 62, 1992), Mercè Ibarz, *Mercè Rodoreda* (Barcelona: Editorial empúries, 1991), and M. Casals, *Mercè Rodoreda: contra la vida, la literatura* (Barcelona: Edicions 62, 1991).

Janet Kaplan's excellent biography and analysis of Remedios Varo's work, *Un-*

expected Journeys (New York: Abbeville Press, 1988) still stands as the most thorough and complete study of this often overlooked surrealist. However, the National Museum of Women in the Arts in Washington, D.C. hosted the first retrospective of Remedios Varo's works in April 2000. The resulting catalog entitled *The Magic of Remedios Varo* (Washington, D.C.: National Museum of Women in the Arts, 2000) contains biographical and analytical essays on Varo and her work that illuminate the thematics, style, and technical prowess of the artist.

Christina Dupláa has written numerous articles on Montserrat Roig and a book-length study entitled *La voz testimonial en Montserrat Roig* (Barcelona: Icaría, 1996). Kathleen Glenn, Mirella Servodidio, and Mary Vásquez edited a collection of essays on the work of Carme Riera that includes a preface written by Riera herself, an interview with the author, and the first English translation of an original Riera play. This important collection is entitled *Moveable Margins* (Lewisburg: Bucknell University Press, 1999).

10. Carme Riera, interview by author, tape recording, Barcelona, 8 October 1998.

11. For accounts of the impact of Roig's death on the literary community see: Maruja Torres, "Una luchadora," *El País* (11 noviembre 1991), 29; "Un millar de personas despidieron a la escritora Montserrat Roig," *El País* (12 noviembre 1991), 41, and "La prematura muerte de Montserrat Roig conmociona al mundo literario catalán," *El País* (11 noviembre 1991), 29.

12. Carme Riera is a native of Mallorca, Spain, where a different version of Catalan is spoken, yet she teaches at the Barcelona Autonomous University and lives in Barcelona.

13. Whitney Chadwick, *Women Artists and the Surrealist Movement* (Boston: Little, Brown, 1985), 11.

14. Susan Rubin Suleiman, *Subversive Intent* (Cambridge: Harvard University Press, 1990), 24.

15. Jaume Martí-Olivella, forward to *Women, History and Nation*, special issue of *Catalan Review* 7, no. 2 (1992): 15. Roig describes in detail her feminism in "La mirada bòrnia," in *Digues que m'estimes encara que sigui mentida* (Barcelona: Edicions 62, 1991), 61–90.

16. Catherine Davies, *Contemporary Feminist Fiction in Spain* (Oxford: Berg Press, 1994), ix.

17. Robert Belton, *The Beribboned Bomb: The Image of Women in Male Surrealist Art* (Calgary: University of Calgary Press, 1995), xiv.

18. Aurora Gómez Morcillo, "Feminismo y lucha política durante la II República y la Guerra Civil," in *El feminismo en España: Dos siglos de historia*, ed. Pilar Folguera (Madrid: Pablo Iglesias, 1988), 65.

19. Sigmund Freud, *Interpretation of Dreams*, trans. A. A. Brill (New York: Macmillan, 1950).

20. Mary Nash, *Defying Male Civilization: Women in the Spanish Civil War* (Denver: Arden Press, 1995), 184.

21. For a concise overview of the actors and ambience of the *movida*, see Kathleen Vernon and Barbara Morris, *Post-Franco, Postmodern* (London: Greenwood Press, 1995). For a more extensive presentation of the movement, see José Luis Gallero, ed., *Sólo se vive una vez: Esplendor y ruina de la movida madrileña* (Madrid: Ardora, 1991).

22. Hélène Cixous, "Laugh of the Medusa," in *New French Feminisms*, ed. Elaine Marks and Isabelle de Courtivron (New York: Schocken, 1981), 245.

23. For a detailed explanation of *écriture féminine*, see Cixous, in ibid., 245–64. Also see Luce Irigaray, *Speculum of the Other Woman* (Ithaca: Cornell University Press, 1984) and Julia Kristeva, "Woman Can Never Be Defined," in Marks and de Courtivron, *New French Feminisms*, 137–41.

24. Xavière Gauthier defends this position in her landmark work *Surréalisme et sexualité* (Paris: Gallimard, 1971).

25. Cadenas calls the novel a "contra-saga" because normally the role assigned to women is reduced to the mere "accompaniment to the masculine world" but in Roig's novel the women take center stage and the men serve as the screen or backdrop onto which their lives are projected. C. B. Cadenas, "Historia de tres mujeres," *Nueva Estafeta* 18 (1980): 76–77.

26. Judith Butler discusses the idea of "gender coherence" which is the genealogy of the constructed identity. In line with Foucault she describes sexuality as power fields and thus impossible to assume but only available to imitate. The genealogy is then a gathering of attributes that equal one or the other gender. Her conclusion is that gender is performative. Butler, *Gender Trouble* (New York: Routledge, 1990), 24–25.

CHAPTER 1. MERCÉ RODOREDA AND REMEDIOS VARO

1. Janet Kaplan, *Unexpected Journeys* (New York: Abbeville Press, 1988), 35.

2. Dalí had returned from a one-year suspension for "insubordination" when Varo began her training as a full-time student at the academy, and two years later he would be permanently expelled. Kaplan concludes that at this time the Academia was conservative and strict, discouraging experimentation. Kaplan, *Unexpected Journeys*, 29.

3. Simone de Beauvoir, *The Second Sex* (New York: Vintage, 1974).

4. Emmanuel Guigon, "Imágenes y textos en la obra de Remedios Varo," in *Remedios Varo: Arte y Literatura* (Teruel: Museo de Teruel/Diputación Provincial de Teruel, 1991), 17.

5. Lourdes Andrade, *Remedios Varo: la metamorfosis* (Mexico D.F.: Círculo de arte, 1996), 7.

6. Guigon, "Imágenes," 15.

7. W. J. T. Mitchell, "What is an Image," *New Literary History* 15.3 (spring 1984): 507.

8. Ibid., 530.

9. Margaret Persin, *Getting the Picture: The Ekphrastic Principle in Twentieth-Century Spanish Poetry* (Lewisburg: Bucknell University Press, 1997), 15.

10. Ibid.

11. The interdisciplinary study of verbal and visual expression has played an important part in the development of peninsular literature in the second half of the twentieth century. Rafael Alberti wrote a series of odes to the plastic arts and artists in *A la pintura* [To Painting], a collection of poems published in 1948. Alberti's *Noche de guerra en el Museo del Prado* [*Night of War in the Prado Museum*] (1956) is a one-act allegory demonstrating the devastating effects of war on art production. All of the characters in Alberti's play are from paintings by Goya, Velázquez, Rubens, and Titian. Antonio Buero Vallejo, a celebrated Spanish dramatist, wrote a very successful two-act play based on the creation of Velázquez's master-

piece entitled *Las Meninas* (1959). García Lorca's drawings that accompany his book of poetry *Poeta en Nueva York* offer a deeper understanding of the artistic process. For an excellent study of the complex relationship between Lorca's art and poetry see Cecelia J. Cavanaugh, *Lorca's Drawings and Poems*. Chapter 3, "Reading Space and Subject," deals specifically with *Poeta en Nueva York*. Pere Gimferrer has written poetry dealing with the invasion of Hollywood on Spanish cultural awareness and the importance of the visual image in contemporary society. Alberti, *To Painting* (Evanston: Northwestern University Press, 1997). Alberti, *Noche de guerra en el Museo del Prado* (1956; reprint, Madrid: Editorial Cuadernos para el Diálogo, 1975). Buero Vallejo, *Las Meninas* (1959; reprint, Madrid: Espasa Calpe, 1999). García Lorca, *Poet in New York/Poeta en Nueva York*, bilingual edition, trans. Greg Simon and Steven White, ed. Christopher Maurer (New York: Noonday Press, 1998). Cecelia J. Cavanaugh, *Lorca's Drawings and Poems: Forming the Eye of the Reader* (Lewisburg: Bucknell University Press, 1995). Gimferrer, *Apariciones y otras poemas* (Madrid: Visor, 1982). Gimferrer, *Espejo, espacio y apariciones (poesía 1970–1980)* (Madrid: Visor, 1988).

12. Margaret Persin defines in detail the advantages of ekphrastic art for feminist artists as it brings up fundamental issues of Self and Other in terms of the presence in absence of the piece of art defined through words. She draws parallels between women's silent perspective and the "otherness" of the plastic arts in literature as well as the decentering gaze or subject positioning found in ekphrastic literature that ruptures the stability of genre and the canon. Persin, *Getting the Picture*, 24.

13. Emilie Bergmann, "Flowers at the North Pole: Mercè Rodoreda and the Female Imagination in Exile," *Catalan Review* 2, no. 2 (1987): 88.

14. Franz Kafka, *The Metamorphosis*, trans. A. L. Lloyd (New York: Vanguard Press, c1946).

15. Xavière Gauthier, *Surréalisme et sexualité* (Paris: Gallimard, 1971).

16. André Breton, *Manifestoes of Surrealism* (Ann Arbor: University of Michigan Press, 1969), 3.

17. Ibid., 13.

18. Pierre Bourdieu, *Language and Symbolic Power* (Cambridge: Harvard University Press, 1991), 107.

19. Breton, *Manifestoes*, 17.

20. André Breton, *Nadja* (Paris: Librairie Gallimard, 1928). Comments on the importance of the pursuit superseding the object are from Briony Fer, *Realism, Rationalism, Surrealism and Art Between the Wars* (New Haven: Yale University Press, 1993), 183–85.

21. Linda Nochlin, *Women, Art and Power* (New York: Harper and Row, 1988), 149.

22. Roland Barthes, "The Death of the Author," in *Image, Music, Text* (New York: Hill and Wang, 1977), 142.

23. Ibid., 146.

24. Foucault's ideas of power and its occult nature within the social system place as much responsibility on the "victim" as on the oppressor. Therefore, in order for power to assert itself, each player must know his role and act accordingly. His *The History of Sexuality* reveals the different stages of power play and how power becomes institutionalized, or obscured within social constructs, in order to function as an ordering element of society. Foucault, *The History of Sexuality* (New York: Pantheon, 1985).

25. Griselda Pollock, *Vision and Difference: Femininity, Feminism and the Histories of Art* (New York: Routledge, 1988), 2.

26. Ibid., 33.

27. Nochlin, *Women*, 10.

28. *Surrealismo en Catalunya, 1924–1936* (Barcelona: Ediciones Polígrafa, 1988). Lucia Garcia de Carpi, "Una muestra del surrealismo español. La Exposición Logicofobista," *Goya* 185 (marzo/abril 1985): 293–98.

29. Whitney Chadwick, *Women Artists and the Surrealist Movement* (Boston: Little, Brown, 1985). Varo and Péret were both incarcerated for subversive political ties in Europe and eventually exiled with help from American liaisons, notably Peggy Guggenheim. Péret, however, was not allowed into the United States due to his loyalty to the Communist Party and therefore both he and Remedios went to Mexico. Péret later returned to Europe after the Second World War but Varo lived the rest of her life in Mexico.

30. Varo's rejection of Breton's idea of automatism appears in a letter she wrote in French. Varo jokes about the technique saying: "one day . . . having accidentally spilled a quantity of tomato sauce on my pants, I found this stain so significant and moving that I quickly cut the piece of fabric and framed it." Janet Kaplan, *Unexpected Journeys*, 128–29.

31. Kaplan, *Unexpected Journeys*, 149.

32. Beatriz Varo, *Remedios Varo: en el centro del microcosmos* (Mexico D.F.: Ediciones Era, 1994), 113.

33. Ibid.

34. Peter Engel, "The Traveler," *Connoisseur* 218 (February 1988): 98.

35. Butler, *Gender Trouble*, 25.

36. Mario Lucarda, "Mercè Rodoreda y el Buen Salvaje," *Quimera* 62 (1986): 34.

37. Frances Wyers, "A Woman's Voices: Mercè Rodoreda's *La plaça del Diamant*," *Kentucky Romance Quarterly* 30, no. 3 (1983): 302.

38. Bergmann, "Flowers at the North Pole," 93.

39. J. W. Albrecht and Patricia Lunn, "A Note on the Language of *La plaça del Diamant*," *Catalan Review* 2, no. 2 (December 1987): 59.

40. Mercè Rodoreda, *La plaça del Diamant* (Barcelona: H. M. B., 1982), 80. All subsequent citations are from this edition.

41. Stephen Hart, *White Ink: Essays on Twentieth-Century Feminine Fiction* (London: Tamesis, 1993), 22.

42. Sandra Schumm, *Reflection in Sequence* (Lewisburg: Bucknell University Press, 1999), 67.

43. Breton, *Manifestoes*, 26.

44. Gauthier, *Surréalisme*, 247.

45. Gauthier includes a description by Robert Benayoun about the image by Jean Benoît. Benayoun claims that it is "one of the most beautiful tributes that could be made to Sade." Ibid., 247.

46. Persin, *Getting the Picture*, 92.

47. Bourdieu, *Language*, 23.

48. Judith Butler, *Excitable Speech: A Politics of the Performative* (New York: Routledge, 1997), 98–99.

49. Beatriz Varo, *Remedios*, 238.

50. Kaplan, *Unexpected Journeys*, 155.

51. Ibid.

52. Ibid.

53. Jacques Lacan extrapolated Freud's theories on desire in regard to the relationship between the child and the mother and father. Lacan affirms that all language is based on desire and thus the acquisition of the Law of the Father or language sets up boundaries and limits to certain kinds of desire. Lacan's mirror stage, which implies the recognition of the subject as such, ushers the child into social discourse of the self and other. Jacques Lacan, *Ecrits* (New York: W. W Norton, 1977).

The importance of the search for a correct language in *El carrer de les camèlies* stems from the lack of a father figure that reveals the law of language inscribed in a name. The protagonist's search for her father symbolically suggests the search for the Law that defines social order, permits entry into society and consequently formulates identity. Cecília never achieves any of this but manages to arrive at a distinctly nonsocialized peace at the end of the novel.

54. Kathleen Glenn, "The Autobiography of a Nobody: Mercè Rodoreda's *El carrer de les Camèlies*," in *The Garden across the Border: Mercè Rodoreda's Fiction*, ed. Kathleen McNerney and Nancy Vosburg (Selinsgrove: Susquehanna University Press, 1994), 111.

55. Ibid., 117.

56. Ibid., 116.

57. Julia Kristeva, "About Chinese Women," in *The Kristeva Reader,* ed. Toril Moi (New York: Columbia University Press, 1986), 153.

58. Mercè Rodoreda, *El carrer de les camèlies* (Barcelona: Club Editor, 1997), 201. All subsequent citations are from this edition.

59. Lagos-Pope, *Exile in Literature*, 8.

60. David Rosenthal, trans., introduction to *Camellia Street* by Mercè Rodoreda (St. Paul: Graywolf Press, 1993), xvi.

61. Mercè Rodoreda, "Paràlisi," in *Semblava de seda i altres contes* (Barcelona: Edicions 62, 1980), 85.

62. Maryellen Bieder, "La mujer invisible: lenguaje y silencio en dos cuentos de Mercè Rodoreda," in *Homenaje a Josep Roca-Pons: Estudis de llengua i literatura*, ed. Jane White Albrecht, Janet DeCesaris, Patricia Lunn, and Josep Sobrer (Barcelona: Publicacions de l'Abadia de Montserrat, 1991), 93.

63. For more in-depth studies on the "male gaze" and a feminist response to it, see: Linda Nochlin, *Women, Art and Power and Other Essays* (Boulder: Westview Press, 1988) and Griselda Pollock, *Vision and Difference: Femininity, Feminism and the Histories of Art* (New York: Routledge, 1988).

64. Chadwick, *Women Artists and the Surrealist Movement*, 140.

65. Kaplan, *Unexpected Journeys*, 88.

66. Chadwick, *Women Artists*, 131.

67. Neus Carbonell, "In the Name of the Mother and the Daughter: The Discourse of Love and Sorrow in Mercè Rodoreda's *La plaça del Diamant*," in *The Garden across the Border: Mercè Rodoreda's Fiction*, ed. Kathleen McNerney and Nancy Vosburg (Selinsgrove: Susquehanna University Press, 1994), 19.

68. Kathleen Glenn, "La plaza del Diamante: The Other Side of the Story," *Letras Femeninas* 12, no. 1–2 (1986): 60–68.

69. Persin, *Getting the Picture*, 19.

70. Michael Fitzgerald, "The Unknown Picasso: A Revolutionary in Clay," *New York Times*, Sunday, 28 February 1999, Arts and Leisure section, 46.

71. Ana Rueda, "Mercè Rodoreda: From Traditional Tales to Modern Fantasy" in *The Garden across the Border: Mercè Rodoreda's Fiction*, ed. Kathleen McNerney and Nancy Vosburg (Selinsgrove: Susquehanna University Press, 1994), 216.

72. Kaplan, *Unexpected Journeys*, 96.

73. Whitney Chadwick, "Leonora Carrington: Evolution of a Feminine Consciousness," *Women's Art Journal* 7 (spring/summer 1986): 40.

74. Paul Kugler, "Involuntary Poetics," *New Literary History* 15.3 (1984): 491.

75. Kugler cites at length Freud's case of obsession neurosis, the "Rat Man." Freud linked his patient's fear of rats to phonetic associations to other words. This interesting case can be found in Peter Gay's *The Freud Reader* (New York: Norton, 1989).

76. Kugler, "Involuntary Poetics," 493.

77. Ibid., 495.

78. Ibid., 499.

79. Elizabeth Rhodes, "The Salamander and the Butterfly," in *The Garden across the Border,* ed. Kathleen McNerney and Nancy Vosburg (Selinsgrove: Susquehanna University Press, 1994), 162–87.

80. Mercè Clarasó, "The Two Worlds of Mercè Rodoreda," in *Women Writers in Twentieth Century Spain and Spanish America*, ed. Catherine Davies (Lewiston, NY: Edwin Mellen Press, 1993), 53.

81. Janet Pérez, "Metamorphosis as a Protest Device in Catalan Feminist Writing: Rodoreda and Oliver," *Catalan Review* 2, no. 2 (1987): 193.

82. Rueda, "Mercè," 210.

83. Pérez, "Metamorphosis," 192.

84. Ibid., 194.

85. Mercè Rodoreda, "La salamandra," in *Tots els contes* (Barcelona: Edicions 62, 1979), 237. All subsequent citations are from this edition.

86. Rueda, "Mercè," 201.

87. Rhodes, "The Salamander," 168.

88. J. P. Brook-Little, *Boutell's Heraldry* (New York: Vintage Books, 1985), 82.

89. Mercè Rodoreda, *Cartes a l'Anna Murià: 1939–1956* (Barcelona: La Sal, 1985), 84.

90. Rueda, "Mercè," 206.

91. Mercè Rodoreda, "La meva Cristina," in *Tots els contes* (Barcelona: Edicions 62, 1979), 253. All subsequent citations are from this edition.

92. George Ferguson, *Signs and Symbols in Christian Art* (New York: Oxford University Press, 1955 c. 1954), 26.

93. Rueda, "Mercè," 205.

94. Ibid.

95. Michael Walsh, ed., *Butler's Lives of the Saints* (New York: Benzinger Brothers, 1955), 255.

96. Mary-Ann Stouck, *Medieval Saints: A Reader* (Ontario: Broadview Press, 1999), 440.

97. Pedro de Ribadeneyra, *Flos Sanctorum, de las vidas de los santos* (Madrid, 1761), 405.

98. Carme Arnau, *Mercè Rodoreda* (Barcelona: Edicions 62, 1992), 98, 104.

99. Geraldine Nichols writes "La metáfora universal, de la gestación, dirige la

lectura" [the universal metaphor of gestation directs the reading] and discusses at length the symbolic importance of the whale as universal motherhood and the implications of the exile without a homeland in the chapter "El exilio y el género en Mercè Rodoreda" in her book *Des/cifrar la diferencia: Narrativa femenina de la España contemporánea* (Madrid: Siglo XXI Editores, 1992), 130. However, if Rodoreda's whale is to be considered a rendering of Saint Christina the virgin martyr, gestation and motherhood do not figure into the story.

100. Kelly Oliver, *Reading Kristeva* (Bloomington: Indiana University Press, 1993), 56.

101. Julia Kristeva, "Approaching Abjection," in *Powers of Horror*, trans. by Leon S. Roudiez (New York: Columbia University Press, 1982), 2.

102. Ibid., 3.

103. Ibid., 9.

104. Ibid., 15.

105. Kaplan, *Unexpected Journeys*, 190.

106. Beatriz Varo, *Remedios*, 232.

107. Ibid.

108. Ibid., 235.

109. Kaplan, *Unexpected Journeys*, 175.

110. Varo's father worked as a hydraulic engineer and encouraged the young Remedios to perfect her skills of mechanical drawing. The detailed perspective drawings found in her sketchbooks show signs of her talent with miniature detail and suggest her initial interest in mechanical and scientific precision. Kaplan, *Unexpected Journeys*, 14–15.

111. Ibid., 159.

112. Deborah Haynes, "The Art of Remedios Varo: Issues of Gender Ambiguity and Religious Meaning," *Women's Art Journal* 16 (spring/summer 1995): 31.

113. Beatriz Varo, *Remedios*, 238.

114. Kaplan, *Unexpected Journeys*, 90.

115. Ibid., 123.

116. Geraldine Cleary Nichols, "Stranger than Fiction: Fantasy in Short Stories by Matute, Rodoreda, Riera," *Monographic Review/Revista monográfica* 4 (1988): 38.

117. Ibid., 49.

118. Belton, *Beribboned Bomb*, xv.

119. Fini is quoted as saying, "I was hostile first because of Breton's puritanism; also because of the paradoxical misappreciation for the autonomy of women." Chadwick, *Women Artists*, 111.

Hayden Herrera has documented Kahlo's disapproval of Breton's patronizing attitude when he visited Mexico in *Frida: A Biography of Frida Kahlo* (New York: Harper and Row, 1983).

120. Griselda Pollock, ed., introduction to *Generations and Geographies in the Visual Arts: Feminist Readings* (New York: Routledge, 1996), xiii–xiv.

Chapter 2. Familial Exile

1. Hélène Cixous proposes that women write themselves into history in "The Laugh of the Medusa," in *New French Feminisms*, ed. Elaine Marks and Isabelle

de Courtivron (New York: Schocken Books, 1981). Her notion of becoming historical originates from a lack of voice and focus of feminine importance within dominant culture. Julia Kristeva combines sociolinguistics with feminist politics when she states: "It was perhaps also necessary to be a *woman* to attempt to take up the exorbitant wager of carrying the rational project to the outer borders of the signifying venture of men." Kristeva, *Desire in Language* (New York: Columbia University Press, 1980), x. Other major works that incorporate the idea of a metaphorical exile of women particularly from a patriarchal "norm" are Simone de Beauvoir, *The Second Sex* (New York: Vintage, 1974), Luce Irigaray, *The Speculum of the Other Woman* (Ithaca: Cornell University Press, 1984), and Juliet Mitchell, "Women: The Longest Revolution" in *Feminist Literary Theory: A Reader*, ed. Mary Eagleton (New York: Basil Blackwell, 1986), 100–103.

2. Catherine Davies, *Contemporary Feminist Fiction in Spain: The Work of Montserrat Roig and Rosa Montero* (Oxford: Berg Press, 1994), 7.

3. Isolina Ballesteros, "The Feminism (Anti-feminism) According to Montserrat Roig," *Catalan Review* 7, no. 2 (1993): 118.

4. Ibid., 126.

5. Ramón Buckley, "Montserrat Roig: The Dialectics of Castration," *Catalan Review* 7, no. 2 (1993): 130.

6. Ibid., 134.

7. Ibid., 136.

8. Susan Sellers, introduction to *The Hélène Cixous Reader*, ed. Susan Sellers (New York: Routledge, 1994), xxix.

9. Irigaray, *Speculum of the Other Woman*, 142.

10. Ibid.

11. Kristeva, *Desire in Language*, 145.

12. Ibid., 146.

13. Kathleen McNerney, introduction to *On Our Own Behalf: Women's Tales from Catalonia*, ed. Kathleen McNerney (Lincoln: University of Nebraska Press, 1988), 14.

14. Biruté Ciplijauskaité, *La novela femenina contemporánea (1970–1985): Hacia una tipología de la narración en primera persona* (Barcelona: Anthropos, 1988), 34.

15. Augustine Brannigan defines postmodernism as the sensibility that arises when the credibility of certain "master narratives" is questioned including scientific knowledge (Truth), aesthetics (Beauty), and morality (Good). Brannigan, "Postmodernism," in *Encyclopedia of Sociology 3*, ed. Edgar Borgatta and Marie Borgatta (New York: MacMillan, 1992), 1523. Roig's brand of feminism focuses on deconstructing the historical hegemonic idea of prosperity, which she sees as patriarchal. Brannigan says that "postmodernity is sometimes referred to as post historical" because "history as a struggle for the gradual liberation of humanity and progressive evolution of more human societies is dismissed . . . as mythic." Ibid. However, Fredric Jameson warns against the idea of History as one "master code among many" and his intent is a "retextualization of History" that considers History not as "some new representation" or "vision" . . . but as the formal effects of what Althusser, following Spinoza, calls an "absent cause." Jameson, *The Political Unconscious*, (Ithaca: Cornell University Press, 1981), 102. Roig seems to agree with Jameson in her intent not to insert women into History or into a historical vision but to amplify the range and degree of "formal effects" taking women's experience into account.

16. Ciplijauskaité, *La novela*, 37–38.

17. Ibid., 38.

18. Ibid., 50.

19. Ibid.

20. Juliet Mitchell, "Women: The Longest Revolution," in *Feminist Literary Theory*, ed. Mary Eagleton (New York: Basil Blackwell, 1986), 100.

21. Montserrat Roig, *L'hora violeta* (Barcelona: Edicions 62, 1980), 219.

22. Montserrat Roig, "La ciutat de Barcelona: Una mirada femenina," *Memorial Montserrat Roig: Cicle de Conferències* (Barcelona: Institut Català de la Dona, 1993).

23. Maryellen Bieder, "The Woman in the Garden: The Problem of Identity in the Novels of Mercè Rodoreda," in *Actes del segon col.loqui d'estudis catalans a Nord Amèrica,* ed. Manuel Duran, Albert Porqueras-Mayo, and Josep Roca-Pons (Barcelona: Publicacions de l'Abadia de Montserrat, 1982), 356.

24. Patrícia Gabancho, *La rateta encara escombra l'escaleta: Cop d'ull a l'actual literatura catalana de dona* [*The Mouse Still Sweeps the Stairs: A Look at Contemporary Catalan Women's Writing*] (Barcelona: Edicions 62, 1982), 13.

25. Ibid., 14.

26. Ibid., 15.

27. This very important aspect of the feminist movement that realizes the limiting powers of privileged class and race on feminine reality appears only sporadically and fleetingly in Roig's work. Benchmark studies published on this topic include bell hooks, *Ain't I a Woman: Black Women and Feminism* (Boston: South End Press, 1981) and Gayatri Spivak's "Can the Subaltern Speak?" in *Marxism and the Interpretation of Culture*, ed. C. Nelson and L. Grossberg (Basingstoke: MacMillan, 1988). Both of these works question the systematic categorization of minority women, their invisibility and inablility to express a unique voice due to the clouding and tainting of their situation by dominant culture and language. Hooks claims "the white American woman's experience is made synonymous with *the* American woman's experience." hooks, 137. She goes on to cite racism as the primary cause of what she considers the failure of feminism in the United States.

28. Gabancho, *La rateta*, 17.

29. Montserrat Roig, "¿Por qué no ha habido mujeres genio?" in *¿Tiempo de mujer?* (Barcelona: Plaza y Janes, 1980), 149. Roig published *¿Tiempo de mujer?* in Castilian originally, therefore I will cite from the original text and not translate the passages into Catalan.

30. Ibid.

31. Ibid., 151.

32. Simone de Beauvoir explains that girls displace their sense of "otherness" in a doll in order to identify with, in essence, an objectified version of themselves. de Beauvoir, *The Second Sex*, 700–701. Therefore, we can conclude that girls' fascination with dolls has little to do with institutionalized assumptions of budding maternal instincts and more with an underdeveloped sense of self. Judith Butler rigorously explores the idea of performing a gender and not "being" a gender in *Gender Trouble* (New York: Routledge, 1990).

33. Gayatri Spivak explores the "unrecognized contradiction within a position that valorizes the concrete experience of the oppressed, while being so uncritical about the historical role of the intellectual." The intellectual's attempt to "disclose and know the discourse of society's Other" reveals the error of an unauthen-

ticated version of the imagined discourse of marginalization compounded by race, gender, culture, and economic status that leads Spivak to the conclusion that "the subaltern cannot speak." Spivak, "Can the Subaltern Speak?" 274–308.

34. Riera describes her alliances with Roig: "Como yo misma nos hemos formado ya en la obra de unas madres bastante más concienciadas, incluso hemos buscado a unas abuelas bastante más concienciadas. Hemos leído, pues, ya los textos de las feministas, nos sabíamos de memoria *El segundo sexo*, hemos estado al día de las aportaciones del feminismo internacional, conocíamos muy bien todas las aportaciones de la ginocrítica. Es decir, partíamos de unas bases y desde luego a mí, no sólo en la literatura sino en la vida normal y corriente, me interesa reivindicar los derechos de la mujer. [We were both brought up on works of more conscientious mothers; in fact we have searched for even more conscientious grandmothers. We've read feminist texts, we know *The Second Sex* by heart, we've been up to date on international feminist issues and we got to know very well all of the contributions of gynocriticism. I mean we started from the same basic ideas and of course for me, not only in literature but also in day to day life, I'm interested in vindicating the rights of women]. Carme Riera, interview with author, 6 October 1998.

35. Elizabeth Rogers, "Montserrat Roig's *Ramona, adiós*: A Novel of Suppression and Disclosure," *Revista de Estudios Hispánicos* 20, no. 1 (1986): 115.

36. Mercè Rodoreda, *La plaça del Diamant* (Barcelona: Editorial H. M. B., 1982), 63.

37. Rogers, "Montserrat," 109.

38. Ana María Brenes García, "El cuerpo matrio catalán como ideologema en *Ramona, adéu* de Montserrat Roig," *Anales de la literatura contemporánea* 21, no. 1–2 (1996): 23.

39. Montserrat Roig, *Ramona, adéu* (Barcelona: Edicions 62, 1972), 102. All subsequent citations are from this edition.

40. Brenes García, "El cuerpo," 23.

41. Ramón del Valle-Inclán (1866–1936) formulated the idea of the *esperpento* as a way of describing modern urban life during the first decades of the twentieth century. The *esperpento* refers to the deformation and grotesque underpinnings of social relationships. The image Valle-Inclán uses to illustrate this point is the deformed reflection of the human body as seen in concave mirrors on the Calle de los gatos in Madrid.

42. Christina Dupláa, *La voz testimonial en Montserrat Roig* (Barcelona: Icaría, 1996), 15.

43. Rogers, "Montserrat," 113.

44. Montserrat Roig, *Molta roba i poc sabó i tan neta que la volen* (Barcelona: Editorial Selecta, 1971), 15. All subsequent citations are from this edition.

45. Meri Torras i Francès identifies this voice as that of the youngest Ramona, the granddaughter of the deceased. Torras i Francès, "Montserrat Roig i les veus que no se senten," *Serra d'or* 410 (febrer 1994): 58–61.

While I do think that this voice represents a younger, more aware generation, I agree whole-heartedly with Christina Dupláa who also reads this ending as a brief manifesto of Roig's literary project in the voice of a characterless narrator. Dupláa, *La voz testimonial de Montserrat Roig*, 143.

46. Dupláa, *La voz testimonial*, 143.

47. Ibid., 144.

48. Susan Merrill Squier, introduction to *Women Writers and the City* (Knoxville: University of Tennessee Press, 1984), 5.

49. Ibid., 4.

50. Geraldine Cleary Nichols, *Escribir, espacio propio: Laforet, Matute, Moix, Tusquets, Riera y Roig por sí mismas* (Minneapolis: University of Minnesota Press, 1989), 164–65.

51. Ibid., 157.

52. Catherine Bellver states that "Love for Roig is an all-consuming passion, known primarily to women, that devastates yet gives meaning to life." Bellver, "Montserrat Roig and the Creation of a Gynocentric Reality," in *Women Writers of Contemporary Spain*, ed. Joan Brown (Newark: University of Delaware Press, 1991), 224. I would add that love should be understood here not only as emotional/sexual love, but a love of writing, of memory, and of one's own past.

53. Montserrat Roig, *El temps de les cireres* (Barcelona: Edicions 62, 1977), 10. All subsequent citations are from this edition.

54. Squier, introduction to *Women Writers*, 5.

55. Pierre Bourdieu, *Language and Symbolic Power* (Cambridge: Harvard University Press, 1991), 37.

56. Nichols, *Escribir, espacio propio*, 147.

57. Simone de Beauvoir states: "it is impossible to be *for one's self* actually an *other* and to recognize oneself consciously as object. The duality is merely dreamed. For the child this dream is materialized in the doll; she sees herself in the doll more concretely than in her own body, because she and the doll are actually separated from each other." *The Second Sex*, 700–701.

58. See chapter 1 for a discussion of Julia Kristeva's explanation of the abject.

59. T. S. Eliot, *The Waste Land and Other Poems* (Minneapolis: University of Minnesota Press, 1996), 37–38.

60. Ibid., 50.

61. Montserrat Roig, *L'hora violeta* (Barcelona: Edicions 62, 1980), 64. All subsequent citations are from this edition.

62. Carme Riera, "Montserrat Roig: Una altra mirada de Barcelona," *Lectora: Revista de dones i textualitat* 1 (1995): 15.

63. Ibid.

64. In an interview Roig admits, somewhat sheepishly, that "mis primeros libros eran más autobiográficos. Se aprende con los años" [my first books were more autobiographical. One learns with time]. V. Ll., "Montserrat Roig: La literatura como mentira necesaria," *Leer* 46 (octubre 1991): 61.

65. Montserrat Roig, *¿Tiempo de mujer?* (Barcelona: Plaza y Janes, 1980), 30.

66. C. B. Cadenas, "Historia de tres mujeres," *Nueva Estafeta* 18 (1980): 76.

67. Pep Blay, "Montserrat Roig," *Avui* 3 agosto 1991, sec. Cultura, pp. 1–2.

68. Catherine Davies draws a parallel between Roig's novel and Doris Lessing's *The Golden Notebook* due to the similarity of the chapter divisions. Lessing's novel is divided into four "notebooks" and Roig's into "hours" (The lost hour, the dispersed hour, the open hour). Davies, *Contemporary Feminist Fiction in Spain*, 54. The characters provide further similarities. In Lessing's novel, Anna and Molly are presented in chapters entitled "Free Women," and just as Natàlia and Norma in Roig's novel they experience love triangles, broken marriages, and a fierce determination to be "free." Also the young anarchist in Lessing's novel, Willi Rhodes, who incited Anna to get involved in politics echoes the political fervor of

Jordi Soteras, socialist diehard who ignores his wife Agnès and his lover Natàlia due to his political commitments. Lessing, *The Golden Notebook* (New York: Bantam, 1962), 70. Roig, however, claims in her interview with Nichols when asked about the similarities that she read Lessing's novel after she had finished *L'hora violeta*, but it seems evident that she was familiar with Lessing's text. Nichols, *Escribir, espacio propio*, 161.

69. Catherine Bellver, "Montserrat Roig and the Penelope Syndrome," *Anales de la literatura española contemporánea* 12 (1987): 118.

70. Eliot, *The Waste Land*, 50.

71. Bellver, "Penelope Syndrome," 120.

72. Roig discusses her disillusionment with university politics and patriarchal organizations in an interview with Maria Aurèlia Capmany: "en entrar a la Universitat va ser quan vaig descobrir el masclisme entre els companys . . . la noia que s'aixecava a parlar en públic ja era malmirada pels seus companys." [when I entered university I discovered sexism between my classmates . . . the girl who dared to speak in public was looked down upon by her classmates]. Capmany, "Montserrat Roig, ofici i plaer de viure i escriure," *Cultura* 22 (abril 1991): 17.

73. Montserrat Roig, *Digues que m'estimes encara que sigui mentida: Sobre el plaer solitari d'escriure i el vici compartit de llegir* (Barcelona: Edicions 62, 1991), 14.

74. Mary Nash's comprehensive study about women in the militia and war effort is an excellent resource revealing the abundance of progressive feminist politics and politicians who were active during the Second Republic and during the civil war. Mary Nash, *Defying Male Civilization: Women in the Spanish Civil War* (Denver: Arden Press, 1995).

75. Julia Kristeva's *chora* identifies the rythms and movement of expression outside the realm of language. The *chora* can be defined as an amorphous gel that holds together meaning, albeit free from the syntactical restraints of language. Her examples of the functioning *chora* are architecture and music. Kristeva, *Revolution*, 25–30.

76. Janet Díaz-Pérez writes, "Natàlia's confidante Norma . . . is a mask of the author" in her review of *La hora violeta*. Pérez, "Montserrat Roig: *La hora violeta*," *World Literature Today* 55 (1981): 658–59. Bellver agrees and states that "by making Norma the collector of these facts, Roig leads some to see Norma as her mask." Bellver, "Gynocentric Reality," 229. However, Roig seems to address this very issue at the beginning of *L'hora violeta* when she writes in Norma's voice, "Una persona té més de mil cares . . . I ja és prou si aconsegueixes que, en una novel.la, n'hi surtin tres o quatre" (12) [A person has a thousand faces . . . and it's enough if you manage, in a novel, to show three or four]. Thus, we can conclude that no one character serves as a mask of the author, but she identifies herself with a part of each one.

77. Bellver, "Penelope Syndrome," 119.

78. Paul Ilie, *Literatura y exilio interior* (Madrid: Espiral, 1980), 10.

CHAPTER 3. AUTHROIAL EXILE

1. Carme Riera, *Qüestió d'amor propi* (Barcelona: Planeta, 1987), 27.

2. Linda Kauffman, *Special Delivery: Epistolary Modes in Modern Fiction* (Chicago: University of Chicago Press, 1992), xiii.

3. Elizabeth MacArthur describes the origins of epistolary narrative in the social structure of seventeenth-century France where "letters were part of a codified system of social relations." She points out that "Letters (and sometimes novels) were the only kind of writing women were thought to be able to do well." MacArthur, *Extravagant Narratives: Closure and Dynamics in the Epistolary Form* (Princeton: Princeton University Press, 1990), 36, 43.

4. Luis Racionero, "La maniera gentile de Carme Riera," *Quimera* 9–10 (1981): 14.

5. Akiko Tsuchiya, "The Paradox of Narrative Seduction in Carmen Riera's *Cuestión de amor propio*," *Hispania* 75, no. 2 (1992): 281.

6. Kathleen Glenn, "Las cartas de amor de Carme Riera: El arte de seducir," in *Discurso femenino actual* (San Juan: Universidad de Puerto Rico, 1995), 53–68.

7. Mirella Servodidio, introduction to *Moveable Margins: The Narrative Art of Carme Riera*, ed. Kathleen Glenn, Mirella Servodidio, and Mary S. Vásquez (Lewisburg: Bucknell University Press, 1999), 9.

8. Ibid.

9. Michel Foucault, "What is an Author," in *Critical Theory Since 1965*, vol. 1, trans. Donald F. Bouchard and Sherry Simon, ed. Hazzard Adams and Leroy Searle (Tallahassee: Florida State University Press, 1969), 145.

10. Montserrat Roig, *Digues que m'estimes encara que sigui mentida* (Barcelona: Edicions 62, 1991), 19.

11. Ibid., 12.

12. Roland Barthes, in his essay "The Death of the Author" in *Image, Music, Text* (New York: Hill and Wang, 1977), affirms that the text incorporates multiple layers of cultural discourse and that the reader plays the key role in understanding a text. Fredric Jameson displaces any importance on either the author or reader and looks to repressed revolutions, or moments of shifts and changes in History that exist as a subtext to any narrative. Jameson, *The Political Unconscious* (Ithaca: Cornell University Press, 1981). William Dowling writing about Jameson claims "when we read a novel with Jameson we are always going to be reconstructing the subtext that it generates as the necessary completion of its meaning." Dowling, *Jameson, Althusser, Marx: An Introduction to The Political Unconscious* (Ithaca: Cornell University Press, 1984), 123. Riera draws on these very notions of subtext in order to construct a polysemantic narrative.

13. Roman Ingarden's idea that each individual reader brings "pre-understandings" to a textual experience tries to capture the "context of beliefs and expectations" that help to decipher narrative discourse, yet this assumption remains fixated on the monolithic subject that seeks to manipulate and interpret a text. Terry Eagleton, *Literary Theory* (Minneapolis: University of Minnesota Press, 1996), 67.

14. Jameson, *Political Unconscious*, 110.

15. Dowling, *Jameson*, 91. However, Jameson's clearly Marxist preoccupation and insistence on a totalizing unconsciousness, which incorporates all individual existence as a necessary part of a functioning whole, never directly address the inherent hierarchy established within his totality. The same can be said about Jameson's notion of History and Necessity as ultimate truths that deny the auton-

omy of marginalized histories. Jameson insists that History as the experience of Necessity eludes "thematization or reification as a mere object of representation or as one master code among many others." Jameson, 102. But he also relies dogmatically on Marxism, "which, in the form of the dialectic, affirms a primacy of theory which is at one and the same time a recognition of the primacy of History itself." Jameson, 24. Therefore, any theoretical negotiations between society, its parts, and History that oppose or undermine a Marxist standpoint would seem erroneous to Jameson, even though his totalizing ideas about dialectic cultural development would seem to suggest otherwise. He goes as far as to say, "The affirmation of radical feminism, therefore, that to annul the patriarchy is the most *radical* political act—insofar as it includes and subsumes more partial demands, such as the liberation from the commodity form—is thus perfectly consistent with an expanded Marxian framework." Jameson, 100. To label a given body of cultural theory as legitimate or not according to its adherence to a Marxian framework can be limiting as well as inaccurate. Thus the problem that Jameson sees in Freud's individual consciousness mirrors that of his own privileging of History and of Marxist theory. While I do agree that the text relies on a subtext generated by the repression of a larger social consciousness, which is the political unconscious, I would add that the text vacillates between various histories and various levels of oppression working within specific epicenters of culture. Departing from this standpoint, I consider Riera's texts as exemplary of the splintering of history into multiple past experiences. Instead of a History and its repressed revolutions, Riera's narrative epistolaries embrace the idea of multiple histories, including those histories of oppressed, marginalized Others, not as separate, secretive pasts to be compared to a more legitimate experience, but as a functioning and vital part of any idea of History itself.

    16. Julia Kristeva, *Revolution in Poetic Language* (New York: Columbia University Press, 1984), 118–19.

    17. Ibid., 126.

    18. Ibid.

    19. Riera's novel *Dins el darrer blau* (Barcelona: Alfaguara, 1994) [*In the Furthest Blue*], awarded Spain's National Prize for Narrative in 1995, treats the marginalization of *criptojudíos* living on the island of Mallorca during the seventeenth century. After a failed escape attempt, the group is condemned to burn during an *Auto de fé,* a religious procession popular in Spain during the Inquisition. This novel explores the idea of histories as a hybrid of various narrative voices as well as of narrative forms. The historical novel or fictionalized history deserves detailed analysis but does not figure into the present study as I have decided to look only at Riera's epistolary narrative. For the beginnings of analytic work on Riera's novel see Geraldine Cleary Nichols, " 'Tras su hache mayúscula': Carme Riera and the Exploration of History in *Dins el darrer blau* ," and Neus Carbonell, "The Ethics of Dissidence: Resistance and Relationality in Carme Riera's *Dins el darrer blau,*" both in *Moveable Margins.*

    20. Julia Kristeva, "Women's Time," in *The Kristeva Reader*, ed. Toril Moi (New York: Columbia University Press, 1986), 209.

    21. Mirella Servodidio, "Doing Good and Feeling Bad: The Interplay of Desire and Discourse in Two Stories by Carme Riera," in *Moveable Margins*, 66.

    22. Carme Riera, *Jo pos per testimoni les gavines* (Barcelona: Laia, 1977), 9. All subsequent citations are from this edition.

23. Servodidio, "Doing Good," 66.

24. Luisa Cotoner, ed. and trans. *Te dejo el mar*, by Carme Riera (Madrid: Espasa Calpe, 1991).

25. Cotoner, introduction to *Te dejo el mar*, 31–32.

26. Carme Riera, *Te deix, amor, la mar com a penyora* (Barcelona: Planeta, 1975), 20. All subsequent citations are from this edition.

27. Carme Riera, interview by Kathleen Glenn, in *Moveable Margins*, 42.

28. Jean Baudrillard, "On Seduction," in *Selected Writings*, ed. Mark Poster (Stanford: Stanford University Press, 1988), 162.

29. Servodidio, "Doing Good," 72.

30. Neus Aguado, "Epistolas de mar y sol: Entrevista con Carme Riera," *Quimera* 105 (1991): 32.

31. Catherine Bellver, "Convergence and Disjunction: Doubling in the Fiction of Carme Riera," in *Moveable Margins*, 233.

32. Carme Riera, "Literatura femenina: ¿un lenguaje prestado?" *Quimera* 18 (1982): 12.

33. Using Freud and Lacan as theoretical models, Peter Brooks proposes that narrative "is condemned to *saying* other than what it *would mean,* spinning out its movement toward a meaning that would be the end of its movement." Brooks, "Narrative Desire," in *Reading for the Plot* (New York: Vintage Books, 1985), 56. Thus narrative moves inevitably toward finality and closure. Riera subverts this notion with her ambiguous and provocative ending. The continuation of the narration in "Jo pos . . ." confirms the survival, nondeath, of her previous text.

34. María Pilar Rodríguez concludes that the mirroring of the subject can pertain only to a homoerotic desire. She writes: "El encuentro sexual se articula como reflejo especular de los dos cuerpos femeninos y el lenguage muestra una forma de conocimiento sexual que no reduplica la representación habitual del erotismo fálico." [The sexual encounter is articulated as a mirrored reflection of the two feminine bodies and the language shows a form of sexual familiarity that doesn't reduplicate the standard representation of phallic eroticism]. Rodríguez, "La (otra) opción amorosa: 'Te dejo, amor, el mar como ofrenda,' de Carme Riera," *Confluencia* 11, no. 2 (spring 1996): 47. Rodríguez cites Brad Epps, who also considers the scene an erotics of strictly lesbian desire. Epps writes: "the body of the beloved . . . harbors the secret pulse of being itself . . . lesbian desire assumes proportions at once almost mythic and divine." Epps, "Virtual Sexuality: Lesbianism, Loss, and Deliverance in Carme Riera's 'Te deix, amor, la mar com a penyora'" in *¿Entiendes? Queer Readings: Hispanic Writings*, ed. Emilie Bergmann and Paul Julian-Smith (Durham: Duke University Press, 1995), 326–27.

35. Kathleen Glenn clarifies Maria's dubious reliability: "We do not know if what she tells us is 'true.' She may have blotted out the 'fact' of Marina's marriage because it was too painful a reality for her to bear; she may have invented a suicide that makes Marina always faithful and exclusively hers." Glenn, "Reading and Writing the Other Side of the Story in Two Narratives by Carme Riera," *Catalan Review* 7, no. 1 (1993): 58.

36. Cotoner, *Te dejo*, 26.

37. Carme Riera, "Grandeza y miseria de la epístola," in *El oficio de narrar*, ed. Marina Mayoral (Madrid: Catedra, 1990), 150.

38. It is interesting to note that Riera changed the names of the characters significantly in the Castilian version of the story entitled "Letra de ángel." Antoni

becomes Don Ramón Vendrell Macià and Cèlia becomes Olga Macià. This doubling of characters according to linguistic dimensions furthers the question of
multiple subjectivity in Riera's works and warrants further study. Riera also
changes the dates of the correspondence from 1982–83 in the Catalan version
to 1986–87 in the Castilian version, which coincide more closely with the 1991
publication date of both collections.

39. Carme Riera, *Contra l'amor en companyia i altres relats* (Barcelona: Destino, 1991), 25. All subsequent citations are from this edition.

40. Mary S. Vásquez, "Textual Desire, Seduction, and Epistolary in Carme
Riera's 'Letra de ángel' and 'La seducción del genio,'" in *Moveable Margins*, 179.

41. Ibid., 181.

42. Ibid., 183.

43. Riera, "Grandeza y miseria," 154.

44. Carme Riera, interview by author, tape recording, Barcelona, 6 October,
1998.

45. Nancy Chodorow, *The Reproduction of Mothering: Psychoanalysis and
the Sociology of Gender* (Berkeley: University of California Press, 1978), 8.

46. Carme Riera, "Femenino singular: Literatura de mujer," in *Crítica y ficción literaria: Mujeres españolas contemporáneas*, ed. Aurora and María Angeles
Pastor Lopez (Granada: Universidad de Granada, 1989), 26.

47. Emilie Bergmann, "Letters and Diaries as Narrative Strategies in Contemporary Catalan Women's Writing," in *Critical Essays on the Literatures of
Spain and Spanish America*, ed. Luis González del Valle and Julio Baena (Boulder: Society of Spanish and Spanish-American Studies, 1991), 22.

48. Elizabeth MacArthur, *Extravagant Narratives*, 8.

49. Kathleen Glenn sees the epistolary narrative as an opportunity for Àngela
to reinvent herself through language: "En vez de quedar encerrada y ahogada en
la novela escrita por él, *El canto del cisne*, Àngela se desahoga en un nuevo texto.
El cisne se niega a desaparecer o morir y, como si fuera fénix, resucita y vuelve a
cantar." Glenn, "Las cartas de amor de Carme Riera: El arte de seducir," in *Discurso femenino actual* (San Juan: Universidad de Puerto Rico, 1995), 66. [Instead
of remaining enclosed and suffocated in the novel written by him, *Swan Song*,
Angela vents her frustrations in a new text. The swan refuses to disappear or die
and like the phoenix revives and sings again]. However, language remains a prison
house, to use the formalists' term, and the real liberation may be located in Àngela's renewed connection with her friend Ingrid, the extratextual dialogue that the
epistolary suggests and not language itself.

50. Carme Riera, *Qüestió d'amor propi* (Barcelona: Planeta, 1987), 22. All
subsequent citations are from this edition.

51. Carol Gilligan, *In a Different Voice* (Cambridge: Harvard University Press,
1982), xvii.

52. Tsuchiya, "Paradox," 281–86.

53. Sandra Schumm, "Borrowed Language in Carme Riera's *Cuestión de
amor propio*," *Anales de la literatura española contemporánea* 20, no. 1–2 (1995):
199.

54. Julia Kristeva, "Woman Can Never Be Defined," in *New French Feminisms*, ed. Elaine Marks and Isabelle de Courtivron (New York: Schocken Books,
1981), 141.

55. Ibid., 140. Kristeva has openly expressed her concern with the feminist

movement as an extremist ideology in an interview: "I have many problems with the feminist movement because I am uncomfortable with all militant movements." Kristeva, *Julia Kristeva Interviews*, ed. Ross Mitchell Guberman (New York: Columbia University Press), 7. However, her writings about the problematic influence of dominant culture and power structures do serve as illuminating theories of language and socialized concepts of gender. Her refusal to be labeled as a feminist should not detract from an interpretation of her writings as pro-woman.

56. Margaret Jones, "Different Wor(l)ds: Modes of Women's Communication in Spain's *Narrativa Femenina*," *Monographic Review/Revista Monográfica* 8 (1992): 60.

57. Carme Riera, "Estimat Thomas," in *Epitelis tendríssims* (Barcelona: Edicions 62, 1981), 80. All subsequent citations are from this edition.

58. Geraldine Cleary Nichols, "Stranger than Fiction: Fantasy in Short Stories by Matute, Rodoreda, Riera," *Monographic Review/Revista Monográfica* 4 (1988): 40.

59. Ibid.

60. Brad Epps, "A Writing of One's Own," in *Moveable Margins*, 117.

CONCLUSION

1. David Herzberger, "The Literary Malaise of Post-Franco Spain," in *Literature and Popular Culture in the Hispanic World*, ed. Rose S. Mine (Gaithersburg, MD: Ediciones Hispamérica, 1981), 185.

2. Juan Goytisolo expressed his concern for Spanish letters in "Captives of Our 'Classics,'" *The New York Times Book Review*, 26 May 1985, 24, quoted in *Nuevos y Novísimos*, ed. Ricardo Landeira and Luis T. González del Valle (Boulder: Society of Spanish and Spanish-American Studies, 1987), 7.

3. Mercè Rodoreda, *Cartes a l'Anna Murià: 1939–1956* (Barcelona: La Sal, 1985).

4. Albert Blanco, "El oro de los tiempos," in *Católogo razonado/ Catalogue raisonné* (Mexico D.F.: Ediciones Era, 1994), 8.

5. Paul Ilie, *Literatura y exilio interior* (Madrid: Espiral, 1980), 276.

6. Marguerite Duras, interview by Susan Husserl-Kapit, *New French Feminisms*, ed. Elaine Marks and Isabelle de Courtivron (New York: Schocken, 1981), 174.

Bibliography

Aguado, Neus. "Epistolas de mar y de sol: Entrevista con Carme Riera." *Quimera* 105 (1991): 32–37.

Alberti, Rafael. *Noche de guerra en el Museo del Prado*. 1956. Reprint, Madrid: Editorial Cuadernos para el Diálogo, 1975.

———. *To Painting*. Translated by Carolyn Tipton. Evanston: Northwestern University Press, 1997.

Albrecht, J. W., and Patricia V. Lunn. "A Note on the Language of *La plaça del Diamant*." *Catalan Review* 2, no. 2 (December 1987): 59–64.

Andrade, Lourdes. *Remedios Varo: las metamorfosis*. Mexico, D.F.: Círculo de arte, 1996.

Arnau, Carme. *Mercè Rodoreda*. Barcelona: Edicions 62, 1992.

Avantguardes a Catalunya: 1906–1939. Barcelona: Fundació Caixa de Catalunya, 1992.

Ballesteros, Isolina. "The Feminism (Anti-feminism) According to Montserrat Roig." *Catalan Review* 7, no. 2 (1993): 117–28.

Balsach, Maria Josep. "Apunts entorn de l'obra pictòrica de Mercè Rodoreda." *Revista de Girona* 157 (1993): 84–85.

Barthes, Roland. "The Death of the Author." In *Image, Music, Text*. Translated by Stephen Heath. New York: Hill and Wang, 1977.

Baudrillard, Jean. "On Seduction." In *Selected Writings*. Edited by Mark Poster, 149–65. Stanford: Stanford University Press, 1988.

Beauvoir, Simone de. *The Second Sex*. Translated by H. M. Parshley. New York: Vintage, 1974.

Bellver, Catherine G. "Convergence and Disjunction: Doubling in the Fiction of Carme Riera." In *Moveable Margins*, ed. Kathleen Glenn, Mirella Servodidio and Mary Vásquez, 230–39. Lewisburg: Bucknell University Press, 1999.

———. "Montserrat Roig and the Creation of a Gynocentric Reality." In *Women Writers of Contemporary Spain*, ed. Joan Brown, 217–39. Newark: University of Delaware Press, 1991.

———. "Montserrat Roig: A Feminine Perspective and a Journalistic Slant." In *Feminine Concerns in Contemporary Spanish Fiction by Women*. Edited by Robert Manteiga, Carolyn Galerstein, and Kathleen McNerney, 152–67. Potomac, MD: Scripta Humanistica, 1988.

———. "Montserrat Roig and the Penelope Syndrome." *Anales de la literatura española contemporánea* 12 (1987): 111–21.

Belton, Robert. *The Beribboned Bomb: The Image of Woman in Male Surrealist Art*. Calgary: University of Calgary Press, 1995.

Bergmann, Emilie L. "<Flowers at the North Pole>: Mercè Rodoreda and the Female Imagination in Exile." *Catalan Review* 2, no. 2 (December 1987): 83–99.

———. "Letters and Diaries as Narrative Strategies in Contemporary Catalan Women's Writing." In *Critical Essays on the Literatures of Spain and Spanish America*. Edited by Luis González del Valle and Julio Baena, 19–28. Boulder: Society of Spanish and Spanish-American Studies, 1991.

Bieder, Maryellen. "La mujer invisible: lenguaje y silencio en dos cuentos de Mercè Rodoreda." In *Homenaje a Josep Roca-Pons: Estudis de llengua i literatura*. Edited by Jane White Albrecht, Janet DeCesaris, Patricia Lunn, and Josep Sobrer, 93–110. Barcelona: Publicacions de l'Abadia de Montserrat, 1991.

———. "The Woman in the Garden: The Problem of Identity in the Novels of Mercè Rodoreda." In *Actes del segon col.loqui d'estudis catalans a Nord Amèrica*. Edited by Manuel Duran, Albert Porqueras-Mayo, and Josep Roca-Pons, 353–64. Barcelona: Publicacions de l'Abadia de Montserrat, 1982.

Blay, Pep. "Montserrat Roig." *Avui* (3 agosto 1991) sec. Cultura: 1–2.

Bourdieu, Pierre. *Language and Symbolic Power*. Translated by Gino Raymond and Matthew Adamson. Cambridge: Harvard University Press, 1991.

Brannigan, Augustine. "Postmodernism." In *Encyclopedia of Sociology 3*. Edited by Edgar Borgatta and Marie Borgatta, 1522–25. New York: MacMillan Press, 1992.

Brenes García, Ana María. "El cuerpo matrio catalán como ideologema en *Ramona, adéu* de Montserrat Roig." *Ánales de la literatura española contemporánea* 21, no. 1–2 (1996): 13–25.

Breton, André. *Manifestoes of Surrealism*. Ann Arbor: University of Michigan Press, 1969.

———. *Nadja*. Paris: Librairie Gallimard, 1928.

Brook-Little, J. P. *Boutell's Heraldry*. New York: Frederick Warne, 1950.

Brooks, Peter. *Reading for the Plot*. New York: Vintage Books, 1985.

Brown, Joan L., ed. *Women Writers of Contemporary Spain: Exiles in the Homeland*. Newark: University of Delaware Press, 1991.

Buckley, Ramón. "Montserrat Roig: The Dialectics of Castration." *Catalan Review*, 7, no. 2 (1993): 129–36.

Buero Vallejo, Antonio. *Las Meninas*. 1959. Reprint, Madrid: Espasa Calpe, 1999.

Butler, Judith. *Bodies that Matter: On the Discursive Limits of "Sex."* New York: Routledge, 1993.

———. *Excitable Speech: A Politics of the Performative*. New York: Routledge, 1997.

———. *Gender Trouble: Feminism and the Subversion of Identity*. New York: Routledge, 1990.

Cadenas, C. B. "Historia de tres mujeres." *Nueva Estafeta* 18 (1980): 76–77.

Capmany, Maria Aurèlia. "Montserrat Roig, ofici i plaer de viure i escriure." *Cultura* 22 (abril 1991): 13–26.

Carbonell, Neus. "In the Name of the Mother and the Daughter: The Discourse of Love and Sorrow in Mercè Rodoreda's *La plaça del Diamant*." In *The Garden across the Border: Mercè Rodoreda's Fiction.* Edited by Kathleen McNerney and Nancy Vosburg, 17-30. Selinsgrove: Susquehanna University Press, 1994.

———. *La plaça del Diamant de Mercè Rodoreda.* Barcelona: Editorial Empúries, 1994.

———. "L'exili en 'La meva Cristina' de Mercè Rodoreda: Intertextualitat i imaginació dialògica." *Lectora: Revista de dones i textualitat* 1 (1995): 75–87.

Casals i Couturier, Montserrat. *Mercè Rodoreda: contra la vida, la literatura.* Barcelona: Edicions 62, 1991.

Cassanyes. "Exposició Logicofobiste." *La Vanguardia* 16 mayo 1936.

"Castellet i Miralles van parlar de Rodoreda i la seva obra pictòrica." *El Nou* (9 marzo 1991): 28.

Cavanaugh, Cecelia J. *Lorca's Drawings and Poems: Forming the Eye of the Reader.* Lewisburg: Bucknell University Press, 1995.

Chadwick, Whitney. "Leonora Carrington: Evolution of a Feminine Consciousness." *Women's Art Journal* 7 (spring/summer 1986): 37–42.

———, ed. *Mirror Images: Women, Surrealism, and Self-Representation.* Cambridge, MA: MIT Press, 1998.

———. *Women Artists and the Surrealist Movement.* Boston: Little, Brown, 1985.

Charlon, Anne. *La condició de la dona en la narrativa femenina catalana (1900–1983).* Barcelona: Edicions 62, 1990.

Chodorow, Nancy. *The Reproduction of Mothering: Psychoanalysis and the Sociology of Gender.* Berkeley: University of California Press, 1978.

Ciplijauskaité, Biruté. *La novela femenina contemporánea (1970–1985): Hacia una tipología de la narración en primera persona.* Barcelona: Anthropos, 1988.

Clarasó, Mercè. "The Angle of Vision in the Novels of Mercè Rodoreda." *Bulletin of Hispanic Studies* 57, no. 2 (1980): 143–52.

———. "The Two Worlds of Mercè Rodoreda." In *Women Writers in Twentieth-Century Spain and Spanish America.* Edited by Catherine Davies, 43–54. Lewiston, NY: Edwin Mellen Press, 1993.

Corredor-Matheos, Josep. "ADLAN y el surrealismo." In *Surrealismo en Catalunya, 1924–1936,* 38–50. Barcelona: Ediciones Polígrafa, 1988.

Cotoner, Luisa. Introduction to *Te dejo el mar,* by Carme Riera. Translated by Luisa Cotoner. Madrid: Espasa Calpe, 1991.

Davies, Catherine. *Contemporary Feminist Fiction in Spain: The Work of Montserrat Roig and Rosa Montero.* Oxford: Berg Press, 1994.

Diamond, Irene, and Lee Quimby, eds. *Feminism and Foucault.* Boston: Northeastern University Press, 1988.

Díaz-Pérez, Janet. "Montserrat Roig. *La hora violeta.*" *World Literature Today* 55 (1981): 658–59.

Dowling, William. *Jameson, Althusser, Marx: An Introduction to The Political Unconscious.* Ithaca: Cornell University Press, 1984.

Dupláa, Christina. "Ideologia i estètica de la ciutat a l'obra de la Montserrat Roig." *DUODA: Revista d'Estudis Feministes* 14 (1998): 51–62.

———. *La voz testimonial en Montserrat Roig.* Barcelona: Icaría, 1996.

Eagleton, Mary. *Feminist Literary Theory.* New York: Basil Blackwell, 1986.

Eagleton, Terry. *Literary Theory*. Minneapolis: University of Minnesota Press, 1996.

Eliot, T. S. *The Waste Land and Other Poems*. New York: Harcourt Brace Jovanovich, 1934.

Engel, Peter. "The Traveler." *Connoisseur* 218 (February 1988): 94–99.

Epps, Brad. "Virtual Sexuality: Lesbianism, Loss, and Deliverance in Carme Riera's 'Te deix, amor, la mar com a penyora'" In *¿Entiendes? Queer Readings: Hispanic Writings*. Edited by Emilie Bergmann and Paul Julian-Smith, 317–45. Durham: Duke University Press, 1995.

———. "A Writing of One's Own." In *Moveable Margins*, ed. Kathleen Glenn, Mirella Servodidio, and Mary Vásquez, 104–52. Lewisburg: Bucknell University Press, 1999.

Fer, Briony. *Realism, Rationalism, Surrealism, and Art Between the Wars*. New Haven: Yale University Press, 1993.

Ferguson, George Wells. *Signs and Symbols in Christian Art*. New York: Oxford University Press, 1955 c. 1954.

Fitzgerald, Michael. "The Unknown Picasso: A Revolutionary in Clay." *New York Times*, Sunday, 28 February,1999, Arts and Leisure Section, 46.

Foucault, Michel. "What is an Author?" In *Critical Theory Since 1965*. Vol. 1. Translated by Donald F. Bouchard and Sherry Simon. Edited by Hazzard Adams and Leroy Searle, 138–48. Tallahassee: Florida State University Press, 1969.

———. *The History of Sexuality*. Vol. 1 and 2. New York: Pantheon, 1985.

Freud, Sigmund. *Interpretation of Dreams*. Translated by A. A. Brill. New York: Macmillan, 1950.

Friedan, Betty. *The Feminine Mystique*. New York: Norton, 1963.

Gabancho, Patrícia. *La rateta encara escombra l'escaleta: Cop d'ull a l'actual literatura catalana de dona*. Barcelona: Edicions 62, 1982.

Gallero, José Luis, ed. *Sólo se vive una vez: Esplendor y ruina de la movida madrileña*. Madrid: Ardora, 1991.

Garcia de Carpi, Lucia. "Una muestra del surrealismo español. La Exposición Logicofobista." *Goya* 185 (marzo/abril 1985): 293–98.

García Lorca, Federico. *Poet in New York/ Poeta en Nueva York*. Translated by Greg Simon and Steven F. White. Edited by Christopher Maurer. New York: Noonday Press, 1998.

Gauthier, Xavière. *Surréalisme et sexualité*. Paris: Gallimard, 1971.

Gay, Peter. *The Freud Reader*. New York: Norton, 1989.

Gerling, David Ross. "Montserrat Roig i Fransitorra, *La hora violeta*." *Anales de la literatura española contemporánea* 8 (1983): 243–45.

Gilligan, Carol. *In a Different Voice*. Cambridge: Harvard University Press, 1982.

Gimferrer, Pere. *Apariciones y otras poemas*. Madrid: Visor, 1982.

———. *Espejo, espacio y apariciones (poesía 1970–1980)*. Madrid: Visor, 1988 c. 1978.

Glenn, Kathleen. "The Autobiography of a Nobody: Mercè Rodoreda's *El carrer de les Camèlies*." In *The Garden across the Border: Mercè Rodoreda's Fiction*. Edited by Kathleen McNerney and Nancy Vosburg, 110–18. Selinsgrove: Susquehanna University Press, 1994.

———. "Las cartas de amor de Carme Riera: El arte de seducir." In *Discurso femenino actual.* Edited by Adelaida López Martínez, 53–68. San Juan: Universidad de Puerto Rico, 1995.

———. "*La plaza del Diamante:* The Other Side of the Story." *Letras femeninas* 12, no. 1–2 (1986): 60–68.

———. Mirella Servodidio and Mary S. Vásquez, eds. *Moveable Margins: The Narrative Art of Carme Riera.* Lewisburg: Bucknell University Press, 1999.

———. "Reading and Writing the Other Side of the Story in Two Narratives by Carme Riera." *Catalan Review* 7, no. 1 (1993): 51–62.

———, ed. *Spanish Women Writers and the Essay.* Columbia: University of Missouri Press, 1998.

Guigon, Emmanuel. "Imágenes y textos en la obra de Remedios Varo." In *Remedios Varo: Arte y Literatura*, 15–22. Teruel: Museo de Teruel/ Diputación Provincial de Teruel, 1991.

Hart, Stephen M. *White Ink: Essays on Twentieth-Century Feminine Fiction in Spain and Latin America.* London: Tamesis, 1993.

Haynes, Deborah. "The Art of Remedios Varo: Issues of Gender Ambiguity and Religious Meaning." *Women's Art Journal* 16 (spring/summer 1995): 26–32.

Herrera, Hayden. *Frida: A Biography of Frida Kahlo.* New York: Harper and Row, 1983.

Herzberger, David K. "The Literary Malaise of Post-Franco Spain." In *Literature and Popular Culture in the Hispanic World.* Edited by Rose S. Mine, 185–90. Gaithersburg, MD: Ediciones Hispamérica, 1981.

hooks, bell. *Ain't I a Woman.* Boston: South End Press, 1981.

Ibarz, Mercè. *Mercè Rodoreda.* Barcelona: Editorial Empúries, 1991.

Ilie, Paul. *Literatura y exilio interior.* Madrid: Espiral, 1980.

Irigaray, Luce. *Speculum of the Other Woman.* Translated by Gillian C. Gill. Ithaca: Cornell University Press, 1984.

Jackson, Rosemary. *Fantasy: The Literature of Subversion.* New York: Methuen, 1981.

Jameson, Fredric. *The Political Unconscious.* Ithaca: Cornell University Press, 1981.

Johnson, Roberta. "Voice and Intersubjectivity in Carme Riera's Narratives." In *Critical Essays on the Literatures of Spain and Spanish America.* Edited by Luis T. Gonzalez del Valle and Julio Baena, 153–59. Boulder: Society of Spanish and Spanish-American Studies, 1991.

Jones, Margaret E. W. "Different Wor(l)ds: Modes of Women's Communication in Spain's *Narrativa Femenina*." *Mongraphic Review/Revista monográfica* 8 (1992): 57–69.

Kafka, Franz. *Metamorphosis.* Translated by A. L. Lloyd, New York: Vanguard Press, c. 1946.

Kaplan, Janet. *Unexpected Journeys: The Art and Life of Remedios Varo.* New York: Abbeville Press, 1988.

Kauffman, Linda S. *Special Delivery: Epistolary Modes in Modern Fiction*. Chicago: University of Chicago Press, 1992.

Kristeva, Julia. "About Chinese Women." In *The Kristeva Reader*. Edited by Toril Moi, 150–59. New York: Columbia University Press, 1986.

———. "Approaching Abjection." In *Powers of Horror*. Translated by Leon S. Roudiez, 1–31. New York: Columbia University Press, 1982.

———. *Desire in Language*. Translated by Thomas Gora, Alice Jardine, and Leon S. Roudiez. New York: Columbia University Press, 1980.

———. *Revolution in Poetic Language*. Translated by Margaret Waller. New York: Columbia University Press, 1984.

———. "Women's Time." In *The Kristeva Reader*. Edited by Toril Moi, 187–213. New York: Columbia University Press, 1986.

Kugler, Paul K. "Involuntary Poetics." *New Literary History* 15, no. 3 (1984): 491–501.

Lacan, Jacques. *Ecrits*. New York: Norton, 1977.

Lagos-Pope, María Inés, ed. *Exile in Literature*. Lewisburg: Bucknell University Press, 1988.

Landeira, Ricardo, and Luis T. González del Valle, eds. *Nuevos y novísimos*. Boulder: Society of Spanish and Spanish-American Studies, 1987.

Lessing, Doris. *The Golden Notebook*. New York: Bantam, 1962.

Ll. V. "Montserrat Roig: La literatura como mentira necesaria." *Leer* 46 (1991): 60–61.

Lozano, Luis-Martín. *The Magic of Remedios Varo*. Washington D.C.: National Museum of Women in the Arts, 2000.

Lucarda, Mario. "Mercè Rodoreda y el Buen Salvaje." *Quimera* 62 (1986): 34–39.

MacArthur, Elizabeth J. *Extravagant Narratives: Closure and Dynamics in the Epistolary Form*. Princeton: Princeton University Press, 1990.

Marks, Elaine, and Isabelle de Courtivron, eds. *New French Feminisms*. New York: Schocken, 1981.

Martí-Olivella, Jaume, ed. *Homage to Mercè Rodoreda*. Special issue of *Catalan Review* 2, no. 2 (1987): 1–292.

———, ed. *Women, History, and Nation in the Works of Montserrat Roig and Maria Aurélia Capmany*. Special issue of *Catalan Review* 7, no. 2 (1993): 1–278.

Martin, Biddy. "Femininsm, Criticism, and Foucault." In *Feminism and Foucault*. Edited by Irene Diamond and Lee Quimby, 3–19. Boston: Northeastern University Press, 1988.

Martínez Romero, Carmen. "Relaciones textuales en la novela femenina de la subjetividad: Gaite, Rodoreda y Riera." In *Ensayos de literatura europea e hispanoamericana*. Edited by Felix Menchacatore, 293–97. San Sebastian: Universidad del País Vasco, 1990.

McNerney, Kathleen. "A Feminist Literary Renaissance in Catalonia." In *Feminine Concerns in Contemporary Spanish Fiction by Women*. Edited by Roberto C. Manteiga, Carolyn Galerstein, and Kathleen McNerney, 124–33. Potomac, MD: Scripta Humanistica, 1988.

————, ed. *On Our Own Behalf: Women's Tales from Catalonia*. Lincoln: University of Nebraska Press, 1988.

————, ed. *Voices and Visions: The Words and Works of Mercè Rodoreda*. Selinsgrove: Susquehanna University Press, 1999.

McNerney, Kathleen, and Nancy Vosburg, eds. *The Garden across the Border: Mercè Rodoreda's Fiction*. Selinsgrove: Susquehanna University Press, 1994.

Memorial Montserrat Roig: Cicle de Conferències. Barcelona: Institut Català de la Dona, 1993.

Merrill Squier, Susan. Introduction to *Women Writers and the City*. Knoxville: University of Tennessee Press, 1984.

"Un millar de personas despidieron a la escritora Montserrat Roig." *El País* (12 noviembre 1991): 41.

Mitchell, W. J. T. "What is an Image?" *New Literary History* 15, no. 3 (spring 1984): 503–37.

Moi, Toril, ed. *The Kristeva Reader*. New York: Columbia University Press, 1986.

Möller-Soler, María Lourdes. "El impacto de la guerra civil en la vida y obra de tres novelistas catalanas: Aurora Bertrana, Teresa Pámies y Mercè Rodoreda." *Letras femeninas* 12, no. 1–2 (1986): 34–44.

Morcillo Gómez, Aurora. "Feminismo y lucha política durante la II República y la Guerra Civil." In *El feminismo en España: Dos siglos de historia*. Edited by Pilar Folguera, 57–83. Madrid: Pablo Iglesias, 1988.

Nash, Mary. *Defying Male Civilization: Women in the Spanish Civil War*. Denver: Arden Press, 1995.

Navajas, Gonzalo. "La microhistoria y Cataluña en *El carrer de les camèlies* de Mercè Rodoreda," *Hispania* 74, no. 4 (1991): 848–59.

Nichols, Geraldine Cleary. *Des/cifrar la diferencia: Narrativa femenina de la España contemporánea*. Madrid: Siglo XXI Editores, 1992.

————. *Escribir, espacio propio. Laforet, Matute, Moix, Tusquets, Riera y Roig por sí mismas*. Minneapolis: University of Minnesota Press, 1989.

————. "Stranger than Fiction: Fantasy in Short Stories by Matute, Rodoreda, Riera." *Monographic Review/Revista monográfica* 4 (1988): 33–42.

Nochlin, Linda. *Women, Art and Power and Other Essays*. New York: Harper and Row, 1988.

Oliver, Conxita. "Lluny de la temàtica convensional: La pintura, una faceta inèdita de Mercè Rodoreda." *Avui* (17 d'abril, 1991).

Oliver, Kelly. *Reading Kristeva*. Bloomington: Indiana University Press, 1993.

Palomo, Anna. "Una 'altra' imatge." *El Nou*(9 marzo 1991): 28.

Pérez, Janet. "Metamorphosis as a Protest Device in Catalan Feminist Writing: Rodoreda and Oliver." *Catalan Review* 2, no. 2 (1987): 181–98.

Persin, Margaret H. *Getting the Picture: The Ekphrastic Principle in Twentieth-Century Spanish Poetry*. Lewisburg: Bucknell University Press, 1997.

Piñol, Rosa Maria. "La exhibición de 89 pinturas descubrirá una faceta inédita de Mercè Rodoreda." *La Vanguardia* (3 mayo 1991).

Pollock, Griselda. *Vision and Difference: Femininity, Feminism, and the Histories of Art*. New York: Routledge, 1988.

————, ed. *Generations and Geographies in the Visual Arts: Feminist Readings*. New York: Routledge, 1996.

"La prematura muerte de Montserrat Roig conmociona al mundo literario catalán." *El País* (11 noviembre 1991), 29.

Racionero, Luis. "La maniera gentile de Carme Riera." *Quimera* 9–10 (1981): 12–16.

Rhodes, Elizabeth. "The Salamander and the Butterfly." In *The Garden across the Border: Mercè Rodoreda's Fiction*. Edited by Kathleen McNerney and Nancy Vosburg, 162–87. Selinsgrove: Susquehanna University Press, 1994.

Ribadeneyra, Pedro de. *Flos Sanctorum, de las vidas de los santos*. Madrid, 1761.

Riera, Carme. *Contra el amor en compañía*. Barcelona: Destino, 1991.

————. *Contra l'amor en companyia i altres relats*. Barcelona: Destino, 1991.

————. *Cuestión de amor propio*. Barcelona: Tusquets, 1987.

————. *Epitelis tendríssims*. Barcelona: Edicions 62, 1981.

————. "Grandeza y miseria de la epístola." In *El oficio de narrar*. Edited by Marina Mayoral, 147–58. Madrid: Catedra, 1990.

————. "Femenino singular: Literatura de mujer." In *Crítica y ficción literaria: Mujeres españolas contemporáneas*. Edited by Aurora and María Angeles Pastor Lopez, 27–38. Granada: Universidad de Granada, 1989.

————. *Jo pos per testimoni les gavines*. Barcelona: Laia, 1977.

————. "Literatura femenina: ¿un lenguaje prestado?" *Quimera* 18 (1982): 9–12.

————. "Montserrat Roig: Una altra mirada de Barcelona." *Lectora: Revista de dones i textualitat* 1 (1995): 7–17.

————. *Qüestió d'amor propi*. Barcelona: Planeta, 1987.

————. *Te deix, amor, la mar com a penyora*. Barcelona: Planeta, 1975.

————. *Te dejo el mar*. Translated by Luisa Cotoner. Madrid: Espasa Calpe, 1991.

Rodoreda, Mercè. *La calle de las camelias*. Barcelona: Editorial Bruguera, 1978.

————. *Camellia Street*. Translated by David H. Rosenthal. St. Paul, MN: Graywolf Press, 1993.

————. *El carrer de les camèlies*. 1966. Reprint, Barcelona: Club Editor, 1997.

————. *Cartes a l'Anna Muria: 1939–1956*. Barcelona: La Sal, 1985.

————. "La meva Cristina." In *Tots els contes*. Barcelona: Edicions 62, 1979.

————. *Mi Cristina y otros cuentos*. Translated by José Batlló. Madrid: Alianza, 1982.

————. *La plaça del Diamant*. 1962. Reprint, Barcelona: Editorial H.M.B., 1982.

————. *La plaza del Diamante*. Translated by Enrique Sordo. Barcelona: Edhasa, 1965.

————. *Quanta, quanta guerra*. Barcelona: Club Editor, 1980.

————. *Semblava de seda i altres contes*. Barcelona: Edicions 62, 1980.

————. "La salamandra." In *Tots els contes*. Barcelona: Edicions 62, 1979.

Rodríguez, María Pilar. "La (otra) opción amorosa: 'Te dejo, amor, el mar como una ofrenda' de Carme Riera." *Confluencia* 11, no. 2 (Spring 1996): 39–56.

Rogers, Elizabeth S. "Montserrat Roig's *Ramona, adiós:* A Novel of Suppression and Disclosure." *Revista de Estudios Hispánicos* 20, no. 1 (1986): 103–21.

Roig, Montserrat. *Aprendizaje sentimental*. Translated by Mercedes Nogués. (Molta roba i poc sabó; Castilian translation). Barcelona: Argos Vergara, 1981.

———. *Els catalans als camps nazis*. Barcelona: Edicions 62, 1977.

———. "La ciutat de Barcelona: una mirada femenina." *Memorial Montserrat Roig*, 11–27. Barcelona: Institut Català de la Dona, 1993.

———. *Digues que m'estimes encara que sigui mentida: Sobre el plaer solitari d'escriure i el vici compartit de llegir*. Barcelona: Edicions 62, 1991.

———. *Dime que me quieres aunque sea mentira: sobre el placer solitario de escribir y el vicio compartido de leer*. Translated by Antonia Picazo. Barcelona: Ediciones Península, 1992.

———. *L'hora violeta*. Barcelona: Edicions 62, 1980.

———. *La hora violeta*. Translated by Enrique Sordo. Barcelona: Plaza y Janes, 1980.

———. *Molta roba i poc sabó i tan neta que la volen*. Barcelona: Editorial Selecta, 1971.

———. *Ramona, adéu*. Barcelona: Edicions 62, 1972.

———. *Ramona, adiós*. Translated by Joaquim Sempere. Barcelona: Editorial Argos Vergara, 1980.

———. *El temps de les cireres*. Barcelona: Edicions 62, 1977.

———. *Tiempo de cerezas*. Translated by Enrique Sordo. Barcelona: Plaza y Janes, 1978.

———. *¿Tiempo de mujer?* Barcelona: Plaza y Janes, 1980.

Rosenthal, David H., trans. Introduction to *Camellia Street*, by Mercè Rodoreda. St. Paul: Graywolf Press, 1993.

———. Translator's foreword to *My Cristina and Other Stories*, by Mercè Rodoreda. Port Townsend, WA: Graywolf Press, 1984.

Rubin Suleiman, Susan. *Subversive Intent: Gender, Politics, and the Avant-Garde*. Cambridge: Harvard University Press, 1990.

Rueda, Ana. "Mercè Rodoreda: From Traditional Tales to Modern Fantasy." In *The Garden across the Border: Mercè Rodoreda's Fiction*. Edited by Kathleen McNerney and Nancy Vosburg, 201–22. Selinsgrove: Susquehanna University Press, 1994.

Schumm, Sandra. "Borrowed Language in Carme Riera's *Cuestión de amor propio*." *Anales de la literatura española contemporánea* 20, no. 1–2 (1995): 199–213.

———. *Reflection in Sequence: Novels by Spanish Women, 1944–1988*. Lewisburg: Bucknell University Press, 1999.

Segura i Soriano, Isabel, ed. *Literatura de Dones: Una visió del món*. Barcelona: La Sal, 1988.

Sellers, Susan, ed. *The Hélène Cixous Reader*. New York: Routledge, 1994.

Servodidio, M., ed. *Reading for Difference: Feminist Perspectives on Women Novelists of Contemporary Spain*. Special issue of *Anales de la literatura española contemporánea* 12 (1987): 11–217.

———. "Doing Good and Feeling Bad: The Interplay of Desire and Discourse in Two Stories by Carme Riera." In *Moveable Margins*. Edited by Kathleen Glenn,

Mirella Servodidio, and Mary S. Vásquez, 66–75. Lewisburg: Bucknell University Press, 1999.

———. Introduction to *Moveable Margins*. Edited by Kathleen Glenn, Mirella Servodidio, and Mary S. Vásquez. Lewisburg: Bucknell University Press, 1999.

Spivak, Gayatri Chakravorty. "Can the Subaltern Speak?" In *Marxism and the Interpretation of Culture*. Edited by C. Nelson and L. Grossberg, 271–313. Basingstoke: Macmillan, 1988.

Stouck, Mary-Ann. *Medieval Saints: A Reader*. Ontario: Broadview Press, 1999.

Surrealismo en Catalunya 1924–1936. Barcelona: Ediciones Polígrafa, 1988.

Tabori, Paul. *The Anatomy of Exile*. London: Harrap, 1972.

Torras i Frances, Meri. "Montserrat Roig i les veus que no se senten." *Serra d'or* 410 (febrer 1994): 58–61.

Torres, Maruja. "Una luchadora." *El País* (11 noviembre 1991): 29.

Tsuchiya, Akiko. "The Paradox of Narrative Seduction in Carmen Riera's *Cuestión de amor propio*." *Hispania* 75, no. 2 (1992): 281–86.

Ugarte, Michael. *Shifting Ground: Spanish Civil War Exile Literature*. Durham: Duke University Press, 1989.

Varo, Beatriz. *Remedios Varo: en el centro del microcosmos*. Mexico City: Fondo de Cultura Económica, 1990.

Varo, Remedios. *Catálogo razonado/Catalogue raisonné*. Mexico D.F.: Ediciones Era, 1994.

Vásquez, Mary S. "Epistolaridad, marginación y deseo en un cuento de Carme Riera." *Cuadernos de ALDEEU* 10, no. 2 (1994): 215–20.

———. "Textual Desire, Seduction, and Epistolary in Carme Riera's 'Letra de ángel' and 'La seducción del genio.' In *Moveable Margins*. Edited by Kathleen Glenn, Mirella Servodidio, and Mary S. Vásquez, 177–99. Lewisburg: Bucknell University Press, 1999.

Vernon, Kathleen, and Barbara Morris. *Post-Franco, Postmodern*. London: Greenwood Press, 1995.

Walsh, Michael, ed. *Butler's Lives of the Saints*. New York: Benziger Brothers, 1955.

Wyers, Frances. "A Woman's Voices: Mercè Rodoreda's *La Plaça del Diamant*." *Kentucky Romance Quarterly* 30, no. 3 (1983): 301–9.

Index

Numbers in italics refer to pages with illustrations.